CORA
WILSON
STEWART

CORA WILSON STEWART

Crusader Against Illiteracy

BY WILLIE NELMS

McFarland & Company, Inc., Publishers

Jefferson, North Carolina, and London

To "Miss B"
Who Introduced Me to Cora Wilson Stewart

Cover photograph: A Moonlight School in Alabama;
inset: Cora Wilson Stewart ca. 1920s.

Frontispiece: Cora Wilson Stewart ca. 1935.

All photographs courtesy of the Special Collections Department,
M. I. King Library, University of Kentucky, Cora Wilson
Stewart Papers.

British Library Cataloguing-in-Publication data are available

Library of Congress Cataloguing-in-Publication Data

Nelms, Willie, 1949–
    Cora Wilson Stewart : crusader against illiteracy / by Willie
Nelms.
        p.   cm.
    Includes bibliographical references (p.   ) and index.
    ISBN 0-7864-0334-9 (sewn softcover: 50# alkaline paper) ∞
    1. Stewart, Cora Wilson, 1875–1958.   2. Educators—Kentucky—
Biography.   3. Literacy—United States—History.   4. Adult
education—United States—History.   I. Title.
LA2317.S826N45   1997
370'.92—dc21
    [B]   97-25077
                                                              CIP

Manufactured in the United States of America

McFarland & Company, Inc., Publishers
  Box 611, Jefferson, North Carolina 28640

CONTENTS

PREFACE

I first discovered Cora Wilson Stewart in 1972, when I was a twenty-two-year-old history graduate student at the University of Kentucky. As a native of rural eastern Virginia with a love for reading and an appreciation for education, I was intrigued by the heroic story of the Rowan County, Kentucky, school superintendent who rose to prominence with the establishment of the Moonlight Schools. Long before it became fashionable to decry the lack of reading skills in the United States, Cora Wilson Stewart was leading crusades to eradicate adult illiteracy. Her life spanned eighty-three years from 1875 to 1958, during which she gained national and international fame. The more I read about her, the more I was impressed by the various facets of this extraordinary woman. I was so interested in her in the early 1970s that I spent roughly a year researching her life and writing my master's thesis on her. This work was accomplished under the direction of Dr. Charles P. Roland, my adviser at the University of Kentucky; I thank him for his help on that paper. Luckily for me, Stewart's voluminous papers were in the M. I. King Library, so I had ready access to them while I also worked as an assistant in the library's Special Collections Department.

Since first writing my thesis, I have continued to meet people who knew Cora Wilson Stewart, and this book represents nearly twenty-five years of my research and thoughts about her life. In the intervening years, I have also worked as a public library director and have been involved on the front lines of literacy work. Based on the additional research and my own experience, this book presents a fuller picture of Mrs. Stewart than I was able to provide as a young graduate student.

Since the story of her Rowan County work and the founding of the Moonlight Schools are the best-known parts of Cora Wilson Stewart's life, I have tried to go beyond the details of her Kentucky crusade to examine the personal part of her life as well as to focus on her later years. In my estimation, her career during the 1920s and early 1930s was at least as important as the original work she accomplished earlier in her home state. It was during these later decades that she worked on the national and international scale. It was also during this time that she came into conflict with the fledgling adult education movement.

1

Viewed as a romantic crusader by the well-educated members of the educational establishment who spearheaded the adult education movement, Stewart voiced opinions and ideas that ran counter to the trends of the 1920s and 1930s. I have tried to place her views in the context of this conflict between educational philosophies. Considering current criticisms of public education, her views about the problems of adult illiteracy continue to merit study today.

Wherever appropriate, I have let Cora Wilson Stewart speak in her own words. One of the most eloquent public speakers of her time, her flair for the dramatic made her a colorful character capable of speaking for herself.

In the years since I conducted my original research, the only significant treatment of Stewart has been Florence Estes's unpublished 1988 Ed.D. dissertation, *Cora Wilson Stewart and the Moonlight Schools of Kentucky, 1911–1920.* Estes looked at Stewart's Kentucky crusade through the lens of intellectual history and described certain movements that influenced her. Like similar academic exercises, Estes's work provides a useful perspective on certain aspects of Stewart's life, but it is not a full-scale biography.

I would like to thank all the people who have encouraged me on this project and who graciously shared with me their thoughts about Stewart. Special thanks go to Noi Doyle, Roi Peers and Marion McCrae, all relatives of Stewart who graciously shared their memories of her with me. I would also like to thank Arpha Burrell who talked with me about her association with Stewart. Fred King and James McConkey deserve special mention for their encouragement in my studies of Stewart.

The Cora Wilson Stewart oral history project at Morehead State University also produced interviews with some people who had direct or indirect knowledge of Stewart. These interviews were helpful in the preparation of this book.

To my friends in the Special Collections Department of the M. I. King Library, I owe a great debt of gratitude for their friendship over the years and their assistance in providing access to the Stewart Papers. I would like to especially acknowledge the late Dr. Jacqueline Bull, who first introduced me to the Cora Wilson Stewart Papers when she was head of the Special Collections Department at King Library. It is to her memory that I dedicate this book.

Finally, to my family, including my parents, my wife, and my children, I would like to say thanks for encouraging me to continue work on this book and for being patient with me when I was often not so patient with them.

*I*NTRODUCTION
AND *R*EFLECTIONS

The elderly lady gently took the letter that she had just dictated. Because she was blind, she had to be shown where to begin her signature. Her hands trembled so that her writing, which had been so graceful earlier in life, seemed shaky and uneven. Determined to complete the task, she doggedly persevered; after carefully completing the signature, she rested her pen.

The simple act of signing a letter was a great source of pride for the woman because she was Cora Wilson Stewart. She treasured the elements of literacy because she had helped thousands of adult illiterates learn the basic skills of reading and writing. As she drew near to the end of her life in 1958, she tenaciously clung to the ability to sign her name despite her own blindness and her failing health.

During the first third of the twentieth century, Cora Wilson Stewart had been the most widely known authority on adult illiteracy in the world. She had founded the Moonlight Schools in Rowan County, Kentucky, in 1911, and she had led until 1920 a crusade to eradicate adult illiteracy in her home state. From the Bluegrass State, she had gone on to become a national and international figure. Five times she chaired the Illiteracy Section of the World Conference of Education Associations. She conducted dozens of illiteracy conferences throughout the United States, served on the powerful Executive Board of the National Education Association, and founded the National Illiteracy Crusade in 1926.

Considered one of the best female orators of her day, Stewart made speeches that inspired campaigns to eradicate adult illiteracy throughout the United States, and in 1929 she convinced President Herbert Hoover to establish the National Advisory Committee on Illiteracy. A champion of the most needy, she startled the nation in 1917 when she made public the information that one out of four men who registered for the initial draft of World War I could neither read nor write. She wrote the first readers designed especially for adult illiterates; she persuaded national corporations to fund public service campaigns against illiteracy, she convinced the government to offer literacy training to native Americans, and she talked prison officials across the country into providing classes for illiterate inmates. A woman of uncommon talents, she even received one vote for president of the United States at the 1920 Democratic Convention.

Cora Wilson Stewart was a product of the Progressive era, that period in the early part of the twentieth century when American reformers brought about local, state, and national changes ranging from prohibition to female suffrage. A contemporary of Jane Addams, Carrie Chatman Catt, and Ida Tarbell, she worked with the major political and social leaders of her time.

Stewart's background differed from the backgrounds of other progressive reformers, however. She was born and reared in the mountains of eastern Kentucky at a time when feuds were a fact of life. Raised to believe that ignorance begot violence, she developed an idealistic faith in the power of education. Coming of age at a time when women were just beginning to assert their rights, she refused to subject her abilities to the traditional role expected of women in her mountain environment.

The determination that impelled Stewart to break out of the expected domestic mold of the time produced a private life that also differed markedly from the lives of other females of the Progressive era. A victim of marital abuse, she suffered three failed marriages (two to the same man) at a time when such experience was almost unknown. The failure of her domestic and personal life caused her to seek success in the arena of public affairs. She chose the elimination of adult illiteracy as her mission in life, and she nurtured this adopted cause as surely as any mother ever nourished a child.

Long before it became popular to decry the problems of adult illiteracy, Stewart was exhorting the nation to join a crusade to teach uneducated adults the basic skills of reading and writing. Many of her methods are still instructive during the last decade of the twentieth century. A romantic at heart, she challenged the rising tide of bureaucratization in the field of education, and she humanized the conditions of needy adults at a time when educators were most interested in studying, quantifying, and analyzing the problem of adult illiteracy.

Cora Wilson Stewart would ultimately lose her battle with trained professionals who signed Ph.D. or Ed.D. after their names, but she would never lose her crusading spirit.

1

GROWING UP IN THE ROWAN COUNTY WAR

When John Halley first came across the Kentucky mountains from Virginia, he had no idea that his great-granddaughter would grow up to have a profound impact on the educational life of the region into which he was moving. It was 1838, and John came to Montgomery County with his wife, Nancy Douglas Halley, to begin a fresh life in the Kentucky hills.

John Halley died soon after the move to Kentucky, and Nancy Halley decided to continue the family journey west. She traveled to Missouri and on to Kansas, where she settled and eventually died in 1869 at age 82. John and Nancy's eldest son, Uriah, had chosen, however, to stay in the area when his mother decided to move further west. A farmer like most people in eastern Kentucky, he met and married Sarah Davis. He established himself in his community and served as a magistrate for many years.[1]

Both Uriah and Sarah Halley were devout Christians in a region that took religion seriously. Together, they produced twelve children; the second, a daughter they named Anne Eliza, was born on February 12, 1849. Sharing her parents' devotion to religion, Anne was baptized and became a member of the Church of Christ at Sycamore near Jeffersonville in Montgomery County.

Anne was exposed to classical literature and the stories of the Bible from an early age. Living at a time when rhetoric was prized, she was an expressive person, especially fond of using dramatic statements in everyday speech. For example, instead of saying that someone was not very bright, she would say, "He has never been on Solomon's Porch." When someone was in danger, she would remark, "The sword of Damocles is hanging over his head."[2]

Anne Halley filled her diary with expressions of romance and her views of love. In a typical diary entry entitled "A True Woman's Love," she offered the following:

> A Woman's affections are sacred. They are her life and he who takes upon himself their guardianship assumes a holy and responsible duty. A true woman loves independent of all worldly circumstances.... A true woman loves when she loves truly and tenderly and if she unites with the opposite

5

sex in the bond of holy matrimony and feels assured that her love is appreciated she is ready to lay her life at the feet of the man she loves and if the task could be allotted to her of making the path in which he were to walk it would be straight and sweet and soft as a bed of roses.... Yes, the love of a true woman for her husband is more precious to her than the miser's affection for his hoarded gold. These are my imperfectly expressed ideas of a true woman's love.[3]

This ornate view of romantic love was echoed in other entries Anne Halley made in her diary. Anne's fondness for classical expressions and flowery language were to have a distinct impact on her second daughter, Cora, as was her romanticized view of the world in general and love in particular.

Anne was energetic as well as articulate. She learned early that a high sense of responsibility was expected from her; at the age of 18, she had to settle the estate of her father when he passed away. By the time she was twenty-one years old, Anne was teaching in neighboring Powell County. There she met Jeremiah Wilson, another educator, who was two years her junior. The young people fell in love and were married on December 11, 1870; they settled on a farm left to Anne by her father's estate.[4]

Like his wife's family, Jeremiah Wilson's family was from Virginia. His parents, Isaiah and Sara Jane Wilson, moved to the narrows of Morgan County, Kentucky, from Leesburg, Virginia, in the 1840s. Cora Wilson Stewart would later claim with pride that the family was related to General Robert E. Lee. The portion of Morgan County in which the Wilsons settled eventually became part of Rowan County. Jeremiah was born on June 30, 1852; like his future wife, he was one of twelve children.

A bright, intelligent young man with an inquiring mind, Jeremiah was later remembered by Cora Wilson Stewart for his quick and biting wit. Although she realized that she had inherited traits from each parent, she always believed that she was more like her mother than her father. From her mother, she claimed to have received her gentle and generous nature; she said she resembled her father when she used sarcasm and sharp wit. Jeremiah Wilson was to become one of the best-known individuals in eastern Kentucky, and his children became leading citizens of the area. His fame was not a result of teaching, however; it was earned in the field of medicine. Soon after getting married, he began studying medicine with Dr. Bunyan Spratt, a well-known Montgomery County physician. Jeremiah thought so highly of his mentor that he named one of his sons Bunyan Spratt in his honor.[5]

The Wilsons began their family in 1871 and eventually had twelve children over the course of seventeen years. These included two sets of twins. The death of children was an integral part of life in the nineteenth century, and only seven of the children lived past their twenty-first birthday. After one of several family moves made during the 1870s, Anne gave birth to her third child—a girl—on January 17, 1875. The mother later told the child that she weighed four pounds at birth and deserved no better name than Cora. According to the

Wilson family Bible, Cora was born on the "waters of Sycamore," near Jefferson-ville in Montgomery County.[6] While she was the third child born, she was soon the oldest daughter, because her older sister Viola died in 1878 at age five. Her older brother, Everett, barely lived to adulthood and died in 1892 when he was twenty years old. Thus, in later years, Cora was destined to assume the leadership role of the oldest child in the Wilson family.

The world in which the Wilsons lived was in many ways wild and violent. The Civil War had divided the Kentucky mountaineers between sympathizers with the Union and the Confederacy. Union supporters held a majority in the mountains, but the South also had many backers. Divisions between neighbors were deep and carried over after the end of the war.

Rivalries between backers of the two sides generally were along party lines. The Democrats were Confederate supporters and Republicans were Unionists. The isolation of the mountains produced individuals who were proud, self-reliant, and suspicious of outsiders. The local residents were mostly small farm-ers who scratched a subsistence living from the rocky soil to feed their fami-lies. Accustomed to using guns, they took care of their own families instead of relying on outside help, and they settled their own disputes without govern-mental intervention.

As a result, family disputes often escalated into feuds that placed entire areas under the threat of violence. Because of the isolation of the area, civil lead-ers came to reflect family rivalries, and local politics mirrored these disputes. The conflicts in the mountains were so intense and diverse that one historian compared county politics in eastern Kentucky to political conditions in medieval Italy. This similarity included assassinations, party intrigue, and a general lack of respect for civil authority.[7]

The most famous eastern Kentucky feud was between the Martin and Tol-liver families. This conflict became so intense that it gained the name the Rowan County War and received newspaper coverage in cities as far away as New York. The feud illustrates the violent nature of the area at the time and shows the intermingling of politics and family disputes. It began in the summer of 1884, when both political parties engaged in a particularly bitter political campaign for the office of county sheriff. The Republican candidate, Cook Humphrey, was elected. Following the election, Floyd Tolliver, a prominent local Demo-crat, wounded John Martin, an influential Republican, in a fight at the More-head Tavern.

Several months later Floyd Tolliver was killed by Martin, and the Tolli-vers swore revenge. Sheriff Humphrey arrested Martin and placed him in pro-tective custody in the Montgomery County jail. The Tollivers forged a court order for Martin's release and extradition to Rowan County. He was taken by train to Morehead despite his protests and became a victim of the feud when a group of Tolliver sympathizers dragged him from the railroad car and mur-dered him.

Martin's bloody murder started a two-and-one-half year period of feuding between the two factions. During this time, twenty-seven people were murdered. Three times the state government intervened to restore peace, and violence resumed each time the troops left. The violence became so outrageous that the state general assembly only narrowly defeated a bill that would have abolished the county.

The final resolution to the conflict came in 1887, when the two sides waged a pitched gun battle in the streets of Morehead. In this clash, Boone Logan, whose two brothers had been killed at the hands of the Tollivers, organized a vigilante group that surprised the Tollivers. Craig Tolliver and several of his most powerful associates were killed in the battle. A brief statement from Kentucky's Governor J. Proctor Knott indicated the extent to which the local political scene had degenerated: "A posse acting under the authority of a warrant from the county judge, attacked the Police Judge of Morehead and his adherents on the 22nd of June, killed several of their number and put the rest to flight, and temporarily restored something like tranquillity to the community."[8]

It was in this world that the young physician Jeremiah Wilson raised his family and practiced medicine. By all accounts, Dr. Wilson was a very caring and successful doctor. He traveled throughout the eastern part of the state, tending to the needs of his patients, some of whom were the victims of feuds. These experiences convinced Jeremiah and his wife that they must find a safe haven for their children to mature in peace, and they were determined to provide their children with opportunities that were above the norm for the average citizens of Rowan County.

Quick to take advantage of these offerings, young Cora early displayed a sharp intellect and keen interest in learning. By age four, she had declared her intention to be a teacher; by age five, according to her mother, she was holding mock classes in the Wilson backyard and demanding that her students address her as "Miss Cora." Her father was so amused by his daughter's commanding nature that he dubbed her "the General" when he came home from work one day and found her conducting school for the neighborhood children.[9]

Cora Wilson knew well the details of the Rowan County War. She later claimed that as a child she had heard Boone Logan tell stories of the feud. As an adult, Cora sold an article to London's *Wide World Magazine* entitled "The Rowan County War," in which she drew heavily on her knowledge of the family quarrels. She attributed much of the fighting and jealousy of the Rowan County War to the ignorance and lack of education of the participants. The feud convinced her that ignorance produced violence and brought her to believe that education was the best means of avoiding such conflicts in the future.[10]

In many ways Cora Wilson grew up like other mountain children. She knew the beauty of the woods, loved the stillness of the mountains, and believed in the purity of spirit of the mountain people. Her contemporaries remembered her as a good friend and playmate, who enjoyed children's games.[11] Cora later recalled that she had attended a typical one-room school with other children—a school with a dirt floor, no windows, and limited sessions for the students.

She walked several miles to her first rural school, which was in session only three months out of the year.

Yet Cora knew that she was more privileged than the other mountain youth. Both her parents believed in the value of education, and they were determined to provide their children with proper schooling. In contrast to other mountaineers, her family had books on the shelves for their children, and they exposed them to a level of culture that was beyond the norm for eastern Kentucky. Years later, she would recall: "We had pictures on our walls while other children had none. We had stories. We had books. The difference between our lives and most of the other children in the community was that our parents were educated."

Although it is uncertain exactly when she learned to read, by age seven Cora was an assiduous reader of *The Old Arm Chair*, a fiction periodical purchased by the neighboring Sanford family. The Sanfords were the only magazine subscribers in the area and the only family other than the Wilsons with books to read. After exhausting the meager libraries of her parents and the neighbors, it is reported that Cora once pulled down one of her father's medical books and said that she would have to read the doctor's books if there was nothing else for her to read.[12]

From 1880 to 1885, the Wilsons moved several times as the doctor's practice grew and he built new houses for his growing family. During each of these moves, Anne held various jobs. She taught school, she opened a post office in the family home, and on another occasion, she ran a country store. Cora later boasted that her mother could always sell more goods than her father because she made friends so easily and was so well liked.

Like many country doctors, Jeremiah Wilson accepted a variety of payments for his services. Currency was rare in the mountains during the last quarter of the nineteenth century, so patients often did not have cash to pay him. Instead of money, barter was used, with livestock, vegetables, and even land. Because of this payment system, Dr. Wilson amassed a considerable amount of property compared to the holdings of the average eastern Kentuckian.[13]

Jeremiah Wilson worked hard and traveled continuously to help his patients. It was not uncommon for him to stay with sick clients for several days at a time, and he was never known to refuse to help a sick person when called. He was often away from home and left his family to take care of themselves. Amazingly, Anne continued to work outside the home in addition to caring for the family. At one point, she went back to teaching in the public schools. Needing help while the doctor was away, Anne turned to Cora for assistance in taking care of the house and the younger children. In later years the Wilson family would be financially secure enough to have help in the household, but in the 1880s most of the domestic work fell to Cora and her mother. In adulthood, Cora exhibited an appreciation for the finer things in life. She liked quality clothes, and she enjoyed having household help. Her appreciation for such things was doubtless a response to the demands placed on her as a young child when she was a major source of domestic help for her mother.[14]

Cora assumed her responsibilities eagerly, and she carefully watched her mother carry on the heroic duties of wife, mother, and working person. The young Cora was deeply influenced by her mother's dramatic, expressive nature and her use of classical phrases and quotations from the Bible in everyday speech. The mother's example inspired the young child and provided a model that she tried to emulate in adulthood. Following her mother's example, Cora assumed that a woman could be a mother, wife, and working person. Cora also absorbed the lessons of self-sacrifice and consideration for others exhibited by Anne. She cooked for her younger siblings, washed their clothes, and generally served as a second mother for them.

Young Cora was especially impressed by her mother's piety. In addition to sprinkling her daily conversation with biblical quotes, Anne encouraged her children to pray and to attend church. Her urgings were not lost on Cora, who as early as eight years old began making pilgrimages into the woods to pray. Later, on July 29, 1888, when she was thirteen years old, Cora became a communicant of the Christian Church.[15]

The influence of Dr. Wilson was also important in the shaping of Cora's personality. He recognized that his daughter had a keen mind that could help her rise above the normal life of most mountain girls. As Cora matured, he encouraged her to continue her education, and most significantly, he made certain that his family enjoyed a standard of living above the norm for eastern Kentucky. Dr. Wilson often invited visitors from outside the mountains into his home. With the large family and guests gathered around the bountiful dinner table, the home seemed like a boardinghouse. Cora listened intently to the visitors as they told of places far away from the mountains, and she dreamed of the day when she might visit these exotic locales.

Family demands took on a new dimension for the Wilsons in the late 1880s, when Jeremiah had to go to Louisville to get his diploma in medicine. This was a new state requirement, and it meant that the family had to carry on without him for longer than usual. In his absence, Anne ran the farm and had loads of bark peeled and sent to Louisville to help pay Jeremiah's expenses at the Kentucky School of Medicine. Needing help with household duties during these trying times, she consistently turned to Cora for assistance.

When Jeremiah returned to his family in 1890, he decided to move to Morehead. This was partly because the growing town offered a good location for the doctor's practice and partly because it was the site of the new Morehead Normal School.[16] The Morehead Normal School was begun by Dr. Frank C. Button and his sister Phoebe, who came from Lexington in 1887 to provide higher education for eastern Kentucky. With moral and financial support from the Christian Woman's Board of Missions, they opened a school that offered college preparatory training and a teacher's course. The classes were small, books scarce, and work consisted mainly of daily recitations, plus occasional lectures, but the school was a major constructive influence in Rowan County. Over the years it continued to grow, eventually evolving into Morehead State University.[17]

By the time Jeremiah Wilson moved to Morehead in 1890, the Rowan County War had ended. The doctor established an office in the Galt House in Morehead but later moved his headquarters to a separate space on Main Street. As the railroad expanded, his practice thrived, and he became well known along the Chesapeake and Ohio Railroad line from Mount Sterling, Kentucky, to Huntington, West Virginia.[18]

Morehead's population had expanded from 163 inhabitants in 1880 to 491 by 1890. By the year 1900, the number of residents reached 1100. The mountain environment changed with the influx of people. Lumber companies moved into the area and began cutting timber for the industrial revolution that was beginning to touch the South. These commercial developments brought a higher level of prosperity to the area and challenged the isolation that had bred feuds.[19]

Not long after moving to Morehead, Cora began her teaching career, just prior to her sixteenth birthday. For the next five years, she taught in the public schools. She later recalled that her first principal, a man named Rea Powers, was "wise, noble, and the soul of courtesy."[20] Of her experience in the classroom, she observed: "My classes I always assembled in the entrance hall. Whenever I entered his room, the principal's room, he always stopped and placed a claim for me gallantly. He told his family and my friends 'That girl is worth her weight in gold.'"[21] While she began teaching in the primary grades, Cora also started taking classes at the Morehead Normal School; by age seventeen, she had received her teaching certificate. During this same time, she continued to live at home and helped her mother with the family. She was always available to assist with the younger children, and her father encouraged her to set a good example for them in the area of education.

Not content to limit her schooling to Morehead Normal, Cora attended the National Normal University in Lebanon, Ohio, during 1892 and 1893 between sessions of the Morehead public schools. She displayed prowess in rhetoric at the Ohio school, and she returned for a session in March 1895. By now a mature young woman of five feet five inches, Cora had brown hair and brown eyes. Described by a contemporary as a "handsome" woman, she enhanced her appearance with careful grooming and attractive clothes. She made many friends while in Lebanon and developed a romantic attraction to a young man named J. A. George. Little is known of this relationship, but a friend, Cora Nichols, wrote in her autograph book, "George and Cora took hold of Love's mill and worked away with a right good will."[22]

The times were indeed changing for young Cora, the mountain community in which she lived, and the entire nation. The budding Progressive movement was the source of much of this change. This national trend fostered organizations that sought community improvements and led to reforms ranging from prohibition to woman suffrage. The young Cora was aware of these changes, and she was eager to realize her potential as an individual. Like any young person, she was restless and considered several possibilities for how she would spend her life. When she returned to Morehead from Lebanon, she took a job teaching at the Morehead Normal School, but there were traditional demands also placed on her. At this time, a woman's place in society was tied directly to marriage and to the traditional duties of a wife and mother.

These forces pulled at the young Cora as she thought about the best path to follow. Her ambitions were great, and she even contemplated careers outside the field of education. Her father encouraged her to try medicine and even the legal profession, but Cora showed little interest in these fields; she was always more attracted to the arts. She later recalled that her thoughts ran to possible careers in music, the theater, and writing. Despite these flights of fantasy, however, she always came back to teaching as the avenue for her.

During this time of restlessness, Cora met young Ulysses Grant Carey. A Morehead resident, Carey was the son of the owner of the Galt House in Morehead, the site of Dr. Wilson's first medical office. The two young people courted, and they were married on June 4, 1895, when Cora was twenty. Later remembered as a gentle man of no particularly outstanding characteristics, Carey worked for his father at the Galt House. Few details are known about the marriage, but it is certain that Cora continued her work as a teacher in the Rowan County school system after the marriage.[23] For two years and two months during 1895 and 1896, she worked in rural schools at Corey Chapel, Seas Branch, and Elliottsville. During these times, she drew closer to the Rowan mountaineers. She boarded in their homes and occasionally helped illiterate adults with miscellaneous clerical matters.

It is obvious that Cora was not the docile, domestic wife that was most common in the mountain community, and she soon realized that her marriage to Carey was a mistake. She filed for separation on November 5, 1896, less than a year and a half after the wedding. Grant Carey objected to the separation, but on June 9, 1898, the case came to court and the marriage was "canceled and set aside and held for naught."[24] Cora was granted the return of her maiden name. Grant Carey eventually moved to the Frankfort area, where he remarried and worked for the rest of his life.[25]

After the aborted marriage, Cora continued to explore alternative careers. She went to the Wilbur R. Smith Business College in Lexington, Kentucky. Here she graduated on December 21, 1899, and considered a possible career in business. She did not totally reject teaching, however. She taught briefly at the college, becoming the first female instructor at the school.[26] Less than a year after taking the teaching job, she was called home when her mother became very sick. Within a week after Cora's arrival home, Anne died on September 10, 1900. Some reports indicate that she had typhoid fever, while others claim that she had suffered from consumption for approximately twelve years. In any event, Cora was grief-stricken at the death of the person who had been the main influence on her life. A local news article summarized Anne's life, noting that she was "an eloquent and beautiful writer. She was always ready to sacrifice herself for those she loved. Her ideas of religion were not narrow and sectarian, but were broad and beautiful."[27]

In order to help educate her brothers and sisters, Cora moved to nearby Huntington, West Virginia, where she took a job as a stenographer and book-keeper for the Standard Lumber Company. One can only conjecture how the strong-willed young Cora, who had earned the nickname "the General" as a child, reacted to the demands of clerical work. Apparently she discharged her duties well, however, because she received a letter of recommendation from her supervisor for her performance.[28]

In any event, Cora quickly tired of the work and searched for a chance to return to Morehead. Such an opportunity was not long in coming, as her brother Bunyan Spratt Wilson, elected in 1900 as the first mayor of Morehead, encouraged her to run in the upcoming election for Rowan County school superin-tendent. This opportunity was too good for Cora to ignore, and it changed her life forever.[29]

2

PUBLIC ACCLAIM, PRIVATE SORROW

Cora Wilson's selection as the Democratic candidate for Rowan County school superintendent was not surprising. Her position as a civic-minded school teacher had been well established during the previous ten years. Her father's reputation and the high regard in which he was held by the mountaineers of Rowan also helped her campaign. Jeremiah Wilson was a leading citizen of the community, with growing land holdings and a medical practice that touched the lives of most people in the county. His daughter was bound to benefit from his fame.

Jeremiah was not the only member of the family in a position to help Cora. Her brother, Bunyan Spratt Wilson, was a successful attorney in addition to being the mayor of Morehead. A prominent Democrat, three years younger than Cora, he would go on to represent the Bath–Rowan district as a member of the Kentucky House of Representatives. Bun had attended law school in Louisville, and he would eventually move to Ashland, where he became a member of the board of education and served as a police judge.

When the party nominated Cora on May 11, 1901, however, her victory was uncertain. Rowan had traditionally been a Republican county, and there was little indication that it was ready to change. Furthermore, the opponent in the election was a man, Emmett Martt. The county had never before elected a woman to the office of school superintendent, and the idea of a female in such a position did not appeal to many people. In the mountains of eastern Kentucky, as in the rest of the nation in 1901, women were expected to fill the traditional roles of wives and mothers; school administration was left to men. To further complicate matters, Martt was a beau of Cora's younger sister Stella Wilson. Years later, Cora would laugh at this last coincidence, but it did not seem funny at the time.[1]

Despite these drawbacks, she enthusiastically entered the political fray. Campaigning as "the children's friend," she made herself known throughout the remote areas by vigorously canvassing the county. Her efforts were noted in several newspapers that gave her their endorsements. One of them said: "She

Cora Wilson Stewart in 1901. Photo used during her first campaign for Rowan County superintendant of schools.

is a pleasant young woman, bright and quite thoroughly imbued with the interest of the public schools."[2] In giving its support, another observed: "Miss Wilson continues her studies, is up on all the new methods and knowing the wants
of her people and their abilities will act wisely and bring the schools up to a
higher standard."[3]

As a result of her intensive campaign, Cora was elected superintendent
of Rowan County Schools on November 5, 1901, by a substantial majority. She
was the first woman elected superintendent in a radius of 26 counties, and her
election paved the way for other female superintendents in neighboring Mor-

gan, Elliott, Bath, and Fleming counties. Miss Wilson's victory was a sign of changes occurring throughout the South.

Southern teachers were beginning to acknowledge the poor conditions of the region's schools, and education was becoming viewed as a way that the South might match the economic growth of the North. The need for educational reform was great. In 1900, white illiteracy ranged from 26% in Virginia to 32% in Louisiana and Alabama. Negro illiteracy was 27% of the total population. The U.S. Census Bureau classified as illiterate anyone who could not write in any language, regardless of his or her ability to read. Based on this rough definition of literacy, the number of functionally illiterate people was doubtless much higher than the census reports.

Teaching was one of the few professions open to women at the turn of the century, and female reformers in the Progressive movement often came from the education field. By 1900, female teachers were beginning to predominate in primary and secondary schools. Women were paid less than men, so this gave an additional incentive for hiring more female instructors. At the same time, however, it was assumed that most of these women would be unmarried. The common assumption was that if a woman married, her interest in her students would decline and that for society's good, she should stay at home and devote her attention to her own children once she started a family.

While women took teaching jobs, they rose to the ranks of principal and superintendent very slowly, if at all. A "glass ceiling" may have existed, but Cora Wilson proved that such a barrier was not unbreakable. Clearly ahead of her time, she was an ambitious and able woman who did not fit many of the stereotypes of the day. College education was still not the norm at the turn of the century, and a traditional role for women was expected in most areas of the United States. In eastern Kentucky, which had only recently recovered from the feuds of the Rowan County War, this view was especially prevalent.

Educational reform was a basic part of the Progressive movement, and Cora Wilson shared many characteristics with the female reformers of her day. She came from a family that was above average in income, she had a good education in comparison to most people in her community, and she was a member of the education profession. The one characteristic she did not share with other female Progressive reformers was her point of origin. Most Progressive women reformers came from city backgrounds, while she was raised in a rural environment and a mountain lifestyle. These roots made her unique among the reformers of her day and colored her approach to issues of the time. She would use this fact to her benefit in the future and never lose sight of her origins.

Some of the changes of the Progressive era were a result of the economic developments that were influencing the roles of women. The Industrial Revolution allowed women more leisure time and gave them a chance to look beyond the roles of wife and mother. Morehead, with its new normal school, a growing population, and the commercialization of the community, was similar to many other towns that offered fresh opportunities at the beginning of the new century. Local women enjoyed more leisure time, and they joined organizations that supported civic reform efforts that took them outside the home.

Despite changes in the lives of women in the first decade of the twentieth century, the prevailing public view held that a woman was different from a man—mentally and physically. For most women, the future meant marriage and retirement to her home to nurture a family. In the final analysis, a woman's role in society was to be determined by the prestige and position her husband was able to attain. Her personal reputation was determined by her success as a wife and mother. If a married woman took a job outside the home, she was, in effect, advertising the inadequacy of her husband to provide for the needs of his family. If such a view was widespread in most of the nation, it was gospel in the mountains. For Cora Wilson, this traditional view of women was to have a devastating effect on her future married life.

It was in these conditions that Cora Wilson rose to become superintendent of the Rowan County Schools. At the time, school superintendents were not required to have any special qualifications, only a political ability to get elected. This meant that in many cases Kentucky school superintendents were totally unqualified for their jobs. Cora Wilson was to prove a genuine exception to this rule. She had already shown her ability as a teacher; she was now prepared to demonstrate that she also had the skills to be an effective school administrator.

Wilson threw herself into her new position. For the first time in history, the superintendent's office was opened on a daily basis to the people. She not only opened it up, she cleaned it up, papered the walls, carpeted the floor at her own expense, and placed pictures in the room. She introduced graduation ceremonies for the students for the first time in county history. Drawing on lessons learned from her mother and from her own training in rhetoric, she trained the young public school students to make their own commencement speeches.[4]

At this time, Wilson began developing into an effective public speaker herself. The eloquence of her mother was not lost on the young woman. Having shown a flair for the dramatic from an early age, she cultivated her oratorical skills as superintendent. She often gave talks to local groups regarding educational matters, and she discovered that she had a real talent for public speaking. During her term as superintendent, she also published an educational newspaper for the trustees of the local schools at her own expense. She used this paper as a way to highlight progress in areas of the county, and she challenged the various sections to match the efforts of their neighbors. In 1901 the county was filled with a series of one-room schoolhouses. Each of these schools had a small board of trustees, many of whom had little education themselves. These trustees were responsible for hiring a teacher and seeing to the maintenance of the school under the general supervision of the county superintendent. Wilson showed genuine concern for the role of trustees and inspired them to make the most of the schools under their purview.

Wilson also used her own money to buy song books for the public school pupils, and she played a major role in the effort that gave the children an extra month of school each year. Even before the Federation of Women's Clubs became active in the area, she had similar women's groups organized in Rowan. She consistently rewarded teachers and students for their efforts with such prizes as flags, pictures, and books. Much of this was done at her own expense.[5]

During these early days as superintendent, Wilson also contributed to several local newspapers, including the *Rowan County News*, the *Ashland Daily Independent*, and the *Hazard Herald*. Her articles were not solely on educational themes but included a variety of community improvement themes.

For instance, in one article Wilson noted:

> Some parts of town are a delight to look upon as well as a joy to "pedestranate" along. But when we get in the height of our glory, lo, we step off on a board side walk, the boards go "flippy flop" and our thoughts are divided between wondering whether we will escape without breaking our neck and whether Rowan County has as much stone as she is noted for. We need walks all over the town, we can afford them, we are entitled to them, and we are going to have them.[6]

At another time, Wilson noted the need for street lights in the town, saying: "A town with the intellect, the culture, the thrift, and the religion that Morehead has certainly deserves lights of some kind. It would be better to return to the coal lights we once had than to be in total darkness. Give us lights, be them ever so dim."[7]

Wilson's observations regarding community improvements sometimes extended to the care of the dead as well as the living. For instance, she noted:

> Our cemeteries ought to be fenced this spring and some plan for their care and improvement should be originated. We have three "cities of the dead" that need our attention either in the way of fencing, grassing, or setting out ornamental shrubbery. Each family gives some attention to their own, but these sacred spots belong to us all and a committee should be appointed to see each family and arrange for improvements of the cemetery, not on one corner, or one spot, but as a whole.[8]

Cora Wilson appealed to the civic pride of her neighbors and challenged them to improve the appearance of the community. "Now is the time to repair and clean up. Morehead has the advantage of other towns in being ideally located and surrounded with the most beautiful scenery to be found," she wrote. "We can improve, though, on what we have, and make of our homes regular bowers of beauty. The humblest cottage can be made a poem with a white wash and a handful of morning glory seed. We have a good town, and we could have a beautiful town. Now is the time to begin."[9]

On another occasion, Wilson urged her fellow citizens to take better care of their environment. After noting the purity and beauty of the mountains, she observed: "The Lord made this earth clean and wholesome in the beginning. We have made it filthy and unsanitary."[10] Her speeches were always couched in dramatic terms, as were her writings. At a time when oratorical rhetoric was a valued commodity, she used her talents for maximum effect.

One of Wilson's most popular speeches was "Our Mountain Jewels." In this speech, she compared the young children of the county to rare gems, that were unpolished and unspoiled, awaiting only the refining influence of education to be formed into priceless jewels. Such a topic appealed to local pride and was a great favorite among church, civic, and school groups. Over the years, Wilson refined this speech, and she was called on to repeat it throughout the state. As a native eastern Kentuckian, she possessed firsthand knowledge of the subject about which she spoke, and she expressed this knowledge in dramatic and impressive language that made her talks even more effective.[11]

To further her position in the community, Wilson became an active participant in a variety of local organizations and eventually held leadership roles in most of these. She became a member of the Women's Club, serving as president of the Morehead chapter. She was district director of the Christian Women's Board of Missions, a member of the advisory board of Morehead Normal, and president of the Rowan County division of the Kentucky Sunday School Association.

For someone as publicly active as Cora Wilson, there seemed to be little time for a personal life. Like her mother, however, she was determined to combine her private and public lives. Wilson crossed the path of Alexander Turney Stewart, and together they would develop a relationship that produced great disappointment, sorrow, and tragedy for both of them.

A. T. Stewart was born in Rowan County in 1878. His ancestors came from England in the seventeenth century, and his grandfather Alexander settled in the Shenandoah Valley of Virginia. The elder Alexander eventually moved to Letcher County, Kentucky, where his son William was born. William married Polly Crank, who is said to have been from Harlan County.[12] Members of the family were strong Unionist supporters, and one descendant speculated that the family finally settled around the Morehead area about the time of the Civil War so that they might stay clear of the conflict.[13] The family confirmed their Unionist tendencies by becoming strong supporters of the Republican party after the war.

A. T. had two sisters and three brothers. His father died very early in A. T.'s life, and he was buried near Morehead. Young A. T. showed an interest in education that was nurtured and grew over the years. Like Cora Wilson, he loved to read. Later in his life he would enter the legal profession and become a lawyer. His children said that he should have been a scholar because his happiest moments were spent reading. A. T. loved to use quotations from the Bible as well as works of classical literature. His family later remembered that he would sit at the dinner table and quote for them famous passages from literature and the Bible.

A. T.'s interests did not stop with quotations, however, as he was also capable of very expressive writing. A member of his family later noted that he was able to write beautiful love letters that used eloquent language. He shared this ability with Anne Wilson. A man of strong will, conservative in temperament as well as politics, young A. T. was approximately six feet in height and was slender in build. He attended the Morehead Normal School and was an admirer of its founder, Frank Button. After attending the Morehead Normal School, A. T. began teaching in the Rowan County public schools.[14]

It is uncertain exactly when A. T. and Cora began courting. They doubtless knew each other while they were both teachers in the public schools. In any event, they met, and a romance developed during the first decade of the twentieth century. No letters exist to show what attracted the two young people, but it is easy to see how the articulate and literate young Alexander would have appealed to Cora. His familiarity with classical literature and his expressive writing must have attracted her to him. He also shared with her a devotion to education. His children would later remember that this was one of the most distinct characteristics of the man. He insisted that his children get an education, and he took it for granted that they would all attend college.

Cora Wilson would have undoubtedly appealed to the young Stewart. When they met, she was an attractive and full-figured young woman, who dressed in a neat and stylish manner. She shared a common interest in literature and the classics, and she was also an educator. The romantic nature of both of these young people must have made the match seem natural.

Cora and A. T. were married on September 24, 1902, and settled in a house on the corner of Vinton and Bishop streets in Morehead. On the marriage bond, Alexander listed his occupation as teacher; Cora did not indicate her occupation on the form. A. T. reported his age as 24, and Cora stated that she was 27 at the time of the wedding.[15]

Despite any romantic attractions that existed, troubles developed very early in the marriage. Alexander was a traditional male of the early twentieth century. Like other men of his time, he assumed that his wife would settle down and bear him a large family. He was later described as a Victorian father by one of his sons, so he also expected to be the master of his own house and to have a wife who was dependent on and obedient to him. In the mountain community of Morehead at the turn of the twentieth century, this was very much the accepted ideal for a man and his wife; Alexander doubtless assumed that his family would follow the same model.

A. T. could not have been further wrong. Cora Wilson Stewart was entirely different from any woman he had known. She had been elected superintendent of Rowan County Schools less than a year before the marriage. Since she was superintendent and A. T. was a teacher, she was essentially his superior in employment. It does not take much imagination to think how this fact must have sat with the young A. T.

The active life that Cora led meant that she was out of the home much of the time. Her community activities and her devotion to her job made her the exact opposite of the domestic wife and mother of the time. As her fame rose and she engaged in more activities, her absences increased, making the Stewart house seem less than a home in A. T.'s view.

To further complicate matters, Cora had run as a Democrat for school superintendent. Her family was active in Democratic politics, and her brother Bun was mayor of Morehead. When one recalls the devotion to the Republican party held by the Stewarts, it is easy to see how political differences would have also complicated the marriage. In any event, difficulties surfaced very early, and within a year and a half of the wedding, Cora realized the marriage was a mistake and sued for a divorce. The court accepted her petition and restored Cora to her maiden name of Wilson. The court made A. T. responsible for paying the $25 legal fee Cora had incurred, and the divorce was finalized on March 7, 1904.[16]

This relationship was obviously very complicated, and there is much that is unknown about the attraction of the two people toward each other. No one knows what transpired between March 1904 and June 1904. There must have been some feelings between the two, however, because soon after the divorce was granted, they began to consider reconciliation. This relationship finally resulted in Cora and A. T. remarrying on June 22, 1904, just three months after the granting of the original divorce decree.[17]

The remarriage was a major reason for Cora's decision not to stand for reelection as superintendent of schools. Although she said that the reason she would not run again was that she had received the offer of a better job in Lexington, she was aware of the stress that her activities had put on her marriage. In addition, as a woman with two failed marriages, she must have had concerns about the local electorate's willingness to elect a twice-divorced woman as school superintendent. In any event, she did not go to Lexington to assume the job she claimed had been offered to her. Instead, she remained in Morehead.[18]

Although Cora did not serve as school superintendent, she did little else to restrict her activities outside the home. She continued to be active in community affairs, attending club meetings, giving lectures, and writing for local newspapers. These were trying times for both A. T. and Cora. She was undergoing very conflicting feelings concerning her role in the marriage. Cora remembered her mother's idealized writings, and she doubtless thought that she should be able to combine a career with a domestic life. She knew that the traditional roles of wife and mother were expected of her, and she felt obligated to fulfill them. She also saw great opportunities outside the home, however, and she wanted to use her education and speaking skills for the benefit of the community.

For A. T.'s part, he must have been happy that his wife did not run again as superintendent of schools. He took this to mean that she would lead a more domestic lifestyle and that he could begin the family for which he longed. When Cora continued to travel, give talks, and take such an active role in community life, A. T. faced his own emotional trauma.

Like many couples with marriage difficulties, the Stewarts did not hesitate to start a family, and as with other couples, the birth of a child did not solve their problems. On August 20, 1907, Cora gave birth to a son. He was named William Halley Stewart—Halley was Anne Wilson's maiden name and William was the first name of A. T.'s father. The arrival of the child seems to have made little change in Cora's active schedule. She continued to speak publicly at various educational and social club meetings, further causing strain on the marriage.

Stirrings in Kentucky educational circles in 1907 were to have a profound impact on the state and would draw Cora back into the public school arena, thus increasing her public activity and further sealing the doom of her marriage. John Grant Crabbe, superintendent of public instruction for Kentucky, began his famous "whirlwind campaigns" to arouse public interest to the need of better schools. During short periods of time in 1908 and 1909, speakers canvassed the state on behalf of public education. Leaders of women's clubs, prominent businessmen, newspapers, and civic leaders all gave their support. Rallies and all-day picnics were held, and thousands heard the gospel of education during these feverish efforts.

The campaigns produced a continuous bombardment of educational information regarding the need for better schools. As a result of the "whirlwind campaigns," numerous improvements were made by the state legislature, including the formulation of a county school district law, a compulsory attendance law, and the establishment of a state educational commission to study the school system thoroughly.[19]

Cora Wilson Stewart became a part of this campaign, giving talks with titles such as "That Child and His Parent" to school groups in eastern Kentucky. Everywhere she spoke, she was deemed a great success, and local school administrators requested her to lecture at in-service training programs for their teachers.

As Cora's reputation grew, her personal life deteriorated, however. The health of young William Halley faltered like her marriage. Finally, on June 7, 1908, the baby died from what one news report described as "three fatal diseases."[20] The death of the child caused some local people to question if Cora had paid adequate attention to him. A few went so far as to claim that if she had taken better care of her baby instead of making so many public appearances, the child would not have died. This view was not widely held, and it was never accepted by Cora Wilson Stewart. Yet, it was held by some in the Morehead community, and it doubtless had an impact on the relationship between Cora and her husband.[21]

The death of their only child stood as a symbol of the Stewarts' marriage and marked a new low in the relationship between Cora and A. T. For her part, Cora immersed herself in public affairs. She found release in public appearances, and she saw the effect of the "whirlwind campaigns" initiated by Dr. Crabbe. She would remember his techniques and would later use similar methods in her campaigns against adult illiteracy.

A. T., on the other hand, fell deeper into gloom as he saw the prospects for a large family die with his son. At the same time, he observed his wife's fame increasing as his prospects dimmed. To relieve stress, he turned to alcohol, refused to work, and ultimately wrote the death warrant for his marriage. For her part, Cora truly did not comprehend what was happening to their relationship. Either she could not accept that her approach to the marriage was not working or she refused to change to meet the needs of her husband. In any event, the situation deteriorated to the point that A. T. berated her publicly in front of friends and acquaintances and tried to be a domestic bully, ordering her about and refusing to support the couple.

With the advent of the "whirlwind campaigns," Cora saw a bright future for educational opportunities in Morehead. Wanting to return to the superintendency of the Rowan County Schools, she sought and received the Democratic nomination for the office in 1909. While this decision was truly the final straw that broke the back of the marriage, it is easy to understand why she decided to run for the office. Her husband was not working, and she was forced to support both of them. In addition, she saw that her future in education was bright; she was becoming a fashionable and much sought-after speaker in the school systems surrounding Rowan County. Whatever her feelings for her husband, she was not willing to sacrifice her abilities for a relationship that seemed hopeless. She also believed that she was acting much as her mother had, working outside the home as well as being a wife and mother. A. T.'s abusive behavior and use of alcohol was completely puzzling to her.

Cora fought vigorously for the post of Rowan school superintendent. Her opponent was Lyda Messer, who had earlier been her protégée. Local news articles described Cora's earlier accomplishments as superintendent and commented on her growing fame as a public speaker. Her campaign literature noted:

> The Good Lord endowed her with an extra share of good common sense, and filled her heart full of love for her fellow-beings and gave her plenty of brains and the result of such a combination is a gifted and useful woman. If she possesses any trait that is more noticeable than another, it is her FRIENDLY manner. Everyday in the year you will find her just the same—with a kindly word and a pleasant smile for all. No little boy or girl is ever too ragged for her to pat them on the head and speak to them a word of encouragement. She is a woman who loves the people and loves to serve them, and is one in whom there is not one whit of foolish pride or selfishness.[22]

For her part, Messer used the unusual tactic of claiming that she needed the job as superintendent to support her family. Messer's strategy shows the political tactics of the time as well as the apparently low esteem in which the position of school superintendent was held. Ultimately, Cora Wilson Stewart was successful in her bid for the office. She won a resounding victory in November 1909 and returned again to the office of superintendent of Rowan County Schools.[23]

Cora's political victory was tempered greatly by the tragic domestic situation she faced. The more she tried to bury herself in work and public activities, the further it drove A. T. toward the edge. The breaking point was finally reached on March 21, 1910, when Cora's sister, Stella McGlone, was staying overnight with her. According to sworn court depositions, at midnight A. T. came home in a drunken state and tried to kick in the door to the room in which the two sisters were sleeping. Cora opened the door to let him in, and he said, "I've come now to blow you up." He violently cursed Cora, told her that he detested her, and again threatened to kill her.

While A. T. searched for a gun, Cora sent Stella to get help. Stella fled to the nearby apartment of Mr. and Mrs. C. C. Nichols. Mr. Nichols went to the Stewart home, while Stella ran to the home of C. L. Clayton and asked him to call the town marshal. Left alone with her husband, Cora pleaded with A. T. for her life. He pointed the gun at her and threatened to kill her on at least six different occasions. When the gun was later examined, it was found that the cap of one of the unfired cartridges in the chambers showed the indention of the pistol's hammer. Apparently, he had pulled the trigger at some point while threatening her, and the gun had misfired.

The police arrived and took A. T. away, and Cora filed for a restraining order against her husband. Court depositions reveal that the March 21 incident was only the most recent in a pattern of domestic abuse going back more than a year. She further charged that A. T. had not supported her in four years and that he refused to work. These claims were verified by friends and relatives who lived in the neighborhood and had firsthand knowledge of the relationship.[24]

Ultimately, Cora was granted a divorce from A. T. on June 8, 1910. The divorce decree noted that the judgment was given against A. T. Stewart because of a "confirmed habit of drunkenness of not less than one year's duration, accompanied by a wasting of his estate without any suitable provision for the maintenance of the plaintiff."[25]

This divorce decree was the final unhappy chapter in the marriage of Cora Wilson and A. T. Stewart; there would be no reconciliation this time. For his part, A. T. soon moved to Stanton, Kentucky. He attended Bowling Green Law School, became a lawyer, and remarried in 1915. He gave up the drinking habits he had while married to Cora, and achieved his goal of having a large family. He fathered six children by his second wife, Clemma Lacy. To his satisfaction, all of them earned college degrees. A. T. continued his love of the classics. Always more of a scholar than a trial lawyer, his happiest times were spent sitting in his law office and reading. His children grew up knowing little or nothing about his life with Cora Wilson Stewart, and he went to his grave in 1956 keeping secret his feelings toward the woman he had married as a young man at the turn of the century.[26]

For Cora's part, the divorce was the most traumatic point in her life. At age thirty-five, she had experienced three failed marriages, something almost unheard of in the early twentieth century. Her most recent husband had tried to kill her after abusing her for more than a year. She knew that she had done nothing to deserve such treatment. Yet, like many victims of such abuse, she sometimes questioned her role in the relationship, and it would be nearly two full years before she would come to grips with the events of her marriage. To occupy her mind and to relieve the stress of her failed personal life, she continued the pattern she had followed in the past: she immersed herself in work and took on more public activities than ever before. She wrote articles for newspapers, gave speeches, and worked to gain public acclaim as the best superintendent of schools Rowan County had known.

Public acclaim came to replace the personal success Cora Stewart was unable to know as a wife and mother. In the future, this would be her solution, as she repeatedly replaced her private life with her work. The trauma of her personal life also encouraged her to find public outlets that avoided controversy and would not threaten her personally. These were comfortable accommodations for her. Public relationships were always more formal, more easily controlled, and personally less dangerous than private relationships. Eventually, she learned to give of herself for public good while withholding her personal emotions; in this way, she was able to avoid further personal tragedies.

The public acclaim Cora Wilson Stewart sought came often and in large quantity. Soon after the divorce, she began giving a lecture entitled "The Mountain Girl," in which she extolled the virtues of the female youth of the hills. Always a popular topic, the speech was presented throughout Kentucky. No group was too small; she spoke before church groups, civic clubs, and educational organizations.[27]

The support and recognition she received were an inspiration to Stewart, and provided her with the solace that she needed. Audiences recognized her abilities, and they encouraged her to continue. After hearing her give the "Mountain Girl" speech, one fellow educator noted: "We have a vision of a future for you, your trained mind and powers are now ready for the glory of God. Nor will he or your friends be disappointed in you. So go with PRAYER and CONFIDENCE for your success AND YOU WILL HAVE IT."[28]

On another occasion, D. F. Gray, superintendent of Elliott County Schools, praised Stewart after a particularly effective speech:

> Nothing you said gave me greater pleasure than your statement that the remainder of your life would be devoted to the cause of education. I have been informed that you intend to make the race for State Superintendent. I think it would be real nice to have one of our own home county girls as the head of the educational affairs of our state, and I hope you will not hesitate to take advantage of any opportunity that may come your way.[29]

Despite public acclaim, however, Stewart needed time to work out her emotions and to develop a philosophical accommodation to her failed private life. At times she felt compelled to speak to associates about her doubts and feelings of personal loss. These confessions often surprised the people who knew her professionally but were not aware of her personal turmoil.

On one such occasion, Stewart confided her private woes in a letter to the Fleming County school superintendent, Lutie Palmer, who responded:

> Your letter came as a surprise to me. I feel that you must have found in me something of good or you would not have spoken so freely to me of the matters that must be so closely *[sic]* to your heart. Events of the same character [divorce] have been very closely connected with my own family in touch with my own life. I have for you a great sympathy because I feel that at times this great shadow must come to you. You know it is hard to keep friends with ourselves sometimes and I'm sure that many beautiful thoughts are lost in the shadows, many hours blighted that should have been happy ones. You yourself have been brave enough to tell me, a stranger, of these things of your past. You have my admiration for your earnest striving among your own people. Let no mournful yesterday disturb thy peaceful heart. Nor let tomorrow spoil thy rest with thoughts of coming ill.[30]

Of all Stewart's confidants, none was more supportive or more influential that Mattie Dalton, secretary to the editor of the *Southern School Journal* in Lexington. The *Journal* was the official publication of the Kentucky Education Association and the Kentucky State Board of Education. Stewart had met Dalton when she began contributing to the magazine.

The two women soon struck up a lively correspondence, and Stewart found in Mattie Dalton a woman of uncommon humor and common sense, who lent moral support to her as she worked out her personal problems. Like others, Dalton was at first surprised when Stewart unexpectedly told her about her failed marriage.

After Stewart first disclosed her feelings regarding her personal life, Dalton said:

> Honestly, I did not INTEND to inspect your naked soul. I had asked the question and knew the answer before I realized that I was intruding where I had no right. There are some things, my dear woman, which we cannot afford to do—not because of the anathema of the crowd who would never understand or admit it if they did—but because of the effect on our own souls, or rather I will say because of the psychological effect on self. I have known for something more than three months that you were coming to me for some reason—but what I did not know. I have been expecting you, I know that, and not without a little misgiving, since I did not know you personally at all, and the opinion of other people does not always meet my approbation. I do not know why we are being pulled together by seeming chance, but "There's a reason," as the Postum people would say. I am now of the opinion that one or two of us may be in need of the

quieting influence of sub-conscious association and the result will be qui-
etly and almost unconsciously worked out in the sleeping hours.[31]

Dalton urged Stewart to get in touch with her subconscious to find out
what she was to do in life. While speaking of a night when the two of them
had shared a room together, she said, "I knew you were lying on your back,
staring with wide-opened eyes, trying to get a mental glimpse of the THING,
whatever it is, which shall serve you. I knew you felt 'spooky'—because I
did."[32]

Going on to encourage Stewart to find her role in life, Dalton offered this
advice: "Get used to the idea of aloneness. You have been trying all your life to
LEAN, as Society expected you to do, on props not strong enough for their
OWN support; but after all we must be strong in ourselves, and possibly we
must be sufficient unto ourselves."[33]

When Stewart asked Dalton about her views of marriage, the latter offered
the following observations:

> I think about seven out of ten marriages, looked at from my point of
> view, are little more than legalized prostitution; and the realization that
> such is the case is the cause of the numerous divorces of today. Women
> are thinking a little more and in consequence they value themselves more
> highly than they used to do, when they placidly accepted the valuation
> of their men-folk as being correct.[34]

Regarding divorce, Dalton encouraged Stewart to take a pragmatic view:

> Time was when the idea of divorce horrified me—I was young! when-
> ever man or woman have tried and tried and find it impossible to live
> with another and maintain his or her self-respect and soul integrity then,
> when they shake off the shackles and assume the burden of life alone and
> unhampered, I am thankful. It is right; it is good.[35]

These were indeed comforting words for Cora Wilson Stewart. She found
in Mattie Dalton a woman who had very decided opinions and was on her side.
Dalton spoke her mind and helped Stewart deal with the personal doubts that
haunted her. At a time when Stewart felt she had failed to live up to the prevailing views of society regarding marriage, Dalton's advice was a rescue line
cast out to her. The two women carried on an active correspondence for two
years. During this time, Dalton served as a sounding board for Stewart and gave
her someone to whom she could communicate her feelings.

Dalton was always supportive, and she was ready with advice on almost
any subject. She admired Stewart's talents and encouraged her to be strong in
facing the barbs of society so that she might reach her full potential in life.
After a letter in which Cora had again expressed her doubts about her past
actions and questioned if God ever intended for her to marry, Dalton offered
these observations:

Perhaps you are stronger or sweeter because of your troubles—but for God's sake, Cora, for the work that you ought to do and can do in this world, stop crucifying your soul because of those besotted fools and get married if you find the right man, irrespective of their too-long delayed demise. Say what you please, but I can never believe God is either a fool or cruel. That you or any blameless woman should suffer unnecessarily because of the mistakes of a blind age, is not God-Like to my mind.[36]

To deal with public reaction to her failed marriages, Dalton advised Stewart to develop a strength that was not dependent on the opinions of others. In this regard, she counseled: "Convince yourself that it really doesn't matter—for it doesn't! Let no man, woman or child be hopelessly damned because of a mistake. Cancel personal relations which are not for your mental and especially soul-good. There is no failure until you have failed yourself—so long as you keep hold on self, you are strong."[37]

Guided by Dalton's advice, Stewart became convinced that God had a plan for her. She knew that she had gifts that were praised by her fellow educators. Public acclaim took the place of close personal relationships that carried the risk of rejection, physical and emotional abuse, and heartache. It was not easy for her to reconcile her mother's view of "A True Woman's Love" with this new vision, but practical experience had taught her that personal relationships, with men at least, were not worth the pain and sorrow. Instead, she concentrated on the public side of life and treasured the acclaim given her in this arena. Eventually, she came to accept that the roles of wife and mother were not to be her lot. Instead, she grew to believe that God had called her for service to others; public service would replace the personal side of her life.

Stewart's puzzlement at what had happened in her marriage to A. T. would continue well into the future, and she sought continued assurance that the failure of her marriages had not been her fault. As late as 1923, she would save a clipping from the *New York Tribune* in which a religious columnist from the Federated Council of Churches wrote that any woman who was involved in a relationship with an abusive alcoholic "deserves immediate release. Surely she ought not to have to be prevented from securing her independence if she desires."[38] Cora Wilson Stewart had sought and won independence from her abusive marriage. In the future, she made certain that she would never let herself be hurt in this way again.

3

$\mathcal{B}$EGINNINGS IN THE $\mathcal{M}$OONLIGHT

Cora Wilson Stewart's reputation as a school institute speaker grew after her divorce from A. T. Stewart, and she used her speaking engagements to develop a network of supporters that would help her in future years. Her institute topics included "Should Agriculture and Domestic Science Be Taught in the Public School" and "The County Superintendent as a Factor in Our Educational Scheme." Besides the useful contacts she established, the money she earned provided her with a source of much-needed income to supplement her meager salary as superintendent of the Rowan County Schools.

As in the past, Stewart not only spoke at educational meetings, she also addressed a variety of civic and church meetings, including the state Christian Women's Board of Missions convention in Louisville in 1910. Her talks were always about the mountain people, and she honed her oratorical skills to the point that the Louisville *Courier Journal* praised her elocution, delivery and topic when she presented her talk entitled "The High Country."[1]

It was as superintendent of Rowan County Schools, however, that Mrs. Stewart had her greatest impact. A strong proponent of vocational education, she insisted that such training be part of the curriculum. She knew that the mountain youth needed skills to get jobs in the growing economy. Although she admired a classic liberal education, she was pragmatic in her approach to the education of the mountain schoolchildren. Her efforts to secure training expertise for her students went far beyond the surrounding hills. She contacted Edward H. Reisner, secretary of the National Society for the Promotion of Industrial Education, and sought his advice on the best means of educating the mountain youth. She even contemplated the possibility of sending students to cities for training, but she was encouraged by Reisner to provide the training in Morehead.[2]

Stewart knew that such training could not be accomplished on the meager school budget available in Rowan County. She pursued funding from John D. Rockefeller and discussed with Reisner the best means of approaching the wealthy oil magnate. She also sought advice on vocational training from the

University of Kentucky Department of Agronomy. George Roberts, professor of agronomy, agreed to help her set up clubs for male students to learn how to grow crops effectively. With his help, she organized corn clubs in which students competed to see who could raise the most corn. Vocational training was provided to both boys and girls. Girls learned canning and had poultry clubs in which they were taught improved ways to raise chickens.

Training was not limited to farm work, as boys were taught to use local timber to make wooden bookcases, picture frames, and furniture. When necessary, they even helped with the maintenance of the county schools. She counseled with Dr. D. C. Smith, a horticulturist at Eastern Kentucky State Normal School in Richmond, concerning alternative crops for the area. Dr. Smith recommended that local students be taught to grow fruit trees after he observed that the Rowan County soil was just right for this purpose. Following his advice, Stewart organized fruit clubs for the male students.[3]

All of these efforts paid dividends, as the county youth developed new enthusiasm for the schools. The practicality of the education provided under Stewart's leadership was evident to all. As a result, a new interest was kindled among parents as well as students. This spirit did not go unnoticed. Dr. Roberts, after visiting an agricultural fair in Rowan, wrote to Stewart: "I must say that the demonstration I saw in your county last Monday is unique in my experience in traveling over the State. It shows what I always stated that the mountain people may be counted upon to respond to any good movement when once they have seen that it is really worthwhile and will better their condition."[4]

Stewart's devotion and charisma were the primary reasons for this interest. The mountain people followed her, and they knew that she had their well-being at heart. A natural leader, she worked nonstop for the betterment of the public schools. This leadership was also recognized by the teachers in the county. Stewart sparked a new sense of purpose and pride in their work. This enthusiasm was displayed daily as they sought to involve all eligible students in the schools. As one source noted, "Whether single or married, if they are of school age, there is no chance for them to escape school."[5]

Teacher loyalty was to prove essential when Stewart began her work with adults. She convinced local educators that the success of the school system would be assured if they could get parents involved in the education of their children. She knew that agricultural fairs and other social events held at the schools were a good means of building this much-needed support. As a result of her efforts, by mid–1911, the local population was alert to the needs of the schools and was awakening to the advantages that a good educational system could provide. Such conditions would provide the springboard for the illiteracy movement that Cora Wilson Stewart was about to launch.

News of Cora Wilson Stewart's success in Rowan County spread across the state. She often received correspondence from teachers, principals, and superintendents applauding her work. R. S. Eubank, editor of the *Southern School Journal*, voiced the view of many when he wrote to her, "I think the spirit manifested by your people is indication of the fact that they are willing to follow your suggestions and I believe you will be glad that you were called to head educational affairs in Rowan at this time."[6]

Public acclaim from her peers led Stewart to consider running for the presidency of the Kentucky Education Association. She was encouraged by the insightful Mattie Dalton, who kept her informed about educational politics in the state. In addition to passing on educational news from her position as secretary to R. S. Eubank, Dalton regularly encouraged Stewart to seek state-level leadership roles.

Many of Stewart's boosters were women who believed that it was time for a female to lead the state educational association. For instance, M. O. Winfrey, superintendent of Middlesborough School wrote to her, "I am glad that you have awakened to the fact that there is a crying need for a WOMAN at the head of the K.E.A. who is EQUAL TO THE OCCASION and WHO CAN PRESIDE. You are that woman, and there will never be a happier moment in all the born days of my life than the moment in which I nominate you for that office."[7] Reinforcing this opinion, Dalton told her, "Now the folks who wish you to run for President and be elected wish it because they know you would be the PRESIDENT OF THE K.E.A. when on duty in that capacity, irrespective of your political preference. This year, in particular, it seems desirable to eliminate political notions as much as possible in the K.E.A. line-up."[8]

Part of Stewart's reluctance to run for the K.E.A. presidency arose from a fear that her domestic misfortunes would become a campaign issue. She dreaded the thought that her three failed marriages might be discussed in public. Despite her reservations, however, she finally overcame this concern and sought the office. Stewart had developed her network of supporters since she became the first woman to be elected county superintendent in eastern Kentucky. She had often campaigned for women candidates for school superintendent, and she was finally rewarded by being elected the first woman president of the Kentucky Education Association on June 29, 1911.

Stewart's victory was hailed by female educators throughout the state. Jessie O. Yancey, superintendent of the Maysville schools, noted: "Your election was a victory for all of us [women]. I never heard your domestic troubles referred to."[9] Another supporter noted, "I want to congratulate you on being elected President of the K.E.A. I feel that 'OLD ROWAN COUNTY' is not coming to the front it is ALREADY in the LEAD."[10] J. H. Booth of the Eastern Kentucky State Normal School wrote to her, "You have now accomplished one of the objects of your life's ambition, an honor that comes to but few—you are the first woman to receive it."[11] Speaking euphemistically, Everett L. Dix wrote from Richmond: "Please accept my sincerest congratulations on your election as president of the K.E.A. We are sure you are 'the man for the place.'"[12] After learning of Stewart's election, leading Kentucky female rights proponent Madeline Breckinridge wrote to enlist her support in the broader cause of women's suffrage, saying, "Don't you want to help me by having your teachers distribute school suffrage leaflets for me?"[13] Mrs. Stewart was indeed support-ive of the franchise for women, but she was not a rabid proponent of women's rights. Her skill at earning respect from men as well as women was a major rea-son she was elected; she was genuinely respected by both sexes. Proof of this ability was voiced by Edgar C. Riley, superintendent of the Boone County Schools, when he wrote to her:

> Again, let me suggest that you get away from the idea that what you do you shall accomplish for your sex. I believe that you bring that element less into your work than other women. I praise you for it. I feel that you understand me when I say that too many women in public are always holding before themselves that they are doing something to make the peo-ple recognize woman is coming to her own. I believe that I am for woman suffrage, but I am telling you the way to bring it about. I am sure that some women in their zeal are the worst enemies of the movement.[14]

Riley did not have to worry about Cora Wilson Stewart. She favored women's suffrage, but she had attained her success locally and on the state level without alienating male supporters. She was comfortable in the working world of men and held herself to the same level as her male counterparts. From this perspective, she should be viewed as a moderate "feminist" of the time.

Cora Wilson Stewart also differed from other female Progressive reform-ers in other ways. Her focus was on the mountain people of her time, unlike the urban reformers of the day. She saw an inherent dignity in the people she championed because she was one of these people. She had grown up in the mountains, and she knew firsthand the lifestyle of the mountaineers. Her dra-matic nature and her eloquence made her a natural champion for the moun-taineers. Because of her education and privileged background in comparison to most Rowan County residents, she was also accepted in more formal society. Thus she was able to bridge the gap between the educated and the uneducated.

Stewart's ability to fit into both worlds proved to be a great asset for her. She romanticized the lifestyle and potential of her mountain neighbors at a time when outsiders disparaged them. They loved her because she gave voice to their virtues as well as their needs. Stewart expressed these ideas in language that eastern Kentuckians understood—the oratory of the religious revivalists of the time. In a manner similar to articulate black activists of a later day, like Mar-tin Luther King and Jesse Jackson, she was able to instill pride in her people with noble words. She also had an abiding faith in the power of education, and she was becoming a powerful public figure. She had substituted public acclaim for private satisfaction, and by 1911 she was prepared to begin the movement that was ultimately to bring her international attention.

It was the Moonlight Schools that brought Cora Wilson Stewart to the attention of the nation. The name is symbolic of the woman who started them. The term sounds romantic, and the schools reflected characteristics that their founder admired. They were heroic, they were practical, they were idealistic, and, most of all, they were a great popular success.

Cora Wilson Stewart claimed that three separate incidents gave her the inspiration for the Moonlight Schools. Each occasion concerned a mountaineer with a thirst for knowledge. The first circumstance involved Mollie McGlothin, an illiterate mountain woman, bent with age, who came into her office one morning with a letter from her daughter who had moved to Chicago. The daughter's letters were a bright spot in the life of the old woman, who often went to the home of a neighbor to have the letters read to her.

Occasionally, Mollie would come to Cora Wilson Stewart to get her to read a letter. On this particular day, Stewart, noticing the letter in the hand of the old woman, assumed that she had again come to have a letter read. When she asked Mollie if she wanted her to read the new letter, old Mollie responded, "No, I have learned to read and write, and am going to answer it myself."

When questioned about this matter, Mollie responded that she had found that neighbors were often too busy to read to her, so she had gone to the store and bought a speller. She stayed up at night until midnight and sometimes until daylight until she had learned to spell, to read, and to write. As evidence of her accomplishment, she sat down and wrote her first letter to her daughter Jane.

In Stewart's words, this was "an achievement that pleased her immeasurably, and which must have pleased the absent Jane even more."[15]

The second incident that inspired Stewart to develop the Moonlight Schools involved a mountain man. Several months after her encounter with Mollie McGlothin, this man came to the superintendent's office. While he was waiting for her, she noticed that he was looking at some books. Knowing firsthand the lack of reading material in the county, she offered to loan the man a book. According to Stewart, he replied with tears in his eyes: "No, I cannot read or write. I would give twenty years of my life if I could."

A short time after this incident, a six-foot tall mountain lad of twenty-one years stepped out and sang a tender ballad with enthusiasm at a school function. Upon hearing the strength and power of the song, Stewart asked the young man for a copy of the song and told him it was worth publishing. He answered sadly that he had thought up hundreds of such songs, but was unable to write down a single one because he could neither write nor read.[16]

These three individuals, according to Cora Wilson Stewart, provided the inspiration for her life's work. In them, she found the meaning for a cause that offered her the romanticism and challenge that she needed in her life. With the problem of adult illiteracy, she met an issue that appealed to her nature. It was a cause with which she could identify. It was a challenge that needed a champion, and it dealt with her people.

Stewart later noted that the three incidents combined the world of art, business, and motherhood for her. She wrote:

I interpreted them to be not merely the calls of the individuals, but a call of the different classes; the appeal of illiterate mothers, separated from their absent children farther than sea or land or any other condition than death had power to divide them; the call of the middle-aged men, shut out from the world of books, and unable to read the *Bible* or the newspapers or to cast their votes in secrecy and security; the call of illiterate youths and maidens who possessed rare talents, which if developed might add treasures to the world of art, science, literature, and invention.[17]

If any statistical justification was needed for such work, one need look no further than the 1910 Census. The U.S. Census showed that there were 5,516,163 illiterates in the United States—7.7% of the population. These figures might not seem particularly high until one remembers that a person was considered illiterate if he could not write his name in any language. This rudimentary definition meant that the actual number of people who did not have literacy skills adequate to function in society was much higher.

In Kentucky the situation was even worse than the national average. According to the Census Bureau's simple test, Kentucky had 108,084 adult illiterates, representing 12.1% of the state's population. The Bluegrass State ranked 37th among the 48 states in literacy. The state had more illiterates than the states of Wyoming, Idaho, Utah, Nevada, North Dakota, South Dakota, Washington, Oregon, Iowa, Kansas, and Nebraska combined. In terms of Negro illiteracy, Kentucky ranked 7th from the bottom among the 48 states. Among whites, the state placed 5th from the bottom.[18]

In Rowan County, 1,152 people (18% of the population) were listed as illiterate in the 1910 census. Considering the mountainous nature of the county, the travel limitations of the time, and the reluctance of the mountain people to talk with federal officials of any type, the actual number of illiterates in the county was doubtless larger.[19]

Local residents recognized the need for better reading and writing skills as the county became more commercial. The population became more mobile, families were separated, and written communication was necessary to keep in touch with relatives who had moved to other areas. The days when a person could live in isolation, tending a few acres of land and seldom coming in contact with neighbors, were vanishing. A new commercial world requiring reading and writing skills was at hand, and people saw the need to meet the changes of the future.

With these facts in mind, Cora Wilson Stewart recognized that she had discovered a problem that appealed to her spirit and crusading nature. She became determined to help the less fortunate citizens of Rowan County gain the basic literacy skills they needed. Having found her cause, she still had to convince others that this battle was worth fighting, however. Naturally, she first turned to the public schools, her greatest source of power. She thought that perhaps the public schools could be opened for adult illiterates to get an education. These buildings were already in use by children during the daytime, however, and there was not time for the adults to attend during daylight hours. With this situation in mind, she conceived the idea of opening the public schools during the evening hours. As a resident of Rowan County, however, she knew that many people remembered the feuds that had torn the county apart in the 1800s. These individuals were leery of venturing out at night because of the threat of violence. The answer, she thought, was to hold the schools initially on moonlit nights. Thus reluctant students could have the light of the moon to show their way to class.

Having chosen the time to hold the schools, Stewart still had to find instructors. Here she turned to the teachers of the county. The teachers were her strongest supporters, but she did not know if they would be willing to give up their evenings to teach adults after they had dealt with children during the daytime. She decided to appeal to their basic self-interest: she told them that teaching the parents would encourage interest in the public schools. If parents were interested in the schools, they would see that the children attended during the day, and they would support the county schools. With this inducement, the teachers volunteered without exception to teach the night schools.[20]

Stewart decided to offer classes for eight weeks. Only the most elementary of lessons would be offered, and the first concern would be given to teaching people to write their own names. Her plans were modest but not insignificant because many Rowan County residents signed their names with a mark. The mark, however, was becoming a sign of shame with the growing interest in public education, and it was thought that many people might come to learn to write their own names.

After planning the opening of the first night schools, Stewart sent the teachers of the county to canvass their districts on Labor Day, September 4, 1911. They went to each home in the district and invited the residents to school the next evening. After the completion of the canvass, Cora Wilson Stewart wondered if the adults would respond. She reasoned that her plan would be a success if an average of three pupils came to each school. With fifty schools in the Rowan County, one hundred fifty students would be needed to reach this goal.

On September 5, the schools opened on what Cora Wilson Stewart later called "the brightest moonlight night, it seemed to me, that the world had ever known."[21] The teachers also waited and wondered if the adults would come. To the surprise and joy of all, the people responded in droves. More than 1200 men and women were enrolled the first evening. They came from all parts of the county, and they came from all walks of life.

Stewart later noted:

> They came singly or hurrying in groups, they came walking for miles, they came carrying babes in arms, they came bent with age and leaning on canes, they came twelve hundred strong! There were overgrown boys

Ollie Kiser's Moonlight School in Munson, Rowan County.

who had dropped out of school at an early age and had been ashamed to re-enter the day school and be classified with the tiny tots. These came to catch up again. There were maidens who had been deprived of education, through isolation, invalidism or some other cause, but who felt that there was something better for them in life than ignorance. There were women who had married in childhood, practically, as is so much the wont of mountain girls—but who all their lives had craved that which they knew to be their inherent right—their mental development. By their sides were their husbands, men who had been humiliated when they had made their mark in the presence of the educated and when forced to ask election officers to cast a vote of them for the candidate of their choice. There were middle-aged men who had seen a hundred golden opportunities pass them by because of the handicap of illiteracy, whose mineral, timber and material stores, as well as their time and labor, were in the control of the educated men, making them but beggars, as it were, on the bounty of those whom they enriched. There were women whose children had grown up and vanished from the home, some of them into the far West, and when the spoken word and the hand-clasp had ceased there could be no heart-to-heart communication, for the third person as an interpreter between mother and child is but a poor medium at best. These and other folk—some half-educated and some more—made up these schools. The students ranged in age from eighteen to eighty-six years old. Side by side, they sat in the seats that were occupied by the youth during the daytime. Many of them learned to write their names the first evening and rejoiced at having overcome the need to make their mark. Others asked for the skills necessary to read the Bible.[22]

To teach reading, Stewart insisted that the adults should not have to use texts designed for children. She thought children's readers would be demeaning to the adults, and she prepared a newspaper as a text. Entitled the *Rowan County Messenger*, the paper was filled with simple news about the county. Fulfilling a dual purpose, it was also designed to challenge residents to match the progress being made in other districts of the county. The newspaper contained simple sentences that could be easily memorized. In the parlance of the current day, it can be said that Stewart used the "whole-word approach" to teaching reading. Her major emphasis was to interest adults in the process of reading. The best means of achieving this goal, she thought, was to insure their success by giving them sentences that they could easily learn. Lessons in more sophisticated levels of reading would be left for later. In her opinion, the essential point was to get the adults into the classroom and to give them a sense of success.

To teach writing, Stewart provided grooved pads on which students could trace letters until they learned how to make them on their own. These pads contained all the letters of the alphabet. After the students mastered the grooved pad, they were encouraged to write a letter to Stewart telling her something about themselves. These letters were expected to provide a sense of accomplishment for the students. For each letter received, Stewart sent the writer a small Bible as a reward.

During the initial series of lessons, classes were held from six to eight each Monday through Thursday evening and were attended by both illiterates and semiliterates. Although elementary lessons were taught in numerous subjects, including history, civics, and health, the main goal was to teach adult illiterates to read and write, and the students did not receive a complete primary education.

Stewart spent the eight-week school session visiting the various schools and offering encouragement to participants. She would arrive at the opening session to greet and encourage the adult pupils; then she would ride on horseback to another school to get there by closing time so she could applaud the work of the students. Her travels were often risky. Riding by horseback at night in the mountains as she did was a hazardous proposition. A wrong step by her mount could mean that she might fall down the mountainside in a deserted area with no help available.[23]

Stewart's activities were so demanding that she was often exhausted, and her family worried that her health would be permanently damaged. One of her brothers wrote: "My sister is killing herself. She performs duties during the day then rides until two o'clock at night keeping the teachers and pupils in the 'Moonlight Schools' in good spirits and leading the fight on illiteracy."[24] Stewart was willing to risk her health for her work because the schools confirmed her belief that the mountain people would respond to education if given a chance.

News of the success of the Moonlight Schools soon spread to other counties. George W. Chapman, superintendent of the Paris Public Schools, noted:

Moonlight School at Open Fork, Rowan County, Kentucky.

"What a great thing for Kentucky it would be if every county in the State would do as you have done and you have demonstrated that it can be done!"[25] E. C. McDougle of the State Normal school at Richmond wrote: "I'm indeed proud of you. That Rowan County idea will surely spread."[26]

Most Kentuckians correctly believed that Stewart's work was novel and innovative because it focused on adult illiterates, but many others wrongly assumed that the schools were the first night classes organized in the United States. In reality, evening courses for educated adults had been an established feature in most northeastern states since before 1900.[27] Although Stewart did not copy the procedures of the northern night schools, she was doubtless aware of their existence.

Information about the Moonlight Schools was spread outside her home state when Stewart addressed the Southern Education Association in Houston, Texas, on December 1, 1911. She had been asked to speak before the start of the Moonlight Schools, so her remarks were on the topic of "The Education of the Mountain Child." Her talk was similar to others she had offered about the virtues of the unspoiled mountain child. She described how the children of the mountains were inherently imbued with characteristics such as honesty, pride, originality, ambition, reverence for God, a poetical nature, and oratorical prowess. The youth of the mountains, according to Stewart, were also blessed with a desire for knowledge. She went on to note that natural geographic barriers had long kept mountain children from getting the educational opportunities that

Moonlight School teachers out scouting for students.

were due them. Changes in the mountains, however, were now opening the
outside world for the mountain child, who stood on the brink of a new age.
Now the mountain youths were ready for the instruction so long denied them.
These educational opportunities should involve vocational training, according
to Stewart. She noted that vocational skills were needed so that the mountain
youth could develop their community into an effective economic environment.
Once such training was provided, she said, the mountaineers would move on
to higher educational levels.

Stewart's remarks also indicated that the adults of the area needed at least
the rudiments of an education, and she used this observation to segue into a
description of the Moonlight Schools. Stewart told the story of how she was
inspired to start the schools. She described how the classes were organized and
related the achievements of the first year. She even read some of the letters from
her students who had written to her after finishing their first eight-week session.[28]

In addressing the Southern Education Association, Stewart was talking
with the largest group of public school educators in the South; their response
was encouraging. The group was so impressed by her speech that it endorsed
the Moonlight Schools as the most practical plan for abolishing illiteracy in
the South. Representatives from other states were interested in her story, and
many of them asked her to speak before their state educational associations.

Not all the responses to the Moonlight Schools were positive, however. At
the time, it was conventional wisdom that older adults were incapable of learning once they passed a certain age. The prevailing view was accepted in much

of the academic community and was sanctioned at the University of Kentucky as well. Early on, academicians doubted the effectiveness of the schools and questioned the results. Skepticism among college and university professors was a contentious point for Cora Wilson Stewart, and she always enjoyed showing the college and university professors that they were wrong about this issue. Despite the misgivings of the university community, the success of the first year of Moonlight Schools and the growing interest throughout the South made Cora Wilson Stewart a happy woman. The letters she received from the students of the Moonlight Schools gave her great personal satisfaction, and she saved many of them for posterity. She had found a work worthy of her talents, and the challenge of teaching adults appealed to her nature. It was a daunting task, but she made progress and received praise from her colleagues as well as the students. Putting her personal problems behind her, she focused on the task that would ultimately absorb her life for the next two decades.

4

MOONLIGHT
SCHOOLS SPREAD

The first session of Moonlight Schools had a profound influence on all facets of the Rowan County public schools. One school trustee noted:

> I have lived in this district for fifty-five years and never saw any such interest as we have here now. The school used to drag along and nobody seemed interested. We never had a gathering at the school and nobody thought of visiting it. We had night school but three weeks until we began improvements. We papered the houses, put in new windows, purchased new stovepipe, made new steps, contributed money and bought winter's fuel.[1]

Other school superintendents in Kentucky wanted to know how they could implement Moonlight Schools. Enthusiasm for the schools crossed state lines as well. During early 1912, Stewart spoke to the state educational associations of Alabama, Arkansas, Virginia, and South Carolina. Couching her arguments in eloquent language and arming herself with statistics from the 1910 census, she convinced many teachers of the plight of Southern illiterates. One Alabama educator observed, "I feel sure that the things you have done, which were so beautifully told to us, will prove an inspiration to many an Alabama teacher. Your visit will be long remembered by us."[2]

The news media quickly picked up on the human interest side of the story. Pictures of the students at the schools were published in state and national newspapers and magazines, including the popular *Literary Digest*. Editors of educational journals such as the *Normal Instructor* and *The Progressive Teacher* sought articles from Stewart concerning the Moonlight Schools. These stories inevitably included pictures of the classes and focused on the oldest students.

The success of the first session of the Moonlight Schools also caught the attention of the U.S. Department of the Interior Bureau of Education. Bureau chief P. P. Claxton asked Stewart for her advice on the best means of reaching and teaching adult illiterates. The Bureau's interest would continue in the future as Stewart ultimately became the leading spokesperson concerning adult illiteracy in the United States.[3]

In early April 1912, Stewart again received regional acclaim when she spoke at the National Conference on Education in the South meeting in Nashville, Tennessee. As before, she captivated her audience with the story of the Moonlight Schools. Here she also met educators from across the South, and she began a correspondence with several of them concerning the schools. R. H. Wilson, superintendent of public instruction in Oklahoma and himself a former Kentucky school superintendent, expressed the thoughts of many when he wrote to her: "I appreciate your address very much and I feel that it had a wonderful impact on the audience and that the good you have done in your county is an example of what others may do and will do, and by this act of yours you have placed your name in history."[4]

Because of her growing reputation, Stewart received several job offers that might have lured her from the illiteracy work. Superintendent of Schools Barksdale Hamlett offered her the post of state school supervisor for Kentucky, and she even discussed the possibility of moving to Alabama to work in that state's school office. She took none of these possibilities seriously, however, as she thought her first obligation was to Rowan County.

Besides her work with illiterates, Stewart gained experience in the workings of Kentucky educational politics as president of the K.E.A. She was not a supporter of State Superintendent of Schools Barksdale Hamlett, and she had campaigned against him for the office. Among other issues, she disagreed with him on the matter of consolidated schools. She thought such schools were a good idea, while Hamlett did not share this vision. She also thought Hamlett was guilty of "playing politics" with the educational system. In the future, the accusation of playing politics was a charge that Stewart would often level at opponents who disagreed with her. Similarly, this indictment was used by other Progressive reformers who were so convinced of the correctness of their causes that they viewed their opposition as being less than honorable.

While Stewart was quick to level charges at people who did not agree with her, the condition of the educational system in Kentucky and the personal nature of politics in the state meant that her accusations were often correct. In her position as K.E.A. president, she was able to generate support for her programs, and she proved to be very adept at developing constituencies. She also used the K.E.A. presidency as a forum from which to advocate vocational education in the public schools. In one address to the state education association, she charged that if the need for such training had "been met forty years ago, 75% of the natural resources of the State would not be in the possession of foreign capitalists and the youths whom Kentucky has given to other states would doubtless have remained at home to help solve her problems and to enrich her history."[5]

With the introduction of the Moonlight Schools, Stewart also called on the school systems to play a larger role in the reduction of adult illiteracy. In her 1912 address at the K.E.A. annual meeting in Louisville, she boldly stated: "The greatest stigma which rests upon Kentucky today and the greatest problem which confronts Kentucky educators is her appallingly high percentage of adult illiteracy. Surely this association, which is supposed to inaugurate and to foster all educational reforms in the State, has no more imperative duty than to foster the movement to abolish adult illiteracy from the borders of the Commonwealth."[6] While she conceded that the schools' first duty was to the children of the state, she also proclaimed: "We cannot escape the responsibility of educating for the sake of the child and for the sake of the State, the child's father and mother, as well."[7] She challenged the members of the K.E.A. to answer this call.

Stewart's focus on the education of adult illiterates was new to the state and nation. It proved to be a popular call, however. She appealed to the reform spirit of the time, and she gave voice to a mass of people who were unable to articulate their frustration at not having basic literacy skills.

As the time drew near for the start of the school term in 1912, the future of the night schools was in question. Were they simply a passing fantasy? Would the students return again? There was no need to worry. The people began calling for the resumption of the Moonlight Schools even before day schools resumed. To help in the running of the schools, a Moonlight School teachers' institute was held. The methods of teaching adult illiterates were discussed, as were the best means of reaching reluctant learners. Similar to institutes for the day schools, in-service training was offered to all who came. Stewart organized the training sessions, and teachers from other counties also came to learn about the Rowan experience. As a result, there was greater consistency in the instructional techniques, and a united front was provided by the teaching corps.

The second session of Moonlight Schools surpassed the first year. Sixteen hundred students were enrolled in Rowan. Of this number, 300 were taught to read and write for the first time. Students from the previous year returned to advance on to other elementary lessons. These students came from all occupations and included school trustees, a postmaster, and at least four Baptist preachers. To reach people who were unable to attend the regular session of school, a home department was developed and teachers went into the homes of illiterates to teach individually.[8]

The Rowan teachers were dedicated to the cause Stewart championed. In some cases, married teachers who lived at home and rode on horseback to school each day left their homes when the night schools started and lived with local residents in their districts. Teachers who commuted long distances to work sometimes remained at the schools from the time the day school ended until the night school closed at 9 o'clock in the evening. That they were willing to make this commitment on a voluntary basis is a tribute to their personal commitment and the influence of Stewart. Like her teachers, Stewart put in 13-hour days or longer. She regularly visited the schools, offering encouragement to the instructors and the pupils each evening.[9]

By this time, the Rowan example had spread, and schools were opened in other counties, including Johnson, Mercer, Garrard, Boyle, Martin, and Carter. Many of these schools began after Stewart spoke at institutes in the counties and challenged the teachers to give of their time and talent. These schools were not as well coordinated as the Rowan schools, yet good results were reported. The superintendent of the Lawrence County Schools, Jay O'Daniel, wrote to Stewart: "I am pleased with the manner in which my schools are progressing so far, and I think you were of *immense* benefit to us. Several night schools are already under headway and are doing splendid work."[10]

As in Rowan, a major side benefit of the Moonlight Schools was the interest shown by adults in the public schools. As Stewart was to note later: "There was an awakened, if not trained leadership, a whetted desire for cooperative activity where individualism and stagnation had prevailed. Men and women who had hitherto been divided by contention and strife now worked side by side in concord. They were schoolmates and that is a tie that binds."[11]

Like the previous year, the second sessions of the Moonlight Schools attracted the attention of state and national publications. The Louisville *Courier Journal* praised the movement, noting:

> A few prizes were offered to stimulate teachers and trustees and were to be awarded on the highest enrollment, the largest attendance, and the number of illiterates taught, but teachers and trustees announced that any prizes won by them would be donated to the district for libraries and other needed improvements. The teachers are in the main natives of Rowan County, young in years and in experience deeply in sympathy with the people and their needs, consecrated to the cause of education and determined to wipe out illiteracy from the county and to make of each and every citizen, high or low, an intelligent, active, happy factor in the school.[12]

At the end of the second session of the schools, Mrs. Stewart continued to speak about the Moonlight Schools, addressing teacher institutes as well as civic clubs around the state. Such a hectic schedule of public appearances was taxing on her health; she was often near exhaustion, but she refused to slow down. By early 1913, her commitment to the illiteracy work had deepened to the point that she refused to let other possible callings change her focus. Having discovered her mission in life, she was determined to see it through.

The U.S. Bureau of Education was so impressed with Stewart's work that it published a pamphlet in 1913 describing the Moonlight Schools as a model that should be followed in other states to reduce illiteracy among adults. This bulletin pointed out that contrary to many popular opinions, it was possible for older adults to learn to read and write. Noting that adults could learn these basics in a short time, the pamphlet also stated that given the opportunity, adults would actively try to master literacy skills.[13]

Stewart loved rebutting the popularly held notion that older adults could not learn. She knew that certain educators, especially in the university community, believed that teaching older adults was contrary to the principles of psychology. She chided: "While they [college professors] went around saying it couldn't be done, we went on doing it. We asked the doubters this question, 'When a fact disputes a theory, is it not time to discard the theory?' There was no reply."[14] For her part, Stewart claimed that the Moonlight Schools were proof of a theory expounded by Yale psychologist Dr. Arnold L. Gesell, who held that older adults, regardless of their age, could learn the basics of reading and writing in a relatively brief time.[15]

By the beginning of the school year in 1913, the Moonlight Schools were spreading into other states. Some of the mountain counties of Tennessee opened their schools to adults in the evening, and Arkansas followed suit. In Rowan County, the third year of the schools saw a resolve to wipe illiteracy out of the county by the end of the school session. Local school trustees were persuaded to take a census of illiterates in their districts. This canvass gave Stewart a record of the name and age of each illiterate in the county as well as any background information that could be used to encourage the reluctant learner to attend school. This census was the most complete documentation of illiteracy in a county to date.

The teachers in each district were given the names of the illiterates in their district and told to visit these people and to talk them into coming to the night schools. Not only the teachers took part in this campaign, local businessmen and professionals were also encouraged to help teach illiterates. In reality, the Moonlight School movement in Rowan County had developed into a true crusade against illiteracy by 1913. Not limited to the schools themselves, the theme of eradicating illiteracy was on the lips of many of the citizens.

The high level of organization among the educational forces in Rowan County was evidence of Cora Wilson Stewart's administrative abilities. She was a great organizer, capable of delegating responsibility, formulating effective action plans, and seeing them to fruition. The experience she gained in Rowan County would prove to be invaluable as she advanced to the state and national levels.

By the end of the 1913 school session, Stewart claimed that all but 23 of the 1152 illiterates in the county had learned to read and write to some extent. True to her organized nature, these remaining illiterates were classified: 6 were blind or had defective sight, 6 were mentally handicapped, 2 moved from the county, 4 could not be induced to learn, and 5 were bedridden invalids. While this exact count may be questioned, there is no doubt that the schools achieved definite results.[16]

Throughout Kentucky, the movement was progressing, as twenty-five counties had adopted the idea. In 1913, Fleming, Grayson, Jefferson, and Mason were among the counties to start Moonlight Schools for the first time. Newspapers in the state printed heartwarming stories of the redemption of illiterates and the success of the schools. A typical report noted:

> In the Sandy Valley hundreds have enrolled, 400 in Lawrence County alone. In one district in Boyd County the people responded to the number

of 60. In Madison a school was conducted among the tenant class, and was thronged with eager students. At the close of a two weeks' session all of these tenants could read and write.[17]

The success of the 1913 session of the Moonlight Schools convinced Cora Wilson Stewart that it was time to take the movement to a new level. With this goal in mind, she wrote to Governor James B. McCreary on December 16, 1913, concerning the possibility of state involvement in the fight against adult illiteracy:

> I am taking the liberty of addressing you upon the subject of having an Illiteracy Commission formed by legislative act to study the condition of adult illiterates in our State and to give men and women their freedom from this bondage; also, to place our State in a better light before the world. For years there has been a constant cry about Kentucky's appalling percentage of illiteracy. It has been repeatedly declared that we are near the bottom of the literacy scale.
>
> The purpose of forming such a commission would be to promote voluntary effort on the part of the teachers and others and to cooperate with those who are already making the effort. Many teachers have already volunteered, but they need guidance and inspiration and other teachers need to be called upon to volunteer.
>
> We taught over a thousand men and women in Rowan County during the past three years, and now some twenty-five counties are putting forth an effort along this line. I have hundreds of letters that demonstrate the fact that men and women can learn to read and write in a very short time after their interest is quickened.
>
> I have letters from octogenarians besides many middle-aged and younger men and women. What has been done in Rowan County in three years in reducing and almost wiping out her illiteracy, can be done in Kentucky during the next six years—by the time the Federal census is taken.
>
> This movement started in Kentucky, and Kentucky is the State which should take the initiative and form a commission to advance this important work. I earnestly request that you will include in your message to the Legislature the suggestion that such a commission be formed.
>
> Hoping that you will see the expediency of this matter, and believing that you will stand for the enlightenment of the 208,084 benighted Kentuckians who cannot read or write, I am
>
> Yours most respectfully,[18]
>
> Cora Wilson Stewart

McCreary responded three days later that he concurred with Stewart's request and that he would include a reference to an illiteracy commission in an upcoming speech to the state legislature. In remarks delivered on January 6, 1914, he followed through on his promise and called for the establishment of a state illiteracy commission. He specified that no appropriation of money would be needed; the members of the commission would serve without remuneration because they should be as patriotic in volunteering their services as the teachers who were involved in the work.

Having received the governor's endorsement, Stewart began lobbying the state legislature to make certain the illiteracy commission became a reality. On February 11, 1914, she appeared before the Kentucky Legislature, which was meeting as a committee of the whole to consider the establishment of the illiteracy commission. She was in her usual fine speaking form on this occasion, and she made the most of the opportunity. Primed with figures on illiteracy and offering personal experiences as illustrations, "she completely swept the Legislature off its feet with her eloquence," according to the Lexington *Herald*.[19] The *Frankfort Journal* dubbed her talk, "by far the most eloquent ever delivered in the General Assembly by a woman."[20]

Following Stewart's dynamic speech, in an action that one source called "unprecedented in Kentucky history," the House of Representatives lifted the illiteracy bill from deep down in the calendar and rushed it through with a unanimous vote. Less than a week later, the Senate also unanimously passed its version of the bill and the Kentucky Illiteracy Commission (K.I.C.) received legislative life.

Stewart's eloquent and forceful appeal was the primary reason for the passing of this legislation. She presented indisputable facts and firsthand knowledge that impressed the legislature. That she also did not ask for any funds for the K.I.C. was important to its passage. The legislature thought that the commission could be authorized without funds and that volunteers could take care of the issue. It was not hard for them to vote for something that they thought was going to do great good and not cost the state anything. In this case, Stewart's eloquence and persuasive speech may have worked against her. At the time the bill was coming before the House, friends of the legislation, unbeknownst to Stewart, were working in committee to add an appropriation amendment to the bill that would have provided $10,000 for the legislation. Before the amendment could be reported out of committee, however, the House, after hearing Stewart's speech, rushed the bill through without an appropriation.[21]

For her part, Stewart was most interested in getting the commission started; she truly believed that volunteerism would wipe illiteracy out of the state by 1920. She had seen the effectiveness of volunteers in Rowan County, and she was always willing to sacrifice herself for the cause. Lack of funds would later prove to be a major stumbling block for the K.I.C., but in early 1914, the euphoria of the moment carried the day and Stewart did not worry about money. The Kentucky Illiteracy Commission had been chartered, and the future was bright.

Soon after the passage of the Kentucky legislation, Stewart was honored by being awarded the Clara Barton Medal for her Moonlight School work. Presented by Dr. Julian Hubbell, field secretary of the Red Cross, the medal was a source of great pride for Stewart.[22] She had accomplished the establishment of the K.I.C., and her work was gaining recognition around the country. In her own home state, many of her friends were encouraging her to run for the position of superintendent of public instruction. She gave this possibility careful consideration and did not close the door on such a bid during early 1914.[23]

While in Washington, D.C., to receive the Clara Barton Medal, Stewart was invited to come before the House Committee on Education to report on the illiteracy work in Kentucky. Her testimony reveals the large-scale plans that she was already envisioning for the crusade against illiteracy. Her comments also show some of the problems she would have to face in her crusade.

Stewart appeared before the legislators at the invitation of P. P. Claxton, commissioner of education. Claxton was trying to get Congress to appropriate $10,000 for the Bureau of Education to help local efforts against illiteracy. On March 3, 1914, Stewart told this group of her work in Rowan County, and she invited questions from the committee members. She said that she supported Claxton's idea and hoped that the modest funds requested could be provided so that the federal government could help local campaigns. In her remarks, she noted:

> I understand there has been some question in regard to men and women learning to read or write in a short time. I will explain to this committee how this is accomplished. It might take a considerable time for a man to learn to read and write; but since we are teaching him the thing that of all things the man wants to know—to write his name, to escape from the shame of making his mark, that sting of humiliation which he has felt a hundred times, perhaps when making his mark in the presence of the educated, and when asking the election officers to cast for him a vote for the candidate of his choice—I pledge you my word it is not difficult to teach a man to very quickly learn to write his name, and from that to write other sentences.
>
> We have this plan: We reward them by sending out 10 post cards. They write those 10 post cards to their friends. In sending out the 10 post cards the idea is to give them the opportunity to practice, and not only the opportunity but the incentive to write something of genuine interest to their friends in writing direct to them as a means of practice.[24]

Stewart also observed that by this time, the students were writing fairly legibly and progressed on from this point. As evidence, she shared with the committee some letters received from new writers. When questioned by the committee about the general impact on public education of the work with adult illiterates, she stated that the sense of achievement encouraged the adults to become supporters of the schools for their children and grandchildren.

When asked about the federal role in this work, Stewart observed that the support of the commissioner of education in sharing ideas among people involved in the illiteracy fight would be sufficient to spur the movement on. She supported the idea of the commissioner of education acting as a resource person who could use his office to counsel others on effective measures in schooling adult illiterates.

When queried about possible objections concerning the national government intervening in a matter that had traditionally been left to the states, Stewart responded, "I think they [states] would consider it a matter of valuable support and endorsement and assistance from the United States Commissioner of Education and not an interference."[25] She added that because the commissioner would be asked for advice by the local officials, he would not be interfering.

Commissioner Claxton stated that the appropriation would also be used to produce written material for teachers of adult illiterates. He went on to say that he hoped the federal government could go into localities when invited to help local efforts against adult illiteracy.

An interesting philosophical question arose from the committee regarding the reason adults did not seek education earlier. Stewart quickly corrected any insinuation regarding the ambition or intelligence of illiterates. She told the committee that in many mountain communities public schools were not available when Moonlight School students were young and that the people were isolated from each other by geography. She finished by asking, "Even supposing they were not interested at the time and that they did have an opportunity, but did not grasp the opportunity, is that any reason to deprive them of a chance at the age of 40 or 50 or 60 or 70 years, or whenever they awakened to their need?"[26]

Still skeptical, Kentucky's representative to the House, Caleb Powers, asked Stewart how, once illiteracy was eliminated, she proposed to keep it from coming back because people would obviously in the future continue to choose to reject schooling when it was offered them in their youth. For this problem, Stewart prescribed the following solution:

> First an illiteracy campaign should so awaken the public conscience that it will be a disgrace to be an illiterate. In the next place, we should have such strong compulsory school laws and so carefully enforced that children would attend school; and there would be no opportunity for them to grow up illiterate; and if there should be through invalidism or any other causes some few illiterates, we should have a system of evening schools in the rural districts for at least six weeks in the year, as we have a system of evening school of longer duration in the cities.[27]

Stewart observed that it was a shame for the country that night schools were offered to immigrants in the cities, while the rural population, mostly native-born, did not have similar opportunities. This was especially embarrassing because the 1910 census showed that rural illiteracy was almost double that found in the cities. Her prescription for eliminating illiteracy revealed an idealized faith in the effectiveness of the public schools. The public school movement in the South was only beginning to gain momentum, and possibilities for its success seemed limitless to her. Hindsight shows that her confidence in the ability of public schools to eliminate illiteracy was too great, but she was not privy to this experience and can be forgiven her idealism.

In her final comments to the committee, Stewart described how the Kentucky Illiteracy Commission had been authorized and how the state legislature unanimously passed the bill establishing it. When asked if funds were authorized for the commission, she admitted that none were provided but added that she was confident such an appropriation would be forthcoming in the future.

In response to Stewart's observations, Representative Jacob T. Baker of New Jersey observed wryly: "The amazing thing is how men flee and avoid doing anything in the way of an appropriation of money for the most important thing in all civilization. For war, for the promotion of their prejudice; their superstitions; their amusements, they will go down deep; but when it is proposed to roll away the stone from the door that encloses the light, not a dollar."[28]

In future years, Stewart would come to learn the truth of Representative Baker's statement. In 1914, however, she was happy to have the K.I.C. established, and she was hopeful that funding would come with time.

5

ℬEGINNINGS OF THE *K.I.C.*

During the weeks following her speech before the legislature, Mrs. Stewart received letters of praise for her success. T. J. Coates of Eastern Normal School wrote: "What a wonderful work for any human being to conceive the plan and execute it of lifting, from a whole section of the country, the pall of illiteracy that has hung like a cloud for so many years over the Appalachian Mountains."[1] John Smith of the Normal Department at Berea College noted that the legislative action "has been a personal victory for you. I hope that the blotting out of Kentucky's illiteracy is now in sight."[2]

These supporters realized the sacrifice that Stewart had already made, and they knew that she would be the person to provide leadership for the new commission. Mrs. Lafon Riker, chairman of the Kentucky Federation of Women's Health Committee, expressed the sentiments of many when she wrote to Mrs. Stewart: "Upon you will fall the burden and we must all use our best efforts to assist."[3]

The law establishing the K.I.C. created a five-person commission. Four members were appointed by the governor, and the superintendent of public instruction served as an ex-officio member. The group was incorporated, and the officers included a president and a secretary-treasurer. The commission was empowered to research, collect data, and conduct surveys throughout the state regarding the condition of adult illiteracy. The group was required to report to the general assembly at the end of two years, and it was authorized to interest citizens, corporate entities, and foundations in whatever means it chose for the elimination of adult illiteracy. The law further authorized the K.I.C. to accept and receive funds and to disperse these funds to eliminate adult illiteracy. While the members served without compensation, they could be reimbursed out of any funds that came into the hands of the commission for actual expenses incurred while performing their duties.[4]

As a result of her forceful leadership before the General Assembly, Governor James McCreary wanted Stewart in his administration. He tried to entice her to accept the post of assistant superintendent of the State Reform School. This position would have given her a steady source of income, but it would have also drawn her away from the work she had begun.

In response to McCreary's letter, Stewart wrote: "I thank you sincerely for your consideration of me in connection with the Reform School as Superintendent and feel that it is a work next in importance to the one to which I have concentrated myself—wiping out Kentucky's illiteracy. I am sorry that my obligation to this self-appointed task prevents my acceptance of the offer."[5]

Although McCreary wanted Stewart in the Reform School position, he respected her interest in the K.I.C., and he named her to the commission. Dr. John G. Crabbe, the former superintendent of public instruction who had developed the "whirlwind campaigns" during the previous decade, was also selected. At the time of his appointment, Crabbe was serving as a professor at Eastern Normal School in Richmond. He would be a source of great support for Stewart in the future, as she sought his advice and used his suggestions in the Kentucky illiteracy campaign. H. H. Cherry, president of Western Kentucky Normal School, and Ella Lewis, superintendent of the Grayson County Schools in eastern Kentucky, were the other appointees. The state superintendent of public instruction, Barksdale Hamlett, served as an ex-officio member.

Stewart began laying the groundwork for the work of the commission soon after she was appointed and before the first formal meeting of the group. In April 1914, she got the Kentucky Federation of Women's Clubs and the Kentucky Education Association to endorse the K.I.C. at their annual meetings. The endorsement from the Federation of Women's Clubs marked the beginning of an association with literacy work that would be a cornerstone of Stewart's efforts against adult illiteracy.

The General Federation of Women's Clubs (G.F.W.C.) had been formed in the late 1800s to coordinate the efforts of local women's clubs around the country. A product of the Progressive movement, Women's Clubs sprouted around the United States and served as a vehicle by which women could be involved in local civic affairs. The history of the South is filled with stories of the work these clubs performed in promoting local reform. They were instrumental in establishing public libraries throughout the region and supported a variety of other educational programs. By 1914 the clubs were united in various states and Kentucky was no exception; the Kentucky Federation of Women's Clubs was an affiliate of the national association. Club women would play a vital role in the fight against illiteracy and were to prove the staunchest of allies for Cora Wilson Stewart. Decidedly upper middle class and upper class in composition, the local clubs consisted of women who had time to devote to the literacy cause. The Kentucky Education Association was also a natural source of support for Stewart. She had served as the first woman president of the organization, and her colleagues were more than willing to help her. The organization also represented the teachers of the state, who formed the phalanx of instructors in the Moonlight Schools.

The first meeting of the K.I.C. was held at the Seelbach Hotel in Louisville on May 1, 1914. Stewart was elected president, and Dr. Crabbe was selected secretary-treasurer. The commission set a goal of eliminating illiteracy from Kentucky by 1920. Dr. Crabbe and Stewart were also chosen to serve as the finance committee, and they were charged with the responsibility of raising funds for the work. It was decided that they would approach both individuals and organizations. Soon after the organizational meeting, Stewart spoke before the Kentucky Press Association's annual meeting at Dawson Springs on June 10, 1914. The Association pledged its support for the campaign. If there ever was a case of enlightened self-interest, the newspaper endorsement was such. The editors knew that the eradication of illiteracy was intrinsically good for their local communities, but they also recognized that redeemed illiterates were potential newspaper subscribers.

The combination of enlightened self-interest and civic good made the illiteracy crusade a popular topic among the state's papers, and Stewart could always count on them to spread the word of the commission's work. In her first annual report for the K.I.C., she observed, "No educational movement in this or any other state has ever had such remarkable cooperation from the press."[6] Three days after getting the endorsement of the newspaper association, Stewart spoke to the annual meeting of the Kentucky Society of Colonial Dames. She told of the work that the commission planned and received the endorsement of this patriotic group.

The help of the teachers of the state was essential to the success of the K.I.C.'s work. To insure this support, Stewart turned to her colleagues—the county school superintendents. Assisted by fellow K.I.C commissioner Ella Lewis, she contacted the superintendents and arranged to speak about the commission's plans at their school institutes. Her fellow school administrators did not let Stewart down. She later noted that "many of them [superintendents] have cheerfully taken upon themselves the extra burden of adult education, and have traveled at night, visiting, and promoting the Moonlight Schools. Some of them have even gone down in the trenches and taught at Moonlight Schools."[7]

The offices of the K.I.C. opened in Frankfort on June 30, 1914. Soon thereafter, Stewart began the tiresome work of sending to local newspapers statistics showing the level of illiteracy in each county. These journals printed countless stories about the rate of illiteracy and published numerous editorials supporting the Moonlight Schools. Not all the publicity was favorable, however. A few newspapers challenged the validity of the statistics, and civic pride made some people doubt that the rate of illiteracy was as high as was shown by the 1910 census.[8] Undaunted by this opposition, Stewart set out to provide documentation for the statistics. In an act that would chill the bones of modern civil libertarians, she decided to get the names of the people who had admitted their illiteracy to the 1910 census takers. Using connections she had developed in winning the Clara Barton Medal, she went to Washington, where she met with General W. H. Sears, a former assistant to the Red Cross founder. With the help of Sears, Kentucky Congressman W. J. Fields, and Senator Ollie James, she asked the chief of the Census Bureau to give her the names of the Kentucky illiterates.

The surprised Census Bureau chief responded that such a request had never before been made. Stewart convinced him to release the names and addresses of the illiterates because of the unusual campaign going on in Kentucky. Eventually, a special clerk in the Census Bureau was assigned to this task, and the Bureau withheld only the age of the illiterates from Stewart. With this documentation, she planned to target specific individuals in the campaign.

Of course, such an invasion of privacy would provoke countless lawsuits today. At the time, however, this was such a novel idea that Stewart was able to persuade the Bureau to release the names and addresses to her. For the next fifteen years, she could count on this assistance from the Census Bureau. Without this information, the K.I.C. could not have conducted its campaign with the precision that it demonstrated over the next five years. For her part, Stewart knew that such information was necessary if the state was to wage an effective campaign. She wanted to identify the illiterates so they could be helped, and she did not believe that there was anything wrong with her request.[9]

Returning to Kentucky after her successful mission in Washington, Stewart announced to the public that she had the names of the illiterates, and she continued to spread statistics through the newspapers regarding the level of illiteracy in each county. She followed up with a request to Governor McCreary to prepare a proclamation against illiteracy. Noting that Kentucky had led the way in establishing the Moonlight Schools, she graphically described the impact of illiteracy on society and told of the benefits that would be reaped from redeeming adult illiterates.

McCreary was completing his second term as governor, after having originally served from 1875 until 1879. His second term was marked by a distinct interest in Progressivism that contrasted with the conservatism of his original tenure. Already in his mid–seventies when elected in 1911, he developed a genuine admiration for the gifts of Cora Wilson Stewart. McCreary was moved by her request for a proclamation, and he wrote to her: "I received your interesting letter of 7th instant on the subject of an Illiteracy Proclamation this evening. It was an able and forceful letter that few women in Kentucky could write. It made an impression on me. Perhaps, as I wish to please you, if you will give me your views as to what the proclamation would contain, I may add my views and issue a proclamation."[10]

McCreary issued his public declaration on September 21, 1914. In it, he voiced the ideas of Cora Wilson Stewart, calling on Kentuckians everywhere to take part in the campaign to eliminate illiteracy from the state by 1920. Appealing to state pride, he said: "The instruction of all illiterates in the State will not only give to Kentucky a higher rank, educationally, among the states, but will give her a new and distinct position as the first Commonwealth which has ever attempted to accomplish such a great and important work."[11]

By this time, McCreary and Stewart had become friends. Acknowledging her work as a selfless gesture, he was always available to offer her encouragement when she needed it. McCreary also appreciated her political abilities. She had a strong contingent of followers that was growing with the interest in the illiteracy movement. In addition, the press was almost entirely behind her work, and the governor recognized her influence in the Democratic party. The newspapers hailed McCreary's decree and printed it throughout Kentucky. They went on to encourage their readers to help eliminate illiteracy in Kentucky by 1920. "No Illiteracy in Kentucky by 1920" became the rallying cry of the cause, and it spread across the commonwealth.[12]

A typical newspaper report in the Elizabethtown *News* indicated the impact of illiteracy in the state:

> It is safe to say that there are 100,000 illiterate voters, or that one man in five has to have his ballot marked. This is a deplorable condition for these people. No greater work has ever been undertaken in the State. The school teachers throughout the state are responding splendidly and are volunteering by the thousands to teach Moonlight Schools. In Grayson County last week 101 teachers volunteered in response to a personal appeal by Mrs. Stewart at the teachers Institute. It is estimated that 40,000 of these adults are now in attendance upon [sic] Moonlight Schools.[13]

Because the legislature did not appropriate any funds for the K.I.C., other means of support had to be found. The bulk of the funds for the Commission were raised by the women's clubs during a six-week campaign. Called the Women's Forward Movement, this effort generated $8,000.[14] In addition, the Commission was able to get money for stationery, telephone service, postage, and even a part-time stenographer from the Kentucky Sinking Fund Commission. These funds were granted after Attorney General James Garnett ruled that the K.I.C. was eligible for such assistance.

Stewart spent the latter part of 1914 talking with teachers at school institutes and was able to persuade many of them to teach illiterates in the evening schools. She also spoke to statewide groups to educate them about the status of illiteracy in Kentucky, and she sent statistics to the local newspapers regarding the number of illiterates in each county. The strain on her was tremendous both financially and physically. She supported herself with the school institute work, but much of her income went to pay for K.I.C. expenses. The self-sacrifice she demonstrated was an inspiration to all who knew her, and it made her more dedicated than ever to the cause she championed. Because she sacrificed so much personally for her work, she was often unsympathetic to those who did not share her zeal. She had little patience with people who did not see the evils of illiteracy. Having invested so much of her own energy in the work, she could speak with determination and conviction about the need for the illiteracy campaign. This commitment caused her to have an increasingly narrow focus on life, however. Having given so much, she could not understand others' unwillingness to make similar sacrifices.

When Stewart became despondent about her work, she often turned for encouragement to the elderly Governor McCreary, who had chosen the illiteracy campaign as a part of his administration. Conversely, whenever an issue arose regarding the illiteracy work, he turned to her.[15] Despite the fund-raising success of the Women's Forward Movement, the financial demands of the Kentucky work were a constant challenge for Stewart. She often made trips to Washington, D.C., New York City, and other places out of the state to explore possible sources of funding for the work. In early February 1915, after a speech before a group in Baltimore, she went to Washington, D.C., and met with President Woodrow Wilson, to whom she was introduced by her friend, Congressman W. J. Fields of Kentucky. President Wilson and Stewart immediately established a positive rapport. She explained the methods used in the Moonlight Schools, and the president responded, "You are doing a wonderful work and I wish to compliment you heartily."[16]

Stewart admired Wilson greatly; he was her type of Progressive. The son of a Southern Presbyterian minister, Wilson had been educated at the University of Virginia and was a devoutly religious and idealistic person. He shared many characteristics with Stewart, including a crusading zeal based on his interest in reform. Stewart's admiration for Wilson would grow in the future as her campaign against illiteracy expanded.[17]

By the beginning of 1915, Stewart had developed plans for a major drive to reduce illiteracy in Kentucky. A speakers' bureau, including 120 of Kentucky's most influential citizens, was formed to cover the state in a whirlwind campaign similar to Dr. Crabbe's earlier efforts for the public schools. Drawing on Crabbe's experience, Stewart made certain that the speakers were well briefed on local illiteracy conditions, and she coordinated the speaking campaign from her Frankfort office in the summer of 1915. All but one of these speakers paid their own expenses, and some of them made as many as fifteen speeches for the cause.[18]

No area of the state was ignored by the K.I.C. in 1915. Reaching out to the churches, the commission designated the last Sunday in October to be "No Illiteracy Sunday." Leaflets were provided to ministers with the request that they preach on the subject. Even the prisons of the state were brought into the process; jailers across the state were asked to establish Moonlight Schools and to get teachers for illiterate inmates. According to the K.I.C.'s first annual report: "Ninety percent of the jailers responded favorably, and some of the most successful schools have been conducted in this way."[19] From this part of the campaign, Mrs. Stewart began noticing a correlation between crime and illiteracy, and she developed a deep concern for illiterate inmates that lasted for the next twenty years.

The Women's Clubs of the state supported the campaign with deeds as well as money. In some cases, members taught schools themselves, and the clubs in Elizabethtown and Henderson were cited by the Commission as particularly striking examples of successful programs. Local clubs included "No Illiteracy in Kentucky by 1920" on their stationery, and the members across the state were called on to teach at least one illiterate during 1915. Several of the clubs encouraged volunteer teachers by offering prizes for the best Moonlight Schools in their counties.

The colleges were involved as well. All colleges in the state were asked to appoint illiteracy committees from their student bodies, and most of them honored this request. Graduating classes in high schools and colleges were enlisted to have each graduate teach at least one student to read and write. At the Jefferson County Common School graduation ceremony, all 96 new graduates raised their diplomas and pledged that they would each teach at least one illiterate.

To supplement the information from the U.S. Census, Stewart persuaded the State Department of Education to help with its own census of illiterates. In April 1915, local school trustees were asked to take a census of local illiterates at the same time they listed the children in their districts. This was purely a voluntary matter, and in areas where the school superintendents were actively involved, the census was complete for the county; in areas where the superintendent was not active, it was incomplete. Despite its limitations, the census was useful in showing skeptical trustees and superintendents that there were many illiterates in their districts.

To supplement the work of local school officials, county illiteracy commissions were established. These commissions were charged with coordinating the local campaigns and cooperating with the state commission. As had been done in Rowan County, a Home Department was developed to teach adults who could not attend night classes. This was seen as a vital part of the K.I.C. work, and when it was connected to the regular Moonlight Schools, the teachers did the work themselves. Many other individuals also took part in the Home Department, and the slogan "One for every one" was adopted. A circuit court judge, several legislators, lawyers, ministers, and doctors were among the participants in this part of the campaign.

The bulk of the work, however, fell to the local teachers and school superintendents, who were constantly reminded that the adult classes had a positive impact on the work of the day schools. Educators were also told of the negative impact that illiteracy had on day school attendance. Guided by these ideas and spurred on by the inspiration of Stewart, teachers volunteered in large numbers during 1915.

The reports of the county superintendents to the K.I.C. reveal the level of cooperation that was part of the campaign in 1915. In all, forty-three county school superintendents sent reports to the commission about Moonlight Schools in their counties. Almost universally, these reports were positive. For instance, R. W. Kincaid, superintendent of the Bath County Schools, wrote:

> I am prepared to state that I have never before seen so much interest and enthusiasm manifested by the people of the rural districts in any work. Many of these people who could not read or write can now write legibly

and can read fairly well. I have had many letters from these people telling me what they thought of the work and expressing their gratitude and pride in being able to read and write.[20]

The Clay County superintendent, Luther Hatton, noted: "The Moonlight School enlists the support and cooperation of a class of parents who could never have been reached any other way. Teaching an adult to read a little and to write his name is no great thing, but when you have taught him enough to interest him in his child's welfare, you have added untold wealth to this Common-wealth."[21]

Superintendent Georgia Sledd of Montgomery County reported: "We had as many as seventy-five to learn to read and write in one school alone. We hope to totally eradicate illiteracy from the county before 1920."[22] Jessie O. Yancey, superintendent of Mason County Schools, sent Stewart a letter from one of her teachers that noted: "My attendance [in the Moonlight School] increased each evening until at the close I have seventy enrolled with an average attendance of fifty pupils. It was indeed a revelation and a surprise to me for I never dreamed I could arouse so much interest or do so much good."[23]

J. H. Garvin, supervisor of the Winchester Colored Schools in Clark County, also reported progress among the black population: "The progress they made is remarkable. I am sending under the same cover a bunch of letters writ-ten by those who learned to read and write during the term just closed."[24] The Hardin County superintendent, James A. Payne, observed: "Most of the illit-erates are eager and anxious to be taught and we are eager and anxious to teach them. We hope to see this great work continue to grow until every illiterate person in Kentucky can read and write."[25]

Besides the effectiveness of the Moonlight Schools, many superintendents reported an increased interest in the day schools. For instance, the Ballard County superintendent, J. E. Lane, noted, "We find where the Moonlight Schools are organized, the interest in the regular public school is greatly increased." These sentiments were echoed by other superintendents who shared their observations about the growing support for the day schools.

While comments regarding the effects of the school were positive, the superintendents also noted the need for literacy agents who could direct the work in the counties. They praised the unselfishness of the teachers who vol-unteered their time and talents but noted that more could be accomplished with additional public information and help from the state. W. A. Pardue, super-intendent of the Edmonson County Schools, voiced the thoughts of many when he wrote, "We need a county agent and more agitation as the county superin-tendent has so much to do that he cannot do it all."[26] Cora S. Payne of the Cum-berland County Schools reported that many of her teachers were young and inexperienced and found it difficult to present the work to older men and women. She said: "We need a county agent to organize and start the younger teachers in this work."[27] Powell County's superintendent, Kate S. Bohanon,

Cora Wilson Stewart (center) during the Kentucky Crusade around 1915.

observed, "We need to have the county organized and the matter taken up in a systematic way, and keep continually agitating the subject until the people who are in ignorance of their privileges shall be made to see what those privileges are."[28]

In 1915 the K.I.C. answered the call for help by hiring three county agents to work in various areas of the state. These workers were Lottie Richards in Clay County, Maude Bishop in McCreary County, and James J. Asher in Leslie County. The agents directed the work of teaching illiterates in each county in concert with the local superintendent. Their reports show the outstanding effort put forth in their counties. Lottie Richards observed that "the teachers and citizens of Clay County in this fight on illiteracy have done a work for the illiterates which has built for them a monument in the hearts of the people. Although the teachers have had many difficulties to overcome, they have pushed forward earnestly, and assumed their task with eagerness. The spirit of these teachers has been a great inspiration to me."[29]

In McCreary County, Maude Bishop described how she had coordinated a speakers' campaign, taken a census of the illiterates, and held a Moonlight School rally for the work. She also observed the positive impact on the day schools. "The average attendance in day schools where Moonlight Schools have been taught exceeds that of those where none was taught by 11 percent," she reported.[30]

The most detailed account was provided by the Leslie County agent, James J. Asher, who had given up a principal's job with a yearly salary of $900 to become an illiteracy agent at $300 per year. His report reveals the deep level of commitment among the people of Leslie County, and he provided many anecdotes about his experiences as a K.I.C. agent. In his report, he noted that

a thousand people had enrolled in the Moonlight Schools. Of these participants, six hundred had learned to read and write. At the end of the 1915 session, he was very optimistic about the prospects for the continuation of the work,
observing, "From the results obtained in this one session of Moonlight Schools
in Leslie County, attended by such difficulties as pioneers usually meet, I believe
that with a continuance of the same effort, illiteracy can be wiped out of Leslie
County within two years."[31]

One of the greatest needs in the campaign was for reading material for the
illiterates. Mrs. Stewart had successfully used the *Rowan County Messenger* in
her home county, but there was no similar resource for the K.I.C. work. Recognizing this need, she set out to write the first textbook designed especially
for illiterate adults. During the last half of 1915, when she was not coordinating the work in Kentucky, she prepared the first of what was to become a series
of three readers for illiterates. This was an extremely difficult financial time for
Stewart. She no longer had her superintendent's job, and she received no compensation from the K.I.C. Her main source of support was her work as a school
institute instructor; the strain of the K.I.C. duties, combined with worries about
money, took a heavy toll on her. She became irritable, often lost her temper,
and found work on the reader exasperating because of the constant demands
placed on her. Unable to complete the book in Kentucky because of distractions, she finally left the state and went to Richmond, Virginia, where, after a
brief rest, she finished the work.[32]

Stewart entitled the volume the *Country Life Reader*. Published by B. F.
Johnson Publishing Company of Richmond, the book contained simple sentences, that not only taught illiterates to read and write but also inspired personal and civic responsibility. There were lessons encouraging better health,
Christian living, improved farming techniques, and thrift. In the preface of the
book, Stewart noted that the people attending Moonlight Schools demanded
texts that dealt with the problems and interests of rural life: "The author has
utilized the opportunity when the rural dweller is learning to read to stimulate
a livelier and more intelligent interest in such subjects as agriculture, horticulture, good roads, home economics, health and sanitation and those subjects,
which if taught to him, will make for a richer and happier life on the farm."[33]

The first volume began with a simple lesson using only six words:

Can you read?
Can you write?
Can you read and write?
I can read
I can write.
I can read and write.[34]

Because the reader was the first book designed exclusively for uneducated
adults, the public greeted it enthusiastically. To this first book, Stewart would
eventually add two other *Country Life Readers*. Moonlight School instructors

welcomed them, and they became the basic texts for the schools. Whenever possible, the books were provided free to Kentucky students.

The sale of the first *Country Life Reader* provided Cora Wilson Stewart with much-needed income. The books were sold throughout the United States and were used to teach illiterates for many years. Because of Stewart's development of the *Country Life Reader* and her leadership of the K.I.C., numerous other states became involved in the work to eradicate illiteracy. During 1915, she spoke to groups across the country, and wherever she spoke, the interest in adult illiteracy soared. In 1915 the Alabama Illiteracy Commission was formed; it was modeled after the Kentucky Commission. It began with a proclamation by Governor Emmett O'Neal and established a slogan of "Illiteracy in Alabama—Let's remove it." Stewart had developed a rapport with the Alabama educators following her 1911 speech before the Southern Education Association, and she often counseled with their leaders.

Late in 1914, Dr. J. Y. Joynor, superintendent of public instruction in North Carolina, began to organize an illiteracy campaign in his state. In enlisting the aid of the newspapers at the state press association meeting in Montreat, Joynor told about the success of the Moonlight Schools in Kentucky. Under his leadership, seven thousand North Carolina teachers eventually volunteered to teach Moonlight Schools.[35] Minnesota organized its first Moonlight Schools in 1915, after State Superintendent of Education C. G. Shulz heard a lecture by Stewart.[36] Under the guidance of State Superintendent of Public Instruction R. H. Wilson, a former Kentucky educator and an admirer of Stewart, Oklahoma began several Moonlight Schools in 1914. With his leadership, the state enlisted the help of several thousand teachers for an illiteracy campaign. After his crusade, Wilson noted that "Probably more than 5000 persons were reached by the Moonlight Schools in Oklahoma during the school year 1915–16."[37] In Georgia, State Superintendent of Public Instruction M. L. Brittain began Moonlight Schools in 1915. He cited the example of the Kentucky work and called on the Georgia legislature to address the problem. Meeting little positive response from the elected officials, he directed his five state rural school supervisors to develop Moonlight Schools. Five counties were selected for the experiment, and he reported that "very good results were obtained."[38] He went on to note that in the Tattnall County Schools more than 600 adults were taught to read and write. On the basis of these results, he went back to the legislature, which eventually created an illiteracy commission.[39]

Other states, including Mississippi and New Mexico, also began illiteracy commissions and based their efforts on the Kentucky model. Stewart was proud of the accomplishments of these states and the impact she had on their development. She was also insistent that proper credit be given to the Moonlight Schools origins. In one letter to a fellow worker in Alabama, she urged:

> You Alabama folks must call your schools "Moonlight Schools." I do resent them being called "night schools." That is a northern institution

and a city affair. The "Moonlight Schools" are of southern origin and it [sic] is a rural and small town institution, whose primary aim is to instruct illiterates. There is a difference and all loyal Southerners should call them "Moonlight Schools."[40]

It was not solely ego that caused Stewart to stress the importance of the term *Moonlight Schools*. She knew that northern night schools provided education above and beyond the basic levels of the Moonlight Schools. In addition, the northern schools tried to "Americanize" recent immigrants. She did not want to see the work of basic literacy confused with an institution that was more widely aimed. She feared that broader-based efforts would sap the energy of the campaign against illiteracy. In future years, this issue became a growing concern for her as she tried to keep the focus on the illiterates while others wanted to widen the scope of work with adults.

December 1915 marked the end of the K.I.C.'s two-year authorization, and it was time to assess the accomplishments and failures of the campaign against illiteracy in Kentucky. The crusade was given a positive evaluation by the newly elected superintendent of public instruction, V. O. Gilbert, who was replacing Barksdale Hamlett. Gilbert noted of the illiteracy campaign:

> I say without hesitation or reservation, and from my own personal observation and participation in this work that it is a work that the state cannot afford to lose and should be fostered by every patriotic citizen. So appealing is this work to educators and thinkers that now some sixteen states in the union have taken up this work, using practically, Kentucky's plan. I find the citizens of the state in every section are enthusiastically for the Illiteracy Commission, and its work, and this is especially true in counties where Moonlight Schools have been taught. To fail to foster this work and push it to its ultimate conclusion—the eradication of adult illiteracy in the state—would be almost a public catastrophe, if not a crime, against higher citizenship.[41]

In summarizing the accomplishments of the K.I.C., the 1914–15 commission report conceded that the exact number of illiterates taught could not be ascertained. The report wryly commented that some teachers had not responded to requests for statistics on the number of people taught because "Many have doubtless thought that their volunteer service, teaching at night and trudging the country over in search of illiterates, was sufficient and that it was an imposition to require a report of them."[42]

In determining the number of illiterates taught, the K.I.C. account to the legislature included only information provided for counties where the superintendents of county schools filed reports. Based on these formal responses, it was determined that approximately six thousand schools had been conducted, including rural, town, city, women's clubs, prison, and home department classes. The report noted that extrapolation from the data indicated that about 40,000 illiterates had been taught to read and write.

The superintendents were universally positive about the impact of the night classes on local education, and the K.I.C. report made recommendations for the future of the work. It called for a $20,000 annual appropriation from the legislature so the Commission could reach its goal of eradicating illiteracy by 1920. The report claimed that this mission could be accomplished if the members of the K.I.C. continued to serve without compensation and if the teachers volunteered as they had in the past.

The commission suggested that $15,000 of this $20,000 appropriation be spent to place county agents in the field. It noted that 30 such workers could organize thirty counties each year until the end of the decade. Thus by 1920, all 120 counties in the state could be covered. A portion of the $20,000 would go to clerical help and office expenses. While the amount requested was modest, the report noted that "this is a work in which the spirit of the workers count [sic] most, and Kentucky's teachers, editors, and other men and women have demonstrated that they have the patriotism and heroism necessary."[43] The recommendations also called for an expansion of the speakers' campaign, further development of the prison schools, and growth of the home department work. The last element was seen as essential because many people were unable to attend the schools.

Finally, the report cited the need for an accurate census of the illiterates to be taken in each county under the direction of the state. Such a canvass would not only help the K.I.C. reach the illiterates more easily, it would also show how Kentucky's status regarding adult illiteracy had improved since the 1910 census.[44] This report reflected Stewart's assessment of the illiteracy work. She knew that the teachers had shown a willingness to work, and she believed that this cooperation would be necessary in the future. She also saw, however, that there was a need for better coordination of the crusade. For this reason, she called for hiring county agents. The achievements of the three agents hired in 1915 had shown that such workers could effectively organize local efforts.

Stewart was prepared to donate her own time, and she thought that other civic-minded people would join her. The work of the women's clubs in the state was encouraging, and the club women were proving to be strong political allies as well as good workers. To hire the needed agents, however, money was needed from the legislature. To this point, the state had made no appropriations to the K.I.C., but as 1916 dawned, Stewart prepared to ask the elected officials for these funds.

6

$\mathcal{A}$ $\mathcal{G}$ROWING $\mathcal{C}$RUSADE

In order to take the illiteracy crusade in Kentucky to a new level, Stewart got introduced into the Kentucky Legislature a bill for $20,000 per year for the K.I.C. Her hard-driving efforts in the legislative area did not go unnoticed. Governor McCreary, who had just completed his term in office, said that she was like a general in the field marshaling her forces for the drive that would cause the legislature to provide the needed funds. When she expressed anxiety about the ultimate fate of the act, McCreary offered these encouraging words: "You have not only the state of Kentucky but you have other states whose people are watching your success. If my words could do you any good, you would have them all the time. You will succeed. Your bill is getting stronger all the time. Your eloquence and strong enrollment of facts and convincing words will bring you victory."[1]

In early January, Stewart went to Washington, D.C., for a speaking engagement. While she was out of the state, an ironic twist of events occurred which brought public opinion clearly behind the K.I.C. and increased the likelihood of the appropriation being granted.

Augustus O. Stanley, a Democrat, had succeeded McCreary as governor. A native of Shelbyville and himself a former school teacher, Stanley had represented the second district of Kentucky in the U.S. House of Representatives for six terms. In a tightly contested campaign, he was elected governor by 471 votes over his close friend Republican Edwin P. Morrow. Morrow had run against the alleged extravagances of the McCreary administration. Noting the effectiveness of Morrow's campaign charges, Stanley decided it was time to investigate the efficiency of state government. To achieve this purpose, he appointed several assistant attorneys general to examine various state agencies.[2]

On January 6, one of these examiners, J. C. Duffy, publicly alleged that the K.I.C. had drawn $1,458.82 from the state treasury without authorization. The money was used for postage, telephone expenses, and hiring a stenographer. To complicate matters, part of the charges claimed that Stewart had used K.I.C postage and stationery to actively support her brother-in-law E. B. McGlone's bid for the nomination for state representative from Powell County. McGlone's opponent in the election was none other than her ex-husband A. T. Stewart.

Duffy's report went on to say that the attorney general would not stand for any more use of state funds by the illiteracy commission, which was supposed to be operated without government funding.[3]

When she heard of the report, Stewart was irate. She immediately wired State Inspector and Examiner Nat Sewell, asking him to start a full examination of the K.I.C.'s actions and expenditures.[4] Stewart returned from Washington and urged the investigation to begin so that the K.I.C. funding request would not be jeopardized. Dissatisfied with the pace of Sewell's investigating, she made an important public statement on January 13, in which she acknowledged that the K.I.C. had indeed spent the funds alleged by Duffy. She noted, however, that the funds had been duly authorized by the attorney general at the time, James Garnett, from the state sinking fund. Garnett had construed the law providing supplies and service to state departments to include the illiteracy commission.

Regarding the use of postage and stationery for political purposes, Stewart stated that no funds had passed through the K.I.C. for this purpose, and she added that she had spent her own money for postage and other costs of operating the Commission. She went on to say that she had always reimbursed the K.I.C. for any funds she used in her role as K.I.C. president.[5]

The public reaction to Stewart's statement was swift and convincing. Her friends in the press, as well as state legislators, were incensed at the charges made against her. The *Louisville Herald* noted that if Governor Stanley wanted to cut government spending, "he can easily find better prey than Cora Wilson Stewart."[6] The Frankfort *State Journal* called the charges a "groundless and uncalled for attack."[7]

The Lexington *Herald* said that "the attack on Mrs. Cora Wilson Stewart went up in smoke" before her denial of the charges. The Woodford *Sun* observed:

> It is a pity that the "reformers" selected for their first object of attack the Illiteracy Commission, instead of going after some of the bigger things alleged to have been done without legal justification at the expense of the State Treasury. If the attack was intended to injure Mrs. Stewart and the anti-illiteracy movement, it has had the opposite effect. Both Mrs. Stewart and the cause she represents are stronger with the people than they were before the criticism was published.[8]

The Elizabethtown *News* captured public sentiment best when it noted:

> When the one woman in Kentucky who has stood conspicuously for a great noble and philanthropic work, giving her time and her brilliant mind without compensation to wipe out the darkest blot upon the state— its illiteracy, is made the target of the common politicians, as Mrs. Stewart has recently been pilfered by alleged reformers, it arouses a storm of protest and indignation from every true Kentuckian.

The newspaper further charged that with the K.I.C.'s efforts "a hundred times as much good work has been done for Kentucky as these Assistant Attorneys General do if they live forever." The editor of the *News* finished with a less than glowing assessment of the state's male leaders, noting that the new administration would be better to attack the real wrongdoers in the state "instead of picking on a great woman. Common decency would suggest this, even if Kentucky manhood is deficient."[9]

Support for Stewart also came in the form of letters from friends who urged her not to get discouraged about the charges. Her pal Mattie Dalton wrote:

> Don't you know, girl, that if they confined themselves to something near the truth, and gave you credit for something near the right attitude of mind that they would be much harder to disprove? Don't you worry, your course of action is O.K. so far and I have faith in your intelligence and right intentions steering you through this mess with greater credit to yourself. Every doer has something as bad or worse to put up with. Go right along with your work and pay no attention to them except to block their mean little games whenever possible.[10]

The public reaction to Stewart's response was an encouraging sign for the illiteracy campaign. Stewart was not prepared to take any chances with the appropriation for the K.I.C., however, she learned that McCreary was going to Washington, D.C., to meet with President Wilson, who was planning a speech in Louisville around the time the K.I.C appropriation was set to come before the legislature. Stewart wanted the president to speak to the legislature on behalf of the bill. She persuaded McCreary to ask the president to visit Frankfort after his Louisville speech and to address the state legislature. She also wrote directly to Wilson to ask him to appear in Frankfort. McCreary talked with Wilson about the matter, and the president said he supported the illiteracy campaign but he could not make any other speeches in Kentucky after the Louisville engagement.[11]

Undeterred by Wilson's refusal to come to Frankfort, Stewart forged ahead with plans for the legislative session. With public opinion clearly in her favor because of the Duffy incident, Stewart spoke to the Kentucky Legislature on February 16, 1916. The galleries were packed with women, many of them carrying appropriate anti-illiteracy banners. Some women had to find seats on the floor of the House, which had been opened to the public because of the overflow audience. In an age that appreciated fine oratory, Stewart combined her considerable speaking ability with a careful marshaling of facts. She talked for more than an hour, giving detailed accounts of the work already done and the need for further action. She emphasized the necessity for the $20,000 appropriation to carry out the K.I.C. work, and she met in advance the arguments of potential foes. Vigorous applause followed her remarks, and Representative Hutchcraft of Bourbon County moved that the bill be called before the body for action. Only a hasty motion to adjourn, engineered by friends of Governor Stanley, kept the measure from sweeping through the legislature.[12]

Once again Stewart's eloquence had carried the day. Friends from across the state sent letters of congratulations and expressed confidence that the appropriation bill would pass.[13] The next day after her speech, however, Governor Stanley put a damper on the enthusiasm when he expressed opposition to any appropriation for the K.I.C. Stanley claimed that he supported the illiteracy work but noted that there were other things of more importance in the state. He cited the fight against tuberculosis and the state hospital for the feeble-minded as two more pressing needs. He went on to state his opposition to any new expenditures unless a way was shown to raise the necessary funds.[14]

Stewart feared that the new governor's opposition would doom the appropriations bill. She was disconsolate and told McCreary that she would retire to Morehead if the appropriation was not forthcoming. The former governor sympathized with her and encouraged her not to lose heart:

> I have been afraid all of the time the Governor would apply his statement about appropriations to your bill. He is mistaken in this. You need not talk about returning to the hills of Rowan. So such cheapness as this in your life you never created and you will continue to be a blessing to mankind and womankind. The appropriation will be made but I am afraid it will not reach the maximum sum.[15]

McCreary's prediction was correct; the legislature appropriated $5000 per year for 1916 and 1917. According to the enabling legislation, the funds were to be used for field agents, clerical help, "and other legitimate expenses as may be necessary in the efficient and economic methods of teaching illiterate men and women."[16] The bill stated that the members of the K.I.C. should continue to serve without compensation, and it authorized local school trustees to conduct a census of illiterates in each county. The results of this census were to be forwarded to the K.I.C.

Knowing that the $5000 appropriation would not be adequate for the work she envisioned, Stewart turned again to the women's clubs of the state to help raise money for the K.I.C. She asked these groups to make up the balance of the funds needed for the illiteracy crusade. Again she was forced to rely on the efforts of volunteers, and she was not disappointed. As never before, day school teachers offered their help, and members of civic organizations, especially the Kentucky Federation of Women's Clubs, continued to work with the Commission. Even bankers and traveling salesmen took part in the activities, telling illiterate clients about the Moonlight Schools. As usual, the press was extremely helpful, and nearly all the state's newspapers supported Stewart. Rallies and fairs were held in areas where Moonlight Schools were offered, with prizes given to the teachers who taught the most illiterates.

Most significantly, large numbers of illiterates responded to Stewart's appeal by enrolling in night classes. Reaction among the black population was especially noteworthy. The schools offered many African-Americans an opportunity to make up for the education they had been denied in their youth. One black teacher in Winchester described to Stewart the enthusiasm of her students: "They came in great numbers through a blinding rain storm which continued until nine o'clock. We enrolled forty persons and we expect to have more than two hundred this week. We had 210 in our school last year and we are expecting to double it this year."[17]

Newspapers across the state reported the successes of the Moonlight Schools. These stories focused on the wide range of ages among the students and the enthusiasm shown. Human-interest features with accounts of Moonlight School rallies and social events were also prominent in the press. Furthermore, the newspapers published statistics on the number of illiterates in the communities and challenged all local people to join the crusade.[18]

The national press caught the spirit, and articles about the Kentucky campaign were published in *The Church and the World*, *The Illustrated World*, and *The Journal of Education*. The last-named publication, a Boston school journal, was edited by Dr. A. E. Winship, an admirer and friend of Stewart. In the future, Dr. Winship would be a great help to Stewart.

When she was not directing the crusade, Stewart completed the second *Country Life Reader*. Like the first book, this volume was written primarily for rural residents and dealt with the problems and opportunities of country living. Written on a slightly higher reading level than the first book, it contained further lessons on positive lifestyles. It encouraged diversified farming, thriftiness, forestry, support for good roads, and personal hygiene, and it ended with lessons from the Bible. The book also offered advice on home economics and some elementary lessons about manners and social reforms of the day.

In a day when teaching was supposed to encourage good moral behavior as well as the technical skills of reading and writing, this book was welcomed by the public. It clearly reflected Stewart's beliefs, and it was in tune with Progressive ideas. To help encourage the sale of the second reader, Stewart promoted its use whenever she spoke. She continued to lecture outside Kentucky, traveling throughout the United States to tell the story of the Moonlight Schools. By the end of the year, she had spoken in Georgia, Tennessee, the District of Columbia, New York, Missouri, Pennsylvania, Michigan, California, Wisconsin, Kansas, Colorado, Louisiana, and Massachusetts.[19]

Although she was often out of the state, Stewart continued to conduct school institutes in Kentucky, and this was an important source of her income. She lectured at training sessions in Owsley, Hardin, Lyon, Clark, Owen, Bath, Calloway, and Cumberland counties during the year.[20] As a result of her growing national fame, Stewart was invited to speak before the National Education Association's annual meeting on July 3, 1916. Her topic was "The Elimination of Illiteracy." She held the audience spellbound with the story of the Moonlight Schools. She described the progress made in Kentucky since 1911, and shared her ideas about the need for a national crusade against illiteracy. After relating the story of the origins of the night schools, she chastised people who claimed illiterates did not want to learn:

This is the unkindest cut of all—to deny him [the illiterate adult] his portion and then to say it is done by his own desire. It is unkind, first, because it is untrue. Then it is unkind because, even if he chose to remain in ignorance, his judgment should not be accepted in this any more than in any other matter vital to himself and to the state. But he does not choose to remain in ignorance. He craves to learn. He hungers and thirsts for knowledge. You seldom find an illiterate who does not accept with joy and gratitude an opportunity when that opportunity is offered in a spirit of sincerity and good faith.[21]

Stewart went on to note that the first need in eliminating illiteracy was to remove the doubt of the illiterates that they could learn. She claimed that the best way of eliminating illiteracy was to teach illiterates and the best time to teach them was in the evening since many were involved in day labor. The best place to teach the illiterates was in the Moonlight Schools, which had proven their effectiveness.

In Stewart's opinion, the best people to teach the illiterates were the public school teachers. Here she showed a faith and confidence in the volunteer efforts of teachers based on her experience in the Kentucky crusade. She called on the educators to look at the illiteracy work as a privilege, saying: "The proper persons to teach the illiterates are the public school teachers. They are trained, prepared, and stationed for the work. It is their duty and their privilege and their opportunity for distinguished patriotic service. No paid service to illiterates can equal that of the volunteer teacher."

In a statement that predicted the community college movement, yet held a special place for the teachers of illiterates, Stewart observed:

Some day I expect to see institutions in all communities, rural and urban, where grown men and women receive elementary instruction, and to see them provided with salaried teachers, but I prefer not to see it while the purpose of such schools is solely the emancipation of the illiterates; for I do not believe that there should be a charge for helping a brother out of the ditch, nor for loosing his fetters, nor for unlocking his prison door.[22]

For Cora Wilson Stewart, the teaching of illiterates was not simply a matter of reading and writing; it was a moral obligation. It was a work that went beyond monetary compensation; it was required as a gesture of human compassion, like rescuing a drowning person. This was a high calling for the teachers of the N.E.A., many of whom had never heard the teaching of adult illiterates expressed in such terms.

For her own part, Stewart told the assembly that she had chosen her path and was set on her life's course. In a moving final statement, she said:

Those who delight in transferring to canvas the beauties of earth and sky, in tracing fair form and beauteous color may do it; those who delight in transforming marble block into figures of noble proportion and speaking likeness may do it; those who may delight in perfecting the form and fragrance and color of flowers and in enriching the flavor and hue of fruits may do it; those who delight in impressing first lessons upon the plastic mind of a little child, molding his character and coloring his very soul, may do it.

But let it be mine to carry the light to the illiterate man as he sits in his mental darkness, straining his eyes gazing after his vanished opportunity, and agonizing in his secret soul over the precious thing which he has lost. Let it be mine to bring to him a new opportunity, a new hope, and a new birth. It is a task too holy, too Christ-like for me, I must confess, but I crave that merit and that alone which will fit me for this task.[23]

With these concluding remarks, Cora Wilson Stewart expressed her mission in life. Like the crusaders of old, she had chosen a path that could only be satisfied with sacrifice and commitment. Her mother and father had taught her the value and power of the printed and spoken word. They had also taught her the need to serve her fellow man. She was now applying their teachings on a grand scale. She would no longer worry about the personal satisfactions of a private life. Her personal life, which had contained so much tragedy and so many disappointments, was rapidly fading behind her; she had answered a call that would absorb her life. It was a calling as pure as mankind could imagine. For who could argue with the need to teach adults to read and write? Who could question a cause that opened the eyes of the illiterate to the printed word and revealed to him a world previously unknown? No one could argue with this cause. It was romantic in its quest, it was gigantic in its scope, and it was fulfilling in its results. Each letter she received from a redeemed illiterate was a measure of her success.

At the end of 1916, Stewart assessed her accomplishments for the previous year and looked to the future. In her diary, she noted that the year was filled "with some triumphs, some joy, some sorrow, and some failures." She entered the new year resolved to continue her crusade, writing: "The year is closing. I am in good health and good cheer with a heavy program before me for 1917. I thank the Lord for the blessings of the past year and pray for the strength and courage to meet and discharge the duties of the approaching one."[24]

The new year began with a letter from her publisher, B. F. Johnson. Johnson noted that the second *Country Life Reader* was not selling well. The publisher observed that the first reader had been a great success because of the Kentucky work and said that such a great promotion was needed for the second book.[25]

Stewart replied: "The trouble has been that none of the states had a fund to purchase them and they have not yet learned how to get individuals to do so." She went on to say that an illness in July had kept her from finishing the third reader in the set, and she claimed that the growth of the illiteracy work in the country had produced an effort to imitate her books. "Some are doing it in bulletin form, and some in the form of printed sheets," she told Johnson.[26]

Despite Stewart's disappointment with the sales of the second reader in other areas, her home state was deeply involved in the illiteracy crusade. The newspapers recounted impressive results from the Moonlight Schools. According to these reports, 500 illiterates were redeemed in Cumberland County, and 800 had learned to read and write in two years in Leslie County. In Clay County, 667 had been taught. In Owsley, 200 illiterates had been redeemed, and in Warren County, 100 people were now literate who had not been able to read and write before.[27] Teachers in Barren County had done their part, and as a result, there were schools for illiterates of all races.[28]

In Hart County, R. E. Jaggers was in charge of the school that taught the most illiterates. As a reward for his efforts, he won a trip to Washington, D.C., to meet with President Wilson.[29] During his visit to the nation's capital, Jaggers noted that "the Moonlight Schools, I found, were the pride of Kentucky's statesmen. Many leaders in congress are champions of the cause which Kentucky is leading."[30]

When meeting with President Wilson, Jaggers noted: "He has kept up with the progress of the work, and he said with great earnestness: 'the work of Moonlight Schools is a great work.'"[31] Jaggers reported that Kentucky's Senator Ollie James was proud of the work and that Champ Clark, Speaker of the House of Representatives, "simply bubbled over with enthusiasm on the subject of Moonlight Schools. Every one of Kentucky's Senators and Representatives is an ardent supporter of Moonlight Schools. They have all given prizes in their districts and in the State at large, and have traveled at their own expense and made speeches for the cause and they feel in every way Kentuckian's duty to help."[32]

The spread of Moonlight Schools across the South was a source of great pride for Stewart, as was the acclaim she received from Kentucky's national leaders and President Wilson. For their part, the Democratic political leaders saw her value as a spokesperson for their cause. Although women did not yet have the franchise, the political leaders of the state and nation recognized Stewart as an influential person. Her approach to the illiteracy movement made her appealing to both men and women. She was able to win the support of women, and she supported the idea of suffrage; but she was not a threat to men. Men accepted her work and praised her as a positive example for other women in public life. An editorial in the Owensboro *Inquirer* noted that Stewart was successful because what she advocated was readily recognized as desirable by everyone. It was not partisan, and she was not a radical feminist.[33]

The Christian *Sun* also praised her work, saying: "Who is Cora Wilson Stewart? Is she one of those who 'picket' the White House and spreads woman suffrage banners before Congress trying to force our law makers to yield to certain acts? No, by far! she does not 'picket' the White House, but the hovel of the poor and ignorant. She is a woman of faith and works, of acts and deeds."[34]

The writer went on to observe that Stewart was too busy working for the eradication of illiteracy to engage in what were viewed as radical activities. It was the nature of her work that made Stewart appeal to both men and women. Her cause was acceptable to all people, and she was respected by both sexes. In this way, she was a person to whom conservative men as well as female activists could point as a positive example for women of the time.

By early 1917, Stewart was considered the leading authority on adult illiteracy in the United States. Her movement was spreading across the nation, and she was well known in both Washington, D.C., and Frankfort, Kentucky. Personally, however, the early part of the year brought her sorrow because her father died. Jeremiah Wilson had become a fixture in eastern Kentucky and was a man of substance. His medical practice had brought him land holdings, and his children had grown up to become leading citizens in the community. He had remarried after the death of Anne Halley, and he lived with his second wife, Virginia, in Morehead. He died on April 24, 1917.[35]

While she felt a great sense of personal loss, Stewart had mixed feelings about her father, although she had always admired his intellect and his wit. Jeremiah was proud of his daughter's accomplishments, but she was never as close to him as she was to her mother. Anne was the major influence on her life and she came to idolize her as the years passed.[36] At his death, part of Jeremiah's estate was divided among his first seven children. He fathered two sons by his second wife, and he left the entire family substantial holdings. For Cora Wilson Stewart, her father's bequest left her resources that she badly needed.[37]

Besides coping with the death of her father during the early months of 1917, Stewart struggled to complete the third volume of the *Country Life Reader*. Sales of the second volume had been a distinct disappointment, so she wanted the third book to be the crowning jewel in the series. She wrote her publisher that she was needed in Frankfort during February because there was a special session of the Kentucky Legislature. She hoped to persuade the legislators to provide more money for the K.I.C. work, and she would not be able to finish the third volume until that session was complete. Pressured by B. F. Johnson to complete the series, she pleaded for more time. After describing her many obligations, she ended one letter to the publisher by stating: "I will say if you have a heart you will give me an extension."[38]

Johnson did give Stewart her extra time, so she was able to gather her thoughts and work on the matters at hand. Nationally, the movement against illiteracy was spreading. Governor Charles H. Brough of Arkansas created an illiteracy commission in 1917 with a slogan "Let's sweep illiteracy out of Arkansas." North Carolina continued its work with the schools, and Stewart's friend R. H. Wilson made strides in Oklahoma. Patterned after the Kentucky work, these states promoted public attention and challenged school teachers to reach and teach uneducated adults.[39]

National publications pointed to Stewart as the prime mover in the illiteracy work and praised her efforts on behalf of the uneducated. One of the publications observed, "What Frances E. Willard was with her blue ribbon, what Jane Addams is with her Hull House, what Julia Lathrop is with her anti-child labor slogan, what the Maid of Orleans was to France, Cora Wilson Stewart

A Moonlight School, Latimer County, Oklahoma, 1916.

was to Rowan County, is to every Southern state, and such she will be to all illiterates, native or foreign born."[40]

In Kentucky the press continued to call for the elimination of illiteracy and at least two newspapers, the *Shelby News* and the *Glasgow Times*, devoted regular columns to the Moonlight Schools.[41] On the national level, Stewart convinced Kentucky's Senator Ollie James and her home district congressman, W. J. Fields, to introduce legislation to create a national illiteracy commission. She was instrumental in writing the actual legislation. Although the bill never passed, its introduction indicates the growing attention to illiteracy on the federal level.

After being given the extension she requested, Stewart was able to finish the third *Country Life Reader*. In her opinion, it was the "flower of the series." It included what she called "the best writings dealing with the corn, the pumpkin, the wheat, the hemp, and the various other products of the farm. Emphasis has been laid on those things which relate to the usefulness and dignity of the farmer and the farmer's wife, and the importance of their work in the world."[42]

Written on a third grade level, the book represented the continuation of the series that Stewart had been writing for rural people. She said that she was guided by two purposes in preparing the book. First, she wanted to point out the beauty of country life in objects that were ordinarily considered commonplace, and second, she wanted to guide the reader to authors who wrote about country living. She included writings from a variety of authors, including James Lane Allen, Hamlin Garland, and Gene Stratton-Porter. All of these works celebrated country life and praised the virtues of rural living.[43]

Thus, by midyear, Stewart was recognized nationally as the premier advocate for adult illiterates. Soon international events would focus attention on the problems of illiteracy, and she would be prepared to make further advancements in her crusade.

WORLD WAR I
AND ITS IMPACT

In June 1917, the United States entered World War I. After years of maintaining neutrality, America was drawn into the conflict that had already engulfed much of the globe. The decision to enter the conflict was difficult for President Wilson, who had campaigned in 1916 on the slogan "He Kept Us Out of War." Once the decision was made, however, Wilson set the country on a crusade to make the world safe for democracy.

As an admirer of the president, Stewart became an enthusiastic supporter of the war effort. Personally familiar with crusades, she was readily able to relate to the theme of democracy versus autocracy. During the war years, her work to eliminate adult illiteracy reflected a martial tone, and the war offered her a new opportunity to expand the Kentucky illiteracy work. The U.S. involvement also caused the introduction of the military draft for the first time since the Civil War. From across the country, young men of military age were required to register for possible service. The registration process produced results that also served as a great spur to Cora Wilson Stewart's crusade against illiteracy.

The first registration was for men 21 to 31 years old and took place on June 5, 1917. Not long after the registration date, the U.S. surgeon general reported that approximately 25% of the men registering for the draft were not able to read or write. In all, approximately 700,000 men registered by mark. Finding out about these conditions, Cora Wilson Stewart immediately began figuring how many Kentuckians had registered by mark. She estimated that 30,000 men, the equivalent of 15 regiments, had registered by mark, and she spread this news through newspapers across the state. The impact of such a large number of illiterates being drafted was graphically illustrated by a news story of a young mountaineer who was arrested for failing to sign up for selective service. When brought to trial, he confessed ignorance of the conscription law, admitted that he was illiterate, and said that he had no idea where or even what Germany was.[1]

Cora Wilson Stewart forecast terrible dangers if illiterates were sent to fight overseas. She dramatically described the impact of drafting thousands of soldiers who could not read camp signs, military manuals, or letters from home. Her first step was to call on the federal government to require that all soldiers in military camps be taught to read and write before they were sent overseas. To this end, she worked through Kentucky's Senator Ollie James and Congressman J. Campbell Cantrill. She requested that the War Department issue an order making it compulsory for illiterates in the army to learn to read and write. The secretary of war replied to the Kentucky congressmen: "With reference to your letter transmitting recommendations from Mrs. Cora Wilson Stewart as to the education of illiterates at Army cantonments, I beg leave to inform you that the War Department has heretofore adopted the policy that during the present emergency it will be impractical to attempt any compulsory instruction along general educational lines."[2]

Frustrated in her attempt to persuade the government to offer literacy training for its recruits, Stewart decided to push for classes in her home state. She appointed committees in each Kentucky county to copy from draft registration cards the names of the men who enrolled by mark. By early July, she had a complete list of such people, and she called on the teachers of the state to conduct a special session of the Moonlight Schools for these recruits before they went into service.[3] Her letter to the teachers noted the dangers of having illiterate soldiers in the army as well as the injustice to the recruits: "It is unfair that these young men should be torn from their homes and dear ones and sent across the water to fight your battles and mine without being able to read a letter or to write a line back home." She went on to say: "It is the duty of every public school teacher to volunteer." In another call to the educators, she sounded the following battle cry:

> Shall Kentucky send thirty thousand illiterates to France? God Forbid! Why should she send any? Hasn't she an Illiteracy Commission, 11,000 public school teachers and as patriotic people as ever the sun shone on? To the guns, yes, every man of them—even though with their affliction they might well be exempt from military service, I believe—but to the books first, and then they go to the guns more content and with less embarrassment and less handicap.[4]

Again the teachers answered Stewart's call for help. News reports announced a special session of the Moonlight Schools for draftees, patriotic teachers volunteered faster than they could be placed in the field, and many men were reached before they went into military service. To help with the new students, Stewart prepared two special resources—*The Soldier's First Book* and the Soldier's Tablet. These materials focused on camp life and instilled a sense of patriotic duty in the recruits.[5]

The first lesson in the book was typical of other reading material created by Stewart. It read:

> I go.
> I go to war.

Do you go to war?
Yes, I go to war.
Yes, we go to war.

To fund the special work with soldiers, Stewart called on eleven prominent state leaders to raise $30,000. The figure of $30,000 was chosen because it represented $1 for each illiterate in the state who had registered by mark. Over the years, the K.I.C. had determined that it cost $1 to teach a person to read and write. Called "The Thirty Thousand Committee," the group composed of leaders from each of the eleven congressional districts in the state raised $10,951.19 for the K.I.C. during a campaign of less than ten weeks.[6]

To encourage similar efforts on the national level, Stewart wrote to President Wilson volunteering to direct the teaching of adult soldiers in the sixteen army cantonments. Her desires were also asserted in a letter of Kentucky's Senator J.C.W. Beckham: "There are two things that I am very anxious to bring about: one is that the Secretary of the War Department shall issue an order to have all illiterates in the army taught to read and write, and the next, that I shall be placed in charge of the work of organizing the classes in the various cantonments."[7]

It was neither personal ambition nor ego that caused Stewart to ask that she be placed at the head of the army work. As the pioneer of the Moonlight Schools, she believed that she was the person best qualified to complete this work. Soon after her suggestion, her expertise was recognized by the National War Work Council of the Y.M.C.A., which consulted with her and employed her methods and materials in the various army camps.

Throughout Kentucky, Stewart traveled to tell about the needs of illiterate recruits. She continuously reiterated the claim that 30,000 Kentucky recruits were illiterate and challenged the people of the state to help these men. Many people found the assertion that so many Kentucky draftees were illiterate hard to believe. For the first time since Stewart began her work in Rowan County, her claims were openly challenged in the press. A disbelieving writer in the Hazard *Herald* boasted that Kentucky had more college and high-school graduates than illiterates. The writer further said that the report of 30,000 draftees registering by mark was a slander on Kentucky men and was a means of getting money under false pretenses. The writer went on to charge: "This [the claim of 30,000 illiterate draftees] is not one eight true and the publishers of this lie ought to be publicly rebuked."[8]

A letter to the editor of the Louisville *Courier Journal*, written under the pseudonym Charles Marlowe, also challenged the work of the Moonlight Schools. The writer claimed that the statistics regarding the level of illiteracy in Kentucky were false and asserted that the K.I.C. was advertising the state's ignorance.[9]

Stewart responded promptly and forcefully to these challenges. She replied that, like a farmer or a merchant, the K.I.C. was advertising something it wanted

to get rid of—illiteracy. Furthermore, the U.S. government had already advertised the illiteracy rate in the 1910 census. She said the census reports were the
kind of advertising that hurt, not the campaign to reduce illiteracy. Stewart said
that she only wished that the facts were not true. The K.I.C. leader finished
her rebuttal by stating: "No one by the name of Charles Marlowe or by any
other name except the appointees of the Kentucky Illiteracy Commission has
examined the registration cards in the various counties to determine the number of illiterates among the 187,573 registrants."[10]

These two letters to the press were harbingers of things to come. Stewart
had successfully refuted the claims, and the people of the state believed her,
but some Kentuckians were tiring of the illiteracy crusade. Others saw the campaign as a constant advertisement of ignorance in the Bluegrass State. Local
pride caused many of these people to dispute the claims of the Commission.
There was no ground swell of criticism at the time, but these sentiments would
grow in the future.

In 1917, however, Stewart was too busy with the work at hand to worry
about critics. When the fall session of the Moonlight Schools began, attention
was again given to the men being called to military service. Teachers were provided copies of *The Soldier's First Book* to use along with the *Country Life Reader*
series. Training was provided by both day-school teachers and women's club
members. The public was aroused to the need to help the recruits, and many
rallies were held to enlist teachers for the night schools. At one rally in Mayfield,
the local newspaper reported: "The courthouse was unable to hold all of the
people who desired to hear the address [on the problem of illiteracy among army
recruits] and at the close there were seventy-five teachers who volunteered to
teach Moonlight Schools.[11]

In Hickham, Mr. A.S. Mackenzie, conductor of the Fulton County School
Institute, addressed a large audience about the Moonlight Schools, and according to press reports, "The audience was enthusiastic and 37 people volunteered
for the program."[12] Similar results were reported elsewhere.

When it was apparent that all the men needing schooling could not be
reached before induction into the military, the K.I.C. focused on helping recruits
at Camp Zachary Taylor near Louisville. The Y.M.C.A. was persuaded to take
up the work of the Moonlight Schools, and they dealt with men from Indiana,
Illinois, and Kentucky at the camp. The K.I.C. provided texts for the men, and
classes were organized so that new recruits could learn to read letters from home
and write back to their loved ones while in Europe. Officers in command of
various units showed a keen interest in encouraging the illiterates, and some
made attendance at night school compulsory. Some Moonlight School teachers reportedly followed the men to Camp Taylor and volunteered their time as
instructors.[13]

Stewart was happy that the Y.M.C.A. was taking the lead in this work and
noted: "It gives me great satisfaction to know that the National War Work
Council of the Y.M.C.A., the authority chosen by the government to direct

educational work, is now studying this problem with a view to action. This is the authority under which the work can best be done."[14] She expressed concern, however, that the Y.M.C.A. did not seem to be grasping the magnitude of the illiteracy problems. She was especially concerned because the Y.M.C.A. seemed interested only in teaching, in their terms, "Blacks and poor mountain whites." As a matter of pride, she took exception to the term "poor mountain whites":

> I wonder who it is that coined the term "mountain whites" and how it is that so many intelligent people have such poor taste and judgment to use it. The very term "mountain whites" is an insult to the brave soldier boys from the mountains and to the mothers who have given them to the country, more cheerfully, perhaps, than have any other mothers in all the land. They are American all—with an American's love for freedom, American courage and pluck. They'll go to School if they get the chance—and they'll learn—how they'll learn![15]

Asserting that illiteracy was not a concern of just the South, Stewart charged that illiteracy was a problem in all the army camps. She observed that New York, Pennsylvania, and Massachusetts had led many Southern states in the number of illiterates shown in the 1910 census. The K.I.C. leader said: "Many of the soldiers from these states are illiterates—'foreign born' some may say, but men just the same, and men that Uncle Sam has called into his service, just as he has called the boys from the South."[16]

Stewart urged the army to provide at least six weeks training for all of these men before they were sent abroad; she claimed that such schooling "will relieve the army of a weakness, remove a dead weight and make these soldiers, in some degree, if not altogether, efficient. Surely, these are reasons enough that every man in Uncle Sam's army—north, south, east, and west should be taught to read and write."[17] Despite her concern and exasperation with the Y.M.C.A., she continued to lobby for the expansion of the work among the camps and she was successful. By the end of the war, courses were being offered at Camp Lee in Virginia, Camp Dix in New Jersey, and Camp Shelby in Mississippi.[18] The spread of the work at these cantonments was a direct result of Stewart's constant lobbying.

As the patriotic fervor about the European War grew, Stewart prepared to ask the Kentucky Legislature to make a bigger commitment to the illiteracy crusade. She had introduced a bill in the 1918 session of the state assembly to provide the K.I.C $25,000 per year over a three-year period. This legislation authorized the hiring of illiteracy agents to organize the work in individual counties. Although the agents were to work with the local school superintendents, they would be under the control of the K.I.C. They were also to lend aid to the local superintendents, school boards, and trustees in increasing attendance of children in the day schools. Like earlier legislation, the bill required the members of the Kentucky Illiteracy Commission to serve without compensation. As a final stipulation, the bill called for the expiration of the K.I.C on July 1, 1920.[19]

Again, Stewart gained the support of the state's newspapers. In a letter to Colonel Robert W. Bingham of the Louisville *Courier Journal*, she expressed her appreciation for that newspaper's past assistance and affirmed that she was committed to seeing the bill through the legislature.[20] For Stewart, this was an exciting and challenging time. Not only was she involved with the work in Kentucky, she often made trips to Washington, D.C., to encourage the illiteracy work on a national level. Part of her effort in Washington was in support of the Bankhead Bill that provided federal funds for states fighting illiteracy. By now, she was well known in the halls of Congress, and the Bureau of Education commissioner, P. P. Claxton, regularly turned to her for advice on matters dealing with adult illiteracy.[21]

At this time, Stewart also gained the services of an associate who would loyally help her for the next eight years in the national work to eradicate illiteracy. Lela Mae Stiles came to work in the K.I.C. Frankfort office in 1917. Stiles was a bright, intelligent young woman who would provide the strong clerical support that Stewart needed as she advanced her crusade to a higher level. Miss Stiles would eventually become a secretary at the White House during the Roosevelt administration.

During the 1918 session of the Kentucky Legislature, Stewart was called to Washington, D.C. She had to leave to her local friends the task of seeing through the $25,000 appropriations bill. Because of the groundwork she had already laid and the interest aroused in illiteracy by the war, the bill was successful. On March 3, 1918, Lela Mae wrote to her: "It is now 4 p.m. and the bill has just passed the Senate. I am enclosing the roll call so you can see how each man voted. I shook hands with every senator I could get after the bill passed."[22]

At the time the bill was being considered by the state legislature, U.S. Commissioner of Education P. P. Claxton offered to appoint Stewart to a position as a specialist in adult education in the U.S. Bureau of Education. This attractive position would open new opportunities for her and would allow her to coordinate the illiteracy work of the nation. It would also provide her potential access to the resources of the federal government in promoting her work. She was tempted to accept the position, but her first allegiance was to her current work in Kentucky, as she wrote Claxton: "It seems to be the opinion of all with whom I have conferred about the matter that it would put a damper on the enthusiasm of all concerned and prove a great hindrance to the work in Kentucky and elsewhere were I to accept a position which would take me out of the State at this time. It has also been presented to me that it would appear ungrateful if I left after getting the $75,000."[23]

In years to come, Stewart might look back with regret for not accepting Claxton's offer. She had forgone an opportunity to be part of the federal government's adult education forces. At this time, however, she was already planning to advance her campaign to the national level, where she would be directly involved in larger scale campaigns to help adult illiterates. Her rejection of

Claxton's offer meant that she was destined to conduct these campaigns as an independent entrepreneur outside the educational establishment of the nation.

For the moment, the Kentucky appropriation was uppermost in Stewart's mind, and its passage was a source of great joy for her. The appropriation meant that for the first time the K.I.C. would have, in her view, adequate funds to complete the illiteracy campaign in Kentucky. Yet there was still one hurdle to cross; some officials questioned the legality of appropriating such money from the state treasury for purposes other than helping the day schools. When this challenge was submitted to Attorney General Charles H. Morris, he ruled that the K.I.C. bill was an aid to the common schools because the literacy agents to be hired with the funds would help enforce the local day school attendance law.

The attorney general cited the general difficulty in enforcing the compulsory school attendance law and stated that wherever Moonlight Schools had been held, day school attendance had increased. He finished his review by asserting that the entire act funding the K.I.C. could be seen as a valid police action in eliminating illiteracy.[24] Despite the passage of the Kentucky appropriation, all was not well in the life of Cora Wilson Stewart, however. The influence of World War I had taken the illiteracy campaign to new heights, and it had attracted many new people. This meant that Stewart did not have the control over the work that she had exercised earlier. Never a person who shared authority easily, she often considered opposing ideas to be a personal threat. She had committed so much of her time and energy to the work that she was not willing to compromise with people who had differing views about the illiteracy movement.

Stewart quarreled with Y.M.C.A. officials when they chose another textbook instead of *The Soldier's First Book* for teaching enlisted men. Her reaction was so intense that it generated the following response from a Y.M.C.A. representative:

> I have your letter of the 18th and after reading same carefully have come to the conclusion that due to the tremendous strain you have undergone in the past year in handling and consummating, so far successfully, the gigantic matter of illiteracy, that you have lost sight of some of the smaller details that have been a vital part of this work. Your letter conveys that you feel I have not been honorable. I know what you have gone through and the sacrifices you have made, financing the campaign and damaging your health.[25]

Financial problems were also a cause of Stewart's stress. She continued to have a very limited income from her lectures, inheritance, and royalties from her books. B. F. Johnson had advanced her more than $600 in royalties, and the publisher was requesting repayment. The financial stress was exacerbated by her fondness for the finer things in life. She had to travel widely, and she took part in functions that required a level of dress above the norm. All of this was expensive for a person with her limited means. In addition, in 1917 she joined the

National Arts Club in Washington, D.C. Here she met many people of social prominence who helped her in the work with illiteracy. Her attempt to keep up with the lifestyle of other club members meant, however, that she was constantly having financial problems.[26]

Because of the stress and strain, Stewart came to experience a case of what today would be called "burnout." For seven years, she had tirelessly committed herself to the Kentucky campaign, and it had taken a physical and emotional toll on her. She felt that she was losing her zeal for telling the story of the Moonlight Schools, and she was frightened by this feeling. For so long, the simple story of the schools' beginnings had provided her with the inspiration that she needed to impel herself forward. In the new world, however, with a war raging in Europe, she feared that her story of working in one county in Kentucky would not carry the wide appeal necessary for her future plans.

With these doubts in mind, Stewart decided to develop a new talk about the work with illiterates. In fashioning her speech, she turned to two old friends for advice. She first talked with Dr. A. E. Winship, editor of the *Journal of Education* in Boston. In the past, Stewart had written several articles for Winship, and she valued his opinion about her work. He replied to one of her letters with the following encouragement: "No woman speaks better than you do. I have never heard you when you were not captivating. I was led to writing as I did because your letter seemed to suggest that you were liable to get stale on yourself, not on others."[27]

When asked for advice, Winship offered the following comments:

> The only thing that troubles you is that you do not get the thrill nor *feel* the thrill *everytime* as you did when your story was a *revealation [sic]*. It has been told by you many times and in the magazines and papers until many in the audience can anticipate. You do not need to notice that difference. All that you need to do, all that you can do is to keep in the game in good shape. You saw how Jane Addams fell down. She has lost all the thrill of the Hull House Story and *she* has cooled off.[28]

Stewart also turned for advice to her old friend Dr. J. G. Crabbe, now the president of Colorado State Teachers College in Greeley. Crabbe offered the following suggestions to her:

> Concerning your public address, I make two suggestions—1) I believe that you ought not eliminate from your new address the plain practical stories of the early illiterates in Rowan County as you used to depict them in your early speeches. At least put in sufficient examples. Maybe just a bit more of gestures—plain, practical, pertinent—might help. Don't overdo it for it would spoil an already fine speech.[29]

Stewart valued this advice because she was regularly lecturing to large assemblies of national organizations and she wanted to make the most of her opportunities. On May 7, 1918, she spoke to the annual meeting of the General Federation Of Women's Clubs in Hot Springs, Arkansas. Her topic was "Adult

Illiteracy in America." According to participants, she captivated the audience and was the most successful speaker at the convention. As a result of her talk, the General Federation appointed its own illiteracy committee, and Stewart was named to head it.

Following the Hot Springs convention, Stewart spoke in July 1918 to the National Education Association in Pittsburgh, Pennsylvania. Her topic was "War-Modified Education and Illiteracy." In her remarks, she charged that the large number of illiterates in the nation, especially among native-born citizens, was not only a menace but a disgrace. She pointed out the negative impact of illiteracy on the war effort and in local economic and civic matters. She speculated that it would be much less expensive to educate illiterate adults than to let them continue to be a drain on the country.

As evidence of the problems of illiteracy, Stewart pointed to the high illiteracy rate in Russia in comparison to Germany. She noted that Germany was able to hold the world at bay while Russia was "broken down, disrupted, unable to enjoy her long-coveted and hardly won liberty and unable, we fear, to sustain a democracy now that she has one."[30] She concluded her remarks by stating that at the end of the war, the rest of the world would come to the United States for leadership. She asked, "Shall they find a democracy founded on the sinking sand of the intelligence of part of the people, or founded on the solid rock of the enlightenment of all?"[31] The N.E.A. was so moved by her comments that President Mary C. C. Bradford appointed an illiteracy committee and Stewart was named its first chair. The formation of the N.E.A. Illiteracy Committee was combined with a proclamation calling for the Americanization of the foreign-born population and teaching of the adult illiterates.[32]

The issue of Americanization was sometimes tied into the illiteracy crusade, much to the displeasure of Cora Wilson Stewart. The impact of World War I caused many previously unconcerned people to worry about the number of illiterates in the United States. Special concern was expressed about the foreign-born men and women of the Northeast. To some patriotic Americans, these new residents represented possible sympathizers with foreign governments and alien causes. As a result of these worries, the process of Americanization gained ground. Part of this process involved teaching the foreign-born to read and write, but it also involved making sure the foreign-born accepted the patriots' ideas of "American values."

Because she was involved in the work with adult illiterates, many supporters of Americanization considered Stewart an ally. She was sympathetic to the work because she thought there was a need to teach everyone to read and write. She was not comfortable, however, with the methods and claims of the people involved in Americanization. Many supporters of the movement were most interested in stampeding the masses of foreign-born citizens into an acceptance of patriotic ideas.[33]

Stewart had little experience with the foreign-born population of the Northeast, but she was a staunch opponent of immigration laws that limited the entrance of illiterate aliens into the country. She thought such people should be taught to read and write once they entered the country, not excluded because of their limitations. When it came to native-born Southerners, she was especially peeved with Americanization workers, who classified native-born illiterates with new immigrants. She rebuked anyone who insinuated that Americanization applied to the people of the Southern mountains simply because they could not read or write. She repeatedly noted that the mountaineers were descended from the earliest American settlers, and she rejected any connection between them and the new immigrants.

Stewart distinguished her work from Americanization by explaining that the Moonlight Schools taught native-born citizens because the South did not have many foreign-born inhabitants. She fought hard to keep the Moonlight School movement separate from the Americanization efforts. She expressed these sentiments most precisely in a letter to the New York *Tribune*: "This work [the illiteracy crusade] must not be confused with Americanization. We work entirely with native-born Americans. This comes about because there is practically no foreign-born element in the South compared with the great urban population of the East. Moonlight Schools correspond to the evening schools of the cities, but are conducted for illiterates only."[34]

Thus, by mid–1918, Cora Wilson Stewart was witnessing a burgeoning public awareness of the problems of adult illiteracy. This growing interest was a direct result of America's entry into World War I and Stewart's efforts to publicize the problems of adult illiteracy. As more people became involved in the illiteracy movement, however, the more different were opinions about the proper focus of the crusade and the greater the challenge to Stewart's authority. She did not know it, but her troubles in trying to maintain control over the work with adult illiterates were only beginning; World War I had released the genie from the bottle and there was no way to get him back inside.

8

*H*IGH *T*IDE OF THE *K*ENTUCKY *C*AMPAIGN

In June 1918, fifty newly hired K.I.C. county agents were called to Frankfort for training before being sent into the field. The agents were expected to fill a variety of roles for very little pay. Besides coordinating the county illiteracy campaigns, they acted as the first school attendance officers for the state. They received salaries of $75 per month, significantly less than public school teachers. Out of this salary, the agents were expected to pay their own living and travel expenses.[1]

If their pay was modest, at least the techniques they were expected to apply were stable; by now, the means of organizing and conducting Moonlight Schools were well established. Guidelines for operating the schools were covered at the agents' training session in Frankfort, and these instructions were published by the K.I.C. shortly thereafter. The format of the schools had changed little since Cora Wilson Stewart began them in Rowan County.

Teachers were told to offer classes Monday through Thursday evenings. The first evening was to begin with the singing of a familiar community song. A short scriptural reading and prayer, followed by another one or two stanzas of singing, completed the opening exercises. Teachers were then instructed to classify students according to their education level: adult illiterates, semi-illiterates, and educated persons who desired to review or to improve their education. Once this division was completed, the illiterates used the first *Country Life Reader*, the semi-illiterates used the second book of the series, and the most advanced students used the third book.

Teachers were directed to begin and end class on time. They were discouraged from exceeding the prescribed time limit because long sessions, even if lengthened at the pupils' request, eventually destroyed students' interest. In the words of the guidelines, teachers were commanded to "follow the program to the minute. Only in this way will each subject be assured of its due proportion of time."[2]

The reading technique used for illiterates was the whole word and sentence method. Teachers began by instructing the class, "Ask me if I can read." The students responded, "Can you read?" The students were then shown the first sentence of the book that read, "Can you read?" Similar sentences were taught by the question and answer method, and the students were shown the corresponding readings in the *Country Life Readers*. The words used in the sentences were then included in drills which students learned from the basic vocabulary of the books.

Spelling was not introduced initially because it was believed to hamper progress and to confuse the pupils. Instead, spelling words served as written exercises after the students had learned to form the letters of the alphabet. The first thing an illiterate was taught to write was his or her name. The teaching manual noted: "No other copy will inspire him to strive as will his own name."[3] After students had accomplished this feat, they practiced writing other words using the script copies in the *Country Life Readers*. At this point, the students were assigned the goal of writing a letter. This objective was set as the standard for the second and no later than the third week, and the letter was to be written to an actual person. The student was expected to write the letter, address the envelope, stamp, seal, and mail it. Teachers were told to impress upon the pupil the joy this message would provide the recipient.

Drills were an important part of the evening, and teachers were encouraged to conduct them in a quick, snappy manner. The classes were to be combined at this point, and all took part. The course of study set for the six-week session was ambitious. Beginning readers were expected to complete the first *Country Life Reader* by the end of the term. All men of draft age were given *The Soldier's First Book* as supplemental reading. For people who could read the first *Country Life Reader*, the second book was the text, and they were expected to complete this volume in the six-week session. The most advanced students were expected to complete the third *Country Life Reader* during the term.

Arithmetic was not forgotten. Beginners were first taught to read and write figures to ten, then to read and write larger numbers. The basic skills of adding, subtracting, multiplying, and dividing were encouraged, and problems were to be drawn from daily life. More advanced students were given the chance to learn higher skills in math.[4] This proscribed course of study had been developed over the first seven years of the Moonlight Schools. It was a very ambitious program, with much material expected to be covered in a short six-week span. That such a course was to be taught by volunteer teachers, who had already worked a full day, is a credit to the people who helped in this movement.

The primary records that remain of the courses of study are interviews with people who taught in the Moonlight Schools and letters written to Stewart by redeemed illiterates. From the interviews, it appears that the teachers were able to abide by the program. In addition, evidence of the progress made by students exists in the form of students' letters sent to Cora Wilson Stewart. These letters tell of the pride that each new writer felt at being able to compose such a message. They also express to Stewart the redeemed illiterates' gratitude for the opportunity to learn such basic skills.

Letters from the Moonlight School students were a source of both inspiration and pride for Stewart. She saved many of them for her entire life. Each one represented a verification of her work, and for her, each one stood as a written testimonial to the effectiveness of the Moonlight Schools. Whenever possible, Stewart sent to the new readers a small Bible as a prize for their success. Most of the funds for these rewards were provided by donations, especially the fund-raising drives of the Kentucky Federation of Women's Clubs. State funds were used to send the county agents into the field and were never used for this purpose.

The economy with which the K.I.C. operated and the manner in which it was able to spend its money were laudable. State Inspector and Examiner Nat Sewell conducted an audit of the K.I.C. at the end of 1918. In his report, he observed that the K.I.C. had received $37,413.61 from May 5, 1914, to July 1, 1918. Of this sum, $25,265.39 was received from private gifts and $12,148.22 from the state treasury. Thus more than two-thirds of the work of the commission was conducted with private funds. In a statement that made Stewart smile as she remembered the Duffy investigation of 1916, Sewell observed: "Upon the whole, there cannot be the slightest charge of extravagance made against any of the members or employees of the Illiteracy Commission. Extreme economy in expenditures is evidenced fully by records of the past four years."[5]

Once in the field, the literacy agents reported regularly to Stewart. To assist communications among the workers, Stewart started a small newspaper, *The Moonlighter*. It contained agents' reports and described local conditions regarding the successes and failures of the crusade. A review of these reports gives a good picture of the Kentucky crusade. In Lee County, agent Susan Simrall wrote that a meeting was held among people working in the campaign and a decision was made to focus first on men of draft age.[6] In Clark County, agent Bessie Cartwright related numerous enthusiastic testimonials about the Moonlight Schools and noted: "The interest, even eagerness, of the Negro teachers in town and county, is wonderful."[7]

Other reports from around the state were just as positive. Because of the European war, *The Moonlighter* often employed military language, which was especially favored by Stewart. To spur on the program, she initiated a contest between the eastern and western counties of the state; the agents were challenged to see which section could get the most people involved in the campaign. Points were earned for every teacher's pledge to teach, every Moonlight School organized, and every person taught to read and write. The contest began on August 12, 1918, and ended on November 1; it was won by the western portion of the state.[8]

During this contest, *The Moonlighter* reported: "How the battle rages! Whose blood doesn't tingle? Who can keep out of the fight?"[9] At another time, A. N. May, the agent from McGoffin County, reported, "Everything O.K. County went over the top. Not one slacker so far. Oh! it is glorious on 'the firing line.'"[10]

Along with the positive reports from the local agents, Stewart received some much-needed financial good news. The Overseas Department of the Y.M.C.A. contacted B. F. Johnson publishers in August 1919 and asked to purchase 50,000 *Country Life Readers.*[11] The sale of such a large quantity of readers provided Stewart with substantial royalties. Inspired by the overseas sales, Stewart encouraged Johnson to translate and sell her readers in Russia. She was concerned for the large number of illiterates in Russia, and she was intrigued by the prospect of helping them. The publisher explored this possibility but wrote back that because of the uncertain political situation in Russia and the lack of copyright laws, they would not proceed with the translation. Dissatisfied with this response, Stewart wrote the publisher again and encouraged him to sell the readers in Russia. When Johnson again refused to pursue the matter, however, she dropped the issue.[12]

In late 1918, Stewart became ill. For more than two years, she had experienced periodic bouts of sickness because of the rapid pace at which she lived. She drove herself relentlessly and was often physically exhausted. In 1917 she was diagnosed as having anemia. Her condition grew more severe during 1918; throughout the year, she was troubled by a dull, throbbing ache in her neck and back. At first the pain was attributed to fatigue, but it was later diagnosed as an illness of the nervous system. She eventually traveled to the Mayo Brothers Hospital in Rochester, Minnesota, for an operation, and she remained there until February 1919.[13] The long convalescence allowed her to rejuvenate her body and her spirits. Even while hospitalized, she kept up an active correspondence and looked forward to returning to her usual pace. She also wrote to other individuals about expanding her work after the Kentucky campaign ended.[14] At this point, she was exploring the possibility of joining the Chautauqua circuit and telling of the Moonlight Schools in that arena.

During late 1918 and early 1919, Stewart formulated her plans for the final year of the Kentucky campaign. She knew that she had one year to complete the work in her home state because the K.I.C. commission would expire on June 30, 1920. She also knew this would be no easy task. In a candid letter to the Louisville *Courier Journal*'s Robert W. Bingham, she expressed some of her frustrations with the Kentucky illiteracy campaign. She complained that many people still thought the campaign only worked with eastern mountain people, when, in reality, more illiterates had been taught in the western part of the state during the previous year than in the east. She noted that this misconception angered many mountain people and did a disservice to them. Always defensive about slights to her fellow mountaineers, she resented any effort to demean them. For nearly twenty years, she had sung the praises of the people of eastern Kentucky, and she was angered by efforts to stereotype them.

Stewart also emphasized to Bingham that there were more branches to the illiteracy crusade than the Moonlight Schools. To her credit, she knew that the problems of adult illiteracy had to be met in ways other than night classes. The schools were the cornerstone of the work with adults and they were a proven mechanism, but they were not the only means to reach and teach illiterates. As evidence, she described to Bingham the work with homebound people and the teaching of inmates in state penal institutions.

Stewart told Bingham that the 1919 campaign had to equal the previous five years combined. She also told him that in early 1920, she planned to turn her attention to securing legislation to help the people who had been redeemed from illiteracy by the Kentucky crusade. Stewart expressed the need for short-term evening schools that would operate like the public school system. In her opinion, these schools should offer continuing educational opportunities for redeemed illiterates. She also noted the need for regular truant officers in the public schools to enforce the attendance laws. Despite these long-term goals, however, her sights were still set on more precise objectives, and she reminded Bingham: "Our immediate task, of course, is to wipe out illiteracy, and for a time we must focus the attention of the public on that."[15]

When Bingham queried her about her future ambitions in state politics, Stewart answered frankly, "I shall be culminating during the coming year eight years of continuous effort, from which nothing in the world could divert me, and as to office or position in Kentucky, there is none that I want or would accept."[16]

By this time, Cora Wilson Stewart clearly envisioned illiteracy campaigns beyond the boundaries of the Bluegrass State. Her reputation had grown, and she was preparing to organize her work on a national level. At this point, she was not certain if the next step would involve working with the federal government or with private agencies. She knew, however, that her plans would be influenced by the culmination of the Kentucky crusade. For this reason, she wanted to make certain that the last year of work in her home state was the most effective ever.

Stewart planned her final year well. In April a meeting was held with leaders from the Kentucky Education Association, the County School Superintendents Association, and the General Federation of Women's Clubs. Stewart wanted to make sure that these organizations were committed to putting forth the best possible campaign during 1919. At this meeting, held at the Seelbach Hotel in Louisville, an agreement was reached which acknowledged the K.I.C. as the lead organization in the campaign. Mrs. Lafon Riker, president of the Kentucky Federation of Women's Clubs, represented her organization, and the county school superintendents selected Superintendent R. W. Kincaid of Bath County to work out the final campaign details for them. It was agreed that the crusade would begin during the summer with the training of a new phalanx of county illiteracy agents. The training session would be followed by a whirlwind speaking campaign during July; some of the most effective speakers in the state were scheduled to participate in this program. Following the speakers' series, a six-week session of Moonlight Schools was planned.[17] The Louisville gathering was followed by similar meetings among smaller groups of educators during the spring. These meetings brought together leaders from the universities and the public schools. Stewart attended all of these sessions and encouraged the educators to make a conclusive attack against illiteracy in Kentucky.[18]

In late June, fifty county illiteracy agents came to Frankfort for final training before setting out into the field. Stewart told them the purpose of the 1919 work was to reach and teach the 100,000 adult illiterates that the K.I.C. estimated were still left in Kentucky. Agents were told to recruit teachers from every occupation, not just the public school instructors. Public school teachers were still expected to provide the bulk of the instructors, however.[19]

Seventy counties had requested illiteracy agents, who entered the field on July 1. The speaking campaign was held during the week of July 28, and participants included congressmen, current and former governors, and some of the most gifted leaders of the state. Along with local campaigns coordinated by the illiteracy agents, several other departments were formed. George S. Spears, state banking commissioner, accepted the chairmanship of the bankers' division. Bankers were expected to report the names of people who could not sign their own names to checks and notes. A traveling salesmen section was organized with Will S. Hayes of LaGrange in charge. The salesmen were asked to tell illiterate customers of the Moonlight Schools and to encourage them to attend classes.[20]

The agents who entered the field on July 1, 1919, came from a variety of backgrounds. Some were graduates of the best colleges in the nation. Others had more modest education, but all were enthusiastic and idealistic. Their reports show the diligence with which they approached their work, as well as the achievements and problems of the Kentucky illiteracy campaign in 1919. There were many reports of success. For instance, in Pendleton County, agent Mary A. Norris noted a great deal of enthusiasm among the public when she arrived in the field.[21] In Barren County, agent Ira Pruden reported: "By far the majority of the trustees have shown a fine spirit toward the work."[22] In Knott County, agent Rose Blessing Craft told of a successful school series with more than 107 illiterates in attendance. In Campbell County, agent Irene Houston was so pleased with the progress that she wrote in October: "I feel confident there won't be one illiterate in Campbell County in 1920."

In Clark County, agent Fannie Curry said, "While there are not so many real illiterates in the district, there are others who want to come, so they can get the advantage and have the opportunity which they never had before."[23] In other areas, teachers went into the homes of people who could not come to the night classes, and the agents' accounts contain many heartwarming stories of success.[24]

The reports were not all rosy, however, and they show a subtle but distinct change from the earlier enthusiasm for the illiteracy crusade. Problems arose among the teachers and the illiterates. Some agents observed that it was very difficult to get the uneducated adults to come to the schools. The frustration was expressed succinctly by M. B. Jamison, a teacher, who said of the illiterates: "They seemed slow to come to the Moonlight School, fearing criticism most likely. It has been my hardest task to make them see the necessity of their regular attendance and faithful application."[25]

Others reported similar difficulties, and some stated that many illiterates seemed indifferent to the opportunity offered. These uneducated adults claimed that they had reached their present status in life without being literate and saw no reason to change. In other cases, illiterates would promise to attend the Moonlight School, but they would not come when classes began. This was a major challenge for the agents and the volunteer teachers; they could not teach people who were unwilling to learn.[26] Most significantly, for the first time in the crusade, many teachers seemed to resent having to teach the schools. Some of them complained of being overworked by the day schools and were unwilling to work at night. Monroe County agent Z. T. Osborne reported that one teacher told her, "She wouldn't teach a Moonlight School for $1000."[27] In Menifee County, agent J. C. Williams wrote that another teacher told him that he was paid little enough to teach in the day school, much less the night school. In Todd County, agent J. H. Rust observed that the worst trouble was that so many teachers lived so far away from the schools that it was impossible for them to return for the evening classes after working all day.

Lack of time, the difficulty in getting illiterates to attend, and the lack of pay for the work were among the reasons other teachers gave for not joining the crusade. In some cases, the teachers took the same tack as the illiterates: they volunteered to teach but never fulfilled their pledges.[28] Most success stories were reported where the agents themselves taught the schools. For instance, in Bell County, agent Sallie Ford wrote: "Most delightful evening work I ever did. Taught twelve men to read. This was the fifth evening. We had several visitors and all were delighted with this work!"[29] In Barren County, agent Ora Pruden described how she taught 72-year-old Mrs. Ben Smith to write and spell her name in about 20 minutes. The elderly lady was moved to tears by this feat and said she would be the happiest person in the world if she could learn to read the Bible. Pruden asked if she had a Bible, and the old woman said that she did not have one because she was too poor. According to Pruden, "I promised her if she would go to the Moonlight School and learn to read and write, Santa Claus would bring her a Bible of the largest print that could be found."[30]

The 1919 illiteracy campaign was graphic proof that the program was not meant to benefit solely mountain whites, if such proof was needed; schools were held throughout the commonwealth. The black population was especially receptive to the Moonlight Schools, and some agents reported their greatest successes among the African-American population. In Barren County, Ira Pruden noted that local preachers were very helpful in encouraging attendance. She wrote: "To my pleasure I found a booming Moonlight School among the black population there in the [Union Hill district]."[31]

In Pendleton County, Mary Norris noted that the black teachers enthusiastically volunteered to teach.[32] Elizabeth Baker reported a similar response in Allen County, as did Mason County agent Joseph B. Ross.[33] In Christian

County, agent Herbert Crik observed, "The greatest amusement to be found is with the Negro Moonlight School pupils, who seem whole soul and mind into the work. At a colored school where I visited Thursday night there were seventeen enrolled. Most all had learned to write their names during the few nights of school and can copy much of the script in the reader."[34]

Reasons for the response in the black community are not hard to find. Educational opportunities for African-Americans were as limited in Kentucky as they were elsewhere in the South. Even the meager instruction offered by the Moonlight Schools was a step up for many blacks, who had never had a chance to attend classes. Like the Rowan County mountaineers earlier in the decade, they were making up for lost time.

To her credit, Cora Wilson Stewart did not try to hide the problems of the 1919 illiteracy campaign. She made sure that *The Moonlighter* reflected the bad as well as the good side of the work, but she always tried to put a positive spin on the reports. In one *Moonlighter* editorial in September, she said: "Not all the efforts are producing the immediate results that might be hoped for. Many times we are discouraged when people in high places do not appreciate the work we are doing, but taken as a whole the outlook is encouraging."[35]

Despite the legislative appropriation, money was also still a problem for the K.I.C. After paying the county illiteracy agents, there was little money left to buy the pads, pencils, and books needed to supply the illiterate students. At one point, Stewart decided that an additional $20,000 was needed to provide the necessary supplies for the campaign. To this end, she turned again to her friends in the women's clubs of the state. At their annual meeting in Ashland on June 2–5, the Federation passed a resolution to raise the needed money. Each county club organization was asked to provide $100 to aid the illiteracy campaign.[36]

The K.I.C campaign was at its zenith during late 1919. Trained agents were in the field, and the most comprehensive campaign against adult illiteracy ever attempted was underway. With this concentrated effort, the extent of the problem of adult illiteracy became apparent. Stewart recognized that the teachers were no longer as enthusiastic as they had been in earlier years. She was still as committed as ever to the program, but she knew that it would take more money to finish the work. It was to this subject that she turned her attention in the latter part of 1919.

As great as they were, financial difficulties were not the only troubles Cora Wilson Stewart faced during the latter half of 1919; international events were also affecting her crusade against illiteracy. Because the Russian Revolution occurred in a country populated largely by illiterates, many people feared that uneducated Americans might be susceptible to Communist propaganda. Newspaper editors, government officials, educators, ministers, and other civic-minded citizens pointed to American illiterates, especially the immigrants of the Northeast, as potential Communists. As the impact of the Bolshevik Revolution became clearer, hysteria spread and Americanization became even more important than it had been during the recent world war. Many patriotic organizations, including the Daughters of the American Revolution and the American Legion, joined the movement to make sure that "one-hundred per cent American" ideals were dominant.[37]

Again, as during the war, Stewart was praised by Americanization workers because of her efforts with illiterates. At first, she welcomed these new supporters and accepted the plaudits awarded her. She soon realized, however, that, like the superpatriots of World War I, many Americanization advocates were more interested in homogenizing the population than in teaching illiterates to read and write.

Stewart feared that the Moonlight Schools would be diverted from the simple purpose for which she had intended them. One cannot deny that she advocated teaching moral civic lessons in the Moonlight Schools. The schools, like the *Country Life Readers*, were filled with the middle-class values of the time; Stewart was a civic-minded Christian who would not have had it otherwise. She knew, however, that the assimilation of immigrants advocated by many groups could not be accomplished overnight. Although she was outwardly cordial to the Americanization workers, she feared their impact on the crusade against illiteracy.

Stewart was especially incensed when people lumped together native-born illiterates with recent immigrants who needed to be "Americanized." She also rejected the idea that native-born illiterates were susceptible to Communist propaganda simply because they could not read or write. She had spent her career dealing with native-born Americans who might be illiterate but had better pedigrees than many of the people determined to "Americanize" them. She also knew that her fellow Southerners, even if some of them might be illiterate, were not going to be swayed by the foreign doctrines of Marx and Lenin.[38]

Despite her concern with outside influences, Stewart continued speaking to groups around the country about the need for a national crusade against illiteracy. During this time, she also organized the first-ever Illiteracy Conference of the Southern States. This meeting, under the general sponsorship of the National Education Association, was held in Columbia, South Carolina, December 1–2, 1919. Educators involved in working with adult illiterates in Alabama, Arkansas, Florida, Kentucky, Mississippi, North Carolina, and South Carolina attended the session. The Columbia meeting was Stewart's first experience in planning a regional conference on the subject of illiteracy, but it would not be her last. In the future, she would take a leading role in similar events, either presiding or making major presentations.

The South Carolina conference passed a resolution supporting the Smith-Towner Bill. This federal legislation, introduced by Congressman H. M. Towner of Iowa on January 30, 1919, called for the creation of a Department of Education in the presidential cabinet and consolidation of various educational bureaus in the federal government. Most importantly for the Columbia assembly, the bill called for a $7,500,000 annual appropriation to help the states eliminate illiteracy. Stewart was a proponent of this proposal, and she testified before Congress in support of it. She was delighted when the Columbia conference endorsed the legislation. The Smith-Towner bill would continue to be a favorite of hers, although it would never be passed. It would be more than 50 years before a cabinet-level department of education was established.[39]

Meanwhile in Kentucky, Stewart was making plans for the next phase of her work with adults. Realizing that the $75,000 appropriated by the legislature was not enough to complete the illiteracy campaign, she traveled to New York to seek aid from General Clement Dupont and the Red Cross. Unfortunately, her trip did more harm than good because it was reported in the press that she had gone to New York to buy a fleet of airplanes to use in the Kentucky crusade. Stewart reportedly remarked to a newspaperman that the poor mountain roads in her home state made it impossible to reach all illiterates by automobile, and she hoped to use the planes to carry teachers into remote areas. Stewart later denied this story, and no one can be sure if she actually intended to buy a fleet of planes. She did attempt to buy or rent at least one airplane from Curtiss Aeroplane & Motor Corporation, however, and she even asked Eddie Rickenbacker, an American flying ace of World War I, to be her pilot. One newspaper reported that she planned to take flying lessons herself to carry out her educational work.[40]

This story was reported by national newspapers, including the *Christian Science Monitor*. When the news hit the local press in Kentucky, it shocked many Kentuckians who favored her work, and it further raised the suspicions of people already skeptical about the K.I.C. Some supporters wondered whether state funds were going to the Moonlight Schools or were being used to finance Stewart's travels. The Jackson *Times*, in West Liberty, wrote a scathing editorial which said that it did not doubt Stewart's flying lessons would gather "first page position in the newspapers, with half tone illustrations, which seem to be a penchant for the chairman of the illiteracy commission." The paper also offered its assessment of the K.I.C. in general and the Moonlight Schools in particular. The editor wrote: "The Commission is deliberately traducing the mountain people and advertising them as being on the same level of civilization with the South Sea Islanders and Hottentot savages. The Moonlight School idea is fatuous and its application a joke."[41]

Thus, by the end of 1919, a definite reaction against Stewart and the illiteracy crusade was developing in her home state. But Stewart was oblivious to the strength of her opposition. She continued making plans for the period after June 30, 1920, when the K.I.C. term expired. She proposed forming a State Department of Adult Education to standardize the night school work and to pay night school teachers; the department would be independent of the State Department of Education. In early 1920, she got such a bill introduced in the House of Representatives. While the bill was passing through the legislative process, the public began assessing the effectiveness of the illiteracy crusade.

Stewart claimed that at least 130,000 of Kentucky's 208,084 illiterates had been taught to read and write. She based her figures on reports that she received from county school superintendents, teachers, and former illiterates.[42]

Because the future of the illiteracy work in Kentucky depended on the action of the legislature, Stewart spent the first two months of 1920 working vigorously for the passage of her bill. Her task grew more difficult early in 1920, however, when new Governor Edwin P. Morrow, in his message to the state legislature, called for the consolidation of boards and commissions wherever possible. Like Augustus Stanley four years earlier, he rejected any new appropriations unless a means of funding them was found.[43]

The first Republican elected during Stewart's work with the Moonlight Schools, Morrow had participated in the K.I.C.'s speakers campaign the previous summer. During 1919, when he was contemplating a run for the governorship, he had also asked Stewart for her ideas about the educational needs of the state. Despite these apparent connections to Stewart, Morrow was determined to make changes in state government following years of Democratic leadership. He enjoyed a clear majority in the House, while the Democrats had a two-vote majority in the state Senate.[44]

Despite the governor's avowed opposition, Stewart focused public attention on the night school bill. To arouse the citizenry, she planned to have the Kentucky Federation of Women's Clubs rally at the Frankfort legislature on March 10, the day that the adult education bill was scheduled to come before the House of Representatives. She was helped in this process by the Federation's representative, Mrs. J. C. Layne of Fort Thomas, who was in Frankfort for several weeks prior to March 10, lobbying for the bill. Fearing the rising support from the women of the state, Governor Morrow reiterated his opposition to any new expenditures on March 2. Spurred on by the governor, the opponents of the bill in the House Rules Committee suddenly called the adult education bill up for consideration on March 4 and tabled it. The Republicans had a clear majority in the House, so this action was not difficult for the administration to sustain.[45]

As the Kentucky Federation of Women's Clubs representative, Mrs. J. C. Layne was furious with the action of the House because it was clearly designed to preempt the women's march on the capital. "Thursday, March 4, 1920, will long be remembered as one of the darkest days in Kentucky's history. On that day, Kentucky gave up its leadership in the fight against illiteracy and set the state back 50 years," she charged. "These tactics employed by the administration leaders to prevent Kentucky's patriotic women from gathering here in the interest of a cause they loved and in which they invested $22,000 are unparalleled in history."[46]

Not to be outdone, the Federation of Women's Clubs threatened to have 1000 women march on the capital. Stewart still held out hope for the night school bill because the Democrats held a two-vote majority in the Senate. She did not plan, however, on the actions of the state's new superintendent of public instruction, George Colvin. On March 2, the same day Governor Morrow made his statement about no new expenditures, Colvin sent a survey to local school superintendents. The survey asked the administrators for their opinion of the Moonlight Schools. It also asked what impact an appropriation for night schools would have on teachers' morale if no money was appropriated to provide salaries for the teaching of such schools. A final portion of the survey stated the new superintendent's personal preference regarding education. He said, "I have been insisting that our chief duty is to remove the cause of illiteracy by making our public schools more efficient, by paying the teachers a decent salary, by taking our schools out of politics, by paying school superintendents a living wage, by securing better attendance upon our schools. In my judgment the time to erad-icate illiteracy is in childhood."[47]

The response from the local superintendents was decidedly against pass-ing the adult education bill if it did not provide money to raise teacher's salaries. After six years of asking teachers to volunteer their time and effort to teach Moonlight Schools, the superintendents were not willing to do more, and they did not think their teachers were willing to sacrifice more. The response to Colvin's survey was 11 in favor of the adult education bill and 109 opposed.[48] Colvin made his findings public and sent the results of the survey to the state Senate on March 8.

Encouraged by the opposition of the governor and the state superinten-dent of public instruction, enemies of the legislation called the bill to the Sen-ate floor for debate on March 9, a day before the women were set to march. The opposition was led by Senator Pleasant Hogue, from Governor Morrow's home district. The Lexington *Herald* carried a detailed account of Senator Hogue's remarks that is hard to improve upon:

> The matter was rushed to a vote after Senator Hogue had demonstrated to at least a majority of those present that illiteracy is by no means an essential to success even to the attainment of a seat in the august Senate of the Commonwealth.
>
> The speech of the Senator from McCreary was at once fiery, eloquent and conclusive. Being a herb-and-root doctor in private life, and in his first session of the Senate, he has been heard seldom and but briefly on the floor, and perhaps for that reason his oratorical effort made even a greater impression, if possible than could have been created by virtue of its pure forensic force and soundness of argument.
>
> "I ain't in favor of wastin' no more money of this here fair state of our'n on this thin o'teachin' old people," the Senator began. "It ain't no use and furthermore they don't deserve it."
>
> "How'd I get my education? Why I got it by stickin' a pine knot in the wall, when these here other people was out gallivantin' around. They didn't try to git no education, they didn't and I ain't in favor of spendin' no money on 'em now. This Moonlight School business hasn't got no where, because the people like me that wanted to git educated has got educated."

According to the *Herald*, the senator went on to chastise his fellow legislators who were concerned about the impending clubwomen's march on the capital. "I ain't afeered to vote against this bill, though they's some here that is. They's some weak-kneed politicians that's afeered of the women. I ain't got no use fer these here women that run around with a poodle dog in their arms, and I ain't afeered of 'em," he boasted.[49]

Inspired by the challenge thrown down by Senator Hogue, the senators defeated the bill 19 to 17. The vote was clearly along party lines, with 17 Republicans and 2 Democrats voting against it; 15 Democrats and 2 Republicans supported it.[50]

Cora Wilson Stewart was furious when she learned about the action of the State Senate, and she responded in the press with a scathing letter attacking George Colvin. She charged that the state superintendent had gotten his negative replies from the local school administrators by giving the impression that the evening school bill would endanger an increase in teachers' salaries; in reality, the bill allowed teachers to be paid $2 per night for each session taught. She also said the responses of the superintendents varied markedly from their responses to a survey conducted by the K.I.C. at the end of 1919. She published the responses of the superintendents to Colvin's letter side by side with the corresponding replies of the same people to a K.I.C survey in late 1919. The responses were indeed very different. In all of the K.I.C. accounts, the superintendents were very positive about the Moonlight Schools and their impact on the counties of the state, but in Colvin's surveys, the same administrators emphasized the negative ramifications of the proposed night school bill.[51]

It is difficult to reconcile the two surveys. It must be granted, however, that the teachers and superintendents of the state had long sacrificed for the Moonlight Schools. They were tiring of the constant campaigns against illiteracy. Despite their exhaustion, they had stated their support for the Moonlight Schools in the 1919 K.I.C. survey. When the state superintendent (in effect, the chief administrative public school official in the state) came out against the night school bill, however, it is not hard to understand how their attitudes might have been influenced. If they thought there was to be no compensation for their efforts, they were not willing to sacrifice further. The educators' reservations, combined with the stated opposition of the new Republican administration, sealed the fate of the night school bill.

Stewart's anger was not reserved solely for Colvin. She scolded the state senators for their actions, noting that for years men had come to the legislature in support of favored programs and "for the women of Kentucky to come to the Capitol in the interest of an education measure should not alarm the legislature and surely should not be termed an assault on Capitol Hill."[52]

Following the death of the legislation, the press of the state speculated about the reasons for its failure. One paper noted that apparently the K.I.C. and the Kentucky Federation of Women's Clubs were the only real supporters of the measure. It also noted that "the mountain people resent what they declare

are slanderous misstatements of their alleged conditions."[53] Other editors speculated that many people thought the problem of illiteracy needed to be attacked in early youth, not old age. Some noted the impact of the negative reports of the superintendents and the growing feeling that there were too many commissions and government agencies on the state and national level. It was observed that such commissions had a way of attaching themselves to the public treasury and not letting go.[54] Finally, the news accounts reported that the new department of adult education was to be outside the supervision of the superintendent of public instruction; such a direct threat was bound to be opposed by the superintendent.[55]

All of these explanations contain elements of truth; together they help explain the failure of the night school bill. There was also a yearning in the country for a return to "normalcy" following the First World War. People were tiring of grand crusades, and a general disillusionment had set in. This sentiment produced a turning away from the Progressive reforms of the first portion of the twentieth century; Kentuckians shared this attitude with the rest of the nation. The people of the state admired Stewart and her accomplishments, but they were unwilling to finance her plans further.

Ironically, the people who ultimately ended the Kentucky campaign were the supporters Stewart had relied on most over the years—the public school educators of the state. The teachers had often answered her call for volunteerism and had taught in the Moonlight Schools. By the end of the decade, however, they were tired, overburdened with the work of the day schools, and had lost heart for the fight. No longer willing to give their time and talents free of charge, they thought they deserved compensation. Stewart tried to include such reimbursement in the adult education bill, but the teachers had seen the legislature too often approve the illiteracy crusade without the necessary funds; they had reason to be skeptical about the new Department of Adult Education.

The educational leadership of the state, personified in George Colvin, was also not eager to share power with a commissioner of adult education. Such a department would challenge the public schools for scarce funds. It would be outside the ranks of the budding educational bureaucracy that had developed in Kentucky over the previous decade; such a new bureaucracy did not need competition. Colvin knew that Cora Wilson Stewart was a formidable force in education; he did not want to give her a chance to establish herself as a rival in a battle for educational dollars.

For her part, Stewart was enraged at what she saw as a Republican conspiracy. In an address to the state legislature several weeks later, she lambasted the party for thwarting educational advancement in the state. She accused the superintendent of playing politics with education and expressed concern that "reactionaries" would undo many of the recent advances in Kentucky education. Stewart was a charitable woman, capable of great actions of compassion, but she seldom forgot a wrong done to her. It would be many years before she forgave Kentucky Republicans, and especially George Colvin.[56]

Following the defeat of the adult education bill, Stewart spent the next several weeks preparing the final report of the K.I.C. This review clearly mirrored Cora Wilson Stewart's hopes for the crusade against illiteracy in Kentucky. It said the remainder of Kentucky's illiterates should be provided with an opportunity to learn to read and write, and newly redeemed illiterates should be given a chance to further their schooling. To accomplish this feat, the K.I.C. recommended a series of night schools similar to those of the Northeast. The report called for the paying of teachers who taught in these schools and recommended a department of adult education with a commissioner to build up the night schools. The commission further suggested the establishment of a state school where adults who wanted to attend on a year-round basis could come and complete their education through the equivalent of the eighth grade. Finally, the commission called for the teaching of inmates in the State Reformatory and Penitentiary.[57]

The final K.I.C. report also assessed the effectiveness of the six-year crusade. According to the 1920 K.I.C. report, there were 208,084 illiterates in Kentucky in 1910. Over the six years since that inception of the Kentucky Illiteracy Commission, Stewart estimated that approximately 130,000 illiterates had learned to read and write.[58]

In contrast to the K.I.C.'s final report, the 1920 U.S. census showed that Kentucky still had 155,004 illiterates. This is substantially more than the 90,000 that Cora Wilson Stewart estimated. As in 1910, the measure of literacy in the 1920 census was determined by asking a person if he or she could write in any language. This standard was used by the Census Bureau because it had been found that, generally, a person who could write could also read.[59] Using the Census Bureau measure, it is reasonable to assume that many of the people who attended the Moonlight Schools would reply that they could write, since a high value was placed on this skill in the classroom instruction. From this perspective, it is surprising that more people did not respond that they were literate.

As can be seen, the ultimate impact of the Moonlight Schools on Kentucky is as difficult to measure as the meaning of the term *illiteracy*. A comparison of the illiteracy rates among counties that held Moonlight Schools and those that did not may, however, be a better measure of the effectiveness of the classes. On the basis of reports of newspapers, school superintendents, illiteracy agents, and teachers, the Moonlight Schools were conducted in 70 counties between 1910 and 1920. Forty-nine counties did not report any Moonlight School activities. The census shows that in counties where the night schools were held, the numbers of illiterates decreased an average of 5.1%. In counties where no schools were held, the number of illiterates decreased by 4%. The state average decrease in illiteracy from 1910 and 1920 was 4.6%. This means that the rate of reduction in illiteracy in counties with Moonlight Schools was 27.5% higher than in counties without schools. Did the schools produce this decrease? It is impossible to say. It is obvious, however, that in counties showing the greatest reduction in illiteracy, the Moonlight Schools were conducted.

There is also no doubt that many people did learn to read and write—or at least thought they had learned to read and write. Reports from teachers, school superintendents, illiteracy agents, and newspaper accounts show that people attended the schools and that they made progress. The K.I.C. relied on the reports of teachers and school superintendents to gather its statistics, and these reports should be considered as least as reliable as the answers to census questions. Most significantly, the letters redeemed illiterates wrote to Cora Wilson Stewart telling of their progress speak most dramatically to the achievements of the schools. It cannot be denied that the level of instruction was very basic and the accomplishments were modest but the letters from the former illiterates offer tactile proof that the schools had an impact.

In the final analysis, perhaps the ultimate influence of the Moonlight Schools and the Kentucky illiteracy crusade should not be measured in statistics of illiterates redeemed, hours taught, or even letters written. Maybe its ultimate effectiveness should be measured by the hope the schools gave to the uneducated. Before the inception of the Moonlight Schools, there were no illiteracy campaigns in the United States, there were no illiteracy commissions, and there were no readers designed especially for adult illiterates. Most importantly, there was little or no hope for the adults who resided in the darkness of illiteracy without any prospect of learning how to read and write.

The schools gave uneducated people confidence that they could learn. At the same time, the schools questioned the conventional wisdom of the time among educated people who thought that adults were incapable of learning. The crusade challenged these educated people to help their less fortunate friends and neighbors. These two features alone made the schools worth the very modest price paid by the Commonwealth of Kentucky. The schools insured that, in the future, other efforts, maybe more technical, more precise, maybe even more effective, but clearly no better motivated, would be tried. It is fair to say that today, every time a Laubach literacy tutor teaches a student, every time that a representative of Literacy Volunteers of America meets with a new reader, they can trace their origins back to the Moonlight Schools.

There can be no more fitting witness to the impact of the schools, and Cora Wilson Stewart would not ask for any more proof of the effectiveness of her idea. Like a siren in the night, she had aroused the state to the problem of adult illiteracy, and she had alerted the public to the needs of the uneducated. If in the end the state did not choose to pursue her recommendations and establish a department of adult education, her accomplishments are not diminished. The night school bill defeat did not deter her from continuing her work.

After she completed the final K.I.C. report, Stewart returned to the hills of Rowan County for a brief respite. When a fellow worker asked why she had not heard from her lately, Stewart characteristically replied, "You must not get the impression that I have given up [the illiteracy work]. I am only enlarging it. My aim of ten years service to my state, ten to my nation, and ten to the world is now entering the second chapter."[60]

FREELANCE CRUSADER

Cora Wilson Stewart was disappointed at the actions of her home state legislature, but she was not demoralized. Her vision transcended political conditions in a single state. Momentary setbacks were to be expected, and she was prepared for them. Just because the K.I.C. had expired, the illiteracy work in Kentucky was not over. She helped organize the Kentucky Literacy League to continue a minimal level of work with adult illiterates in her home state. Ever the optimist, she even expressed hope of converting the Morrow administration to her views. As she told several of her friends in other states, "Do not feel disturbed over our failure to get our bill through the Legislature last time. We had a very large program and it takes some time for new men to get the vision."[1]

While Kentucky lost its vigor for illiteracy campaigns, other states were continuing their efforts. In Alabama, Arkansas, South Carolina, and Georgia, local illiteracy battles were ongoing, and Stewart's friends looked to her for support and guidance.[2] In the summer of 1920, she also began writing a book on the Moonlight Schools. Her involvement in the Kentucky illiteracy crusade had not allowed her time to put her story in book form. Several of her friends encouraged her to write about the night schools, and she planned to use the time in Rowan to prepare a manuscript for publication.

The events in the recent session of the Kentucky legislature, the passage of the eighteenth amendment, and the impending adoption of the nineteenth amendment to the U.S. Constitution also influenced Stewart's views about politics. After seeing the success of the prohibition and women's suffrage forces, she concluded that further progress against illiteracy would come through political channels. As she wrote to one of her friends: "I am convinced that the time has come when if our work is to have the fullest extension, we must work through the political channels as the Prohibition and other causes have found that to be the case."[3]

Stewart was not comfortable with the need for political action because she thought that the crusade against illiteracy should be above common politics. She was prepared to make such a commitment if it helped her cause, however. In her mind, a cornerstone to the national illiteracy crusade was the Sterling-

Towner bill, federal legislation which created a cabinet-level department of education and provided money for the states to conduct illiteracy campaigns. She was intent on seeing the passage of this legislation.

The decision to enter the political arena was made easier for Stewart by the fact that 1920 was a presidential election year. Her avowed admiration for Woodrow Wilson, her contacts in the Democratic party, and her recent unpleasant experience with Kentucky Republicans provided additional motivation. Using her standing among Kentucky Democrats, she became a delegate to the National Democratic Convention and set off for its meeting in San Francisco in June 1920.

At the convention, Stewart made the most of her opportunities to network with prominent individuals. Among the people she met was William Allen White, the Emporia, Kansas, newspaper editor, who would later play a key role in her illiteracy work. She was impressed with Governor James B. Cox of Ohio, a candidate for the nomination, and she noted: "He has many of the qualities of Theodore Roosevelt, particularly his strenuous habits, his progressiveness and his magnetism. He also has the reverence and the vision of Woodrow Wilson." After meeting the potential vice-presidential candidate Franklin Roosevelt, she observed that he "is one of the finest young men that the nation has ever produced."[4]

Stewart's enthusiasm for James B. Cox was returned by the supporters of the Ohio governor. Aware of her significant speaking abilities and mindful of the passage of the nineteenth amendment, the Cox contingent wanted her to second his nomination at the convention. Representatives of the governor, along with her old friend General W. H. Sears, met with Stewart at her hotel to ask her to make this speech. Despite her admiration for Cox, Stewart was not totally convinced that he was strong enough on prohibition. She supported a "bone-dry" plank in the party platform submitted by William Jennings Bryan, while Cox was not so firm on this issue. After reviewing Cox's entire record, she told General Sears, "I am not satisfied. I want to talk to some of the Ohio women." Sears escorted her to the St. Francis Hotel, two blocks away, where they met with two women who had led the prohibition fight in Ohio. After frankly discussing Governor Cox's qualifications with the two prohibitionists for half an hour, Stewart was satisfied that Cox was not a "wet" and told Sears she would second the nomination.

J. C. Cantrill, the Kentucky representative who was scheduled to second the nomination, withdrew in deference to Stewart, who made a strong speech on behalf of the Ohio governor. She told the women in the convention hall that she was satisfied with Cox as a presidential candidate. Her remarks were popular with the crowd, and several people later wrote to congratulate her on her forceful speech. The nomination was far from assured, however, and the convention went to forty-four ballots before Cox was selected to be the party's candidate. In recognition of her accomplishments, Stewart's fellow Kentucky delegates cast one vote for her for president on the 36th ballot.[5]

Kentucky delegation to the 1920 Democratic Convention. Cora Wilson Stewart is fourth from left, and future vice president of the United States Alben Barkley is sixth from left.

Stewart's endorsement of Cox significantly influenced the women at the convention. Many of them shared her concern about the governor's stand on prohibition, but they were reassured by her support. As one California educator wrote to Governor Cox, the women of the convention knew that "Cora Wilson Stewart would not have nominated a man whose ideals in this respect and all others were not of the highest."[6]

Part of Stewart's reluctance to nominate Cox was her fear that she might alienate some supporters of the illiteracy crusade with such a partisan gesture. She definitely favored prohibition, as one might expect from her earlier marriage experience, but she knew that the issue of adult illiteracy cut across political lines. Referring to her seconding speech in San Francisco, she later wrote to Brainard Platt, editor of the Louisville *Times*: "I feared that at times that I'd forfeit whatever reputation I might have made in fields where I knew my ground better."[7]

Satisfied that the convention had nominated the right man, Stewart left San Francisco and hurried east to Salt Lake City, where the National Education Association was assembled. She planned to ask the N.E.A. to appropriate $5000 for its Illiteracy Committee, and she also wanted the association to sponsor four illiteracy conferences during November and December. She envisioned regional gatherings similar to the Southern illiteracy meeting she had organized during 1919.

Because the Democratic Convention had lasted so long, Stewart arrived late at the N.E.A. meeting. She missed much of the conference, including the N.E.A. Illiteracy Committee meeting. Because of her late arrival, she was not able to lobby the membership as vigorously as she planned. She did have time, however, to persuade the educators to establish two committees to interview the presidential candidates of the national parties to determine their stands on the problem of adult illiteracy. She also convinced the convention to appropriate $1,000 per year for the N.E.A. Illiteracy Committee. This sum was significantly less than she hoped would be provided, but considering her late arrival at the conference, it was the best she could do.[8]

Later in August, Stewart attended the General Federation of Women's Clubs convention to enlist its support in a national crusade. She was disappointed when the Federation failed to elevate the illiteracy work to the status of a department in its organizational structure, and she was also concerned about the Federation's growing emphasis on Americanization. In a letter to the General Federation's Lida Hafford, she said, "Please don't let them put illiteracy under Americanization. It grossly insults our southern mountain people to speak of Americanizing them."[9]

Returning to Morehead, Stewart resumed work on her book during the summer; she was not aware, however, of the impact that her seconding speech in San Francisco would have on her schedule. The 1920 campaign was the first national election in which women had the vote; no one knew how female voters would cast their ballots, and the political parties did not want to take any chances. The Democratic leadership knew that Cora Wilson Stewart's national reputation, plus her dynamic and forceful speaking style, would help their candidate. She could rival any man on the stump, women respected her endorsement of Cox, and the national party wanted her services.

Stewart's own home state also counted on her to carry the female vote for Cox. Henry V. McChesney, former state superintendent of public instruction and now coordinator for the Democratic speakers, had assumed that she would give most of her time to Kentucky, but national Democratic leader Pat Harrison of Mississippi got to Stewart first. Harrison asked her to commit herself to a national speaking tour on behalf of Cox. Unaware that the Kentucky Democrats also relied heavily on her, Harrison wrote to her in late August, "Remember you promised to give us your time. We are having calls for you in various places. Most of your time will be spent outside Kentucky."[10]

McChesney was sorely disappointed when he heard of Stewart's commitments outside the state. He pleaded with her to save the larger part of her time for Kentucky. When Stewart explained to him that she had already made national commitments, he pressured her: "I am going to say something personal. I don't know whether you have any political ambitions or not. If you do, conditions may come about where it would appear perfectly proper for you to have such ambitions. If your demand among Kentucky Democrats is any indication, I beg you not to overlook this in deciding [where you speak during the campaign]."[11]

Facing conflicts between her original commitment to the national party and allegiance to her home state, Stewart was frustrated. She wrote to one friend:

> I feel that I am being treated like a child about it [the speaking conflict] and what I ought to do really is to just withdraw from it altogether, at least such thoughts come at times. I have offered to give forty days time even though I am just at the close of years of volunteer campaigning against illiteracy. It is not easy from a financial standpoint nor any other. The state attitude is disturbing.[12]

Stewart finally reconciled the problem by giving all but eight days of the campaign to her home state. Her involvement in the presidential election deepened when she was appointed to head the N.E.A. committee to interview Governor Cox regarding his positions on the Sterling-Towner bill. On September 2, she met with Cox along with the other members of the N.E.A. committee. After she described the problem of adult illiteracy, the governor asked her to tell his secretary the type of things she wanted and he would see that they were included in his acceptance speech. Cox then asked her personally to campaign for him.[13]

Another N.E.A. committee was appointed to meet with Republican candidate Warren Harding. Stewart noted later that the Republican candidate refused to endorse the Sterling-Towner bill. He explained that there were four or five interests demanding inclusion in the cabinet, and he could not be expected to know what was needed on all of them. She was disappointed in the Republican candidate's response; Harding's answers made her more certain than ever that Cox should be elected.[14]

After committing to the Kentucky campaign, Stewart actively encouraged women to support the Democrats. She also traveled throughout the United States, making fifty speeches on behalf of Cox during the final three weeks before the election; thirty-four of these talks were in Kentucky. The travel was tiring, and the final four days took an almost superhuman effort on her part.[15] She gave the same effort to her political speeches that she gave to her talks about illiteracy. Each speech was an oratorical event, not a simple endorsement. When she finished the campaign, she felt that she had done her best.

Cox lost the national election in a landslide. Ironically, the much ballyhooed impact of women never materialized. The new influx of female voters did not change the makeup of the election dramatically as had been thought. Kentucky was the only border state to go Democratic, however, and Stewart took pride in this victory. She was glad that Kentucky had been, in her words, "redeemed." She had done her part for the party, and it was no small comfort to her that the Republican success on the national level had not extended to her home state.

Stewart was not dispirited about national results either. Shortly after the election, she observed: "The fact that we did not win in the nation has not diminished my pride or enthusiasm. We were right, and it is more noble to be right and in the minority than ever to be right and in the majority."[16] She consoled a fellow Democratic female with the following advice: "We laid a good foundation this time for the campaign four years hence and I am hoping to come back in the next campaign. The Republicans will split into a thousand pieces and our next fight will be easy. It was a great pleasure and honor to stand up for the Party principles at a time when adversity struck it."[17]

The election of 1920 marked a change in the national mood, although Stewart did not realize it at the time. Many Progressives of the early twentieth century had tired of reform campaigns. The First World War disillusioned the electorate, which wanted a rest from the changes of the previous two decades. This return to "Normalcy" ushered in twelve years of Republican government on the national level. Although Stewart detected a change in the political climate, she did not believe that it marked the end of Progressivism. She reasoned that it would simply take the new men time to get "the vision" as she called it. Instead of becoming a cynic like many prewar reformers, she retained her crusading zeal. She returned to work on her book about the Moonlight Schools and made plans for a national illiteracy crusade.[18]

Stewart's feelings about her book and her confidence about the future were expressed in a letter to fellow illiteracy worker and Alabama educator Sarah E. Luther:

> You ask what I am doing with myself. Why, dear lady, what a question! I'm fighting illiteracy, of course, fighting it with my pen just at the present time. You didn't expect me to stop when Kentucky did—did you? The Republican Administration here did not have enough vision to adopt our program. We are delayed, and while waiting, I have much to write that I had no time to put in form before—and much that will be helpful, I hope. That's why I am here in the quiet of my hills. I was afraid that the action of our Legislature would cripple the work of some others—like you—who are engaged in the violent fight, so I've kept just as quiet as I could. Though I regret the delay, I am not discouraged. The illiterates will have their chance. Progress never goes in a straight line but zig-zag, I'm told.[19]

Stewart began 1921 determined to finish her book, and she delivered it to her publisher, E. F. Dutton, in May. Early in the same year, B. F. Johnson also approached her concerning the prospects for revising the *Country Life Reader* series. The publisher suggested that she consult with others who were involved in the work with adult illiterates when making changes. She was direct in her response saying, "In regard to revising the readers, I shall be very glad to have suggestions and will incorporate every one that is practical or helpful, but if you mean for me to do it under a supervisory group of amateurs, I have a better plan to suggest than revision." With this attitude, one can easily imagine what final solution she might have had for the Richmond publisher.[20] At this point in her career, Cora Wilson Stewart had a national reputation of which she was very protective. There were others involved in this work, but she was selective about the people with whom she was willing to collaborate on such a project.[21]

Besides finishing her book, Stewart made plans for speaking campaigns during the year, as well as arranging several regional conferences. To help her, she hired Lela Mae Stiles as her secretary. Lela Mae had assisted her in the Kentucky campaign, and the two would make a dynamic team during the next several years. Stiles set up an office in Frankfort, while Stewart began planning a series of national lecture tours.

In April, Stewart spoke before the Kentucky Education Association. She used this opportunity to blast the Association for ignoring and excluding women from leadership roles. She observed that the Association had not chosen a woman president since she had been elected ten years earlier. "The K.E.A. has gone from bad to worse in its policy of eliminating women and is conspicuous for the absence of women in its councils," she told the group. "The K.E.A. is composed two-thirds of women, but they make up the audience and have no power. I do not advocate rebellion, but demand equality. We have the vote and should use it. California and Arkansas women formed separate associations and we can if necessary."[22]

This militant call was the first major address Stewart had made before the state's educators since the rejection of the adult education bill the previous year. She no doubt felt relieved to speak her mind before the people who had let her down in 1920. To her satisfaction, two days after her speech, the Association elected as president Mrs. M. L. Hall, superintendent of Shelby County Schools; Stewart seconded her nomination.[23]

During the year, Stewart carried the illiteracy crusade to areas of the country new to her. Educators in the upper Midwest and the Northwest wanted to attack adult illiteracy because they saw such battles as a way to have a national impact on education. In the words of Josephine Corliss Preston, superintendent of schools in Washington State: "We western educators have long since wanted to do some distinctive things as a western movement. With illiteracy, we can make a distinctive contribution, with low illiteracy and our progressive educational conditions."[24] Needing an inspirational speaker to help them carry on a crusade, they called on Stewart.

By mid-year, Stewart had agreed to terms for a series of speaking tours in the Midwest and far West. Among the states she visited were North Dakota, Washington, Wisconsin, and Iowa. In order to maximize the impact of her appearances, she told her schedulers in the Northwest: "I can only pour my soul into one lecture daily. If I only TALKED I could do more, but I make an oratorical effort that means drafting on all my strength and energy." She further advised them that she only needed to give two speeches in a locality: "My first is inspirational. My second is instructive. There's no need to spend a week in a place. One or two days is enough. I'm a campaigner, you know, not so much an instructor."[25]

Stewart did not disappoint her audiences. They were not accustomed to seeing a female speaker with her talents, and she inspired the local populace like a religious evangelist. She encouraged the educational leaders to set goals for eradicating illiteracy within fixed time limits. To help them in this process, she got Lela Mae Stiles to forward statistics on local illiteracy conditions to area newspapers before her arrival. These figures were printed in the press and increased the impact of her speeches.

Her friends planned a vigorous schedule for Stewart, and she loved it. Whenever possible, she traveled by train. The travel was difficult, and she often had to go to remote areas with severe weather. She described a typical trip to Lela Mae Stiles:

> I traveled 28 miles in the snow yesterday in an open car, then took a slow train, made one change, waited for hours at a country station. I spoke, drove 19 miles in the snow, spoke again, attended a tea in my honor, talked all the time at it, spoke at night and drove 39 miles in a deep snow after ten o'clock. We got stuck twice and I thought we would have to stay out all night. This is Armistice day. But no armistice for illiteracy. We'll press it to death.[26]

At these stops, Stewart told the story of the Moonlight Schools and warned against the dangers of adult illiteracy. In her speeches, she incorporated the fervor of a religious revivalist. The audiences were inspired by her account of the mountaineers of eastern Kentucky, and they were challenged to eradicate illiteracy like a plague from their midst. Always popular with her audiences, she spoke to local civic clubs as well as educators. As in the Kentucky campaign, local citizens volunteered to identify and teach illiterates. The word of Stewart's speeches spread across the country, and other state leaders asked her to come offer inspirational remarks. By the end of the year, her reputation as the leading crusader against illiteracy was spread across the Midwest and far West, and it grew with each inspirational speech.

Needing help with the illiteracy statistics, Stewart asked Lela Mae Stiles to get the Census Bureau to release and forward to her figures on illiterates in the various states. The Census Bureau was not as cooperative as it had been during the Kentucky campaign, and Stiles was frustrated by the agency's reluctance to release information. Stewart urged her not to lose heart, writing to her secretary, "Just think how the publication of these statistics in every newspaper is going to help and how many illiterates will be redeemed through your efforts."[27]

Intent on getting the needed statistics, Stewart wrote to Secretary of Commerce Herbert Hoover to help her get the information. She had met Hoover during the Wilson administration, and she had a very high opinion of him. He responded to her entreaties, and he promised to help her get the figures she needed. This correspondence marked the beginning of a mutual admiration that would later result in her becoming an official in Hoover's administration.[28]

While her speaking engagements in the West and Midwest occupied much of her attention, Stewart still found time to organize four regional conferences on illiteracy. The first meeting, for the eastern states, was held November 25-26, 1921, in New York City. Many prominent figures, including Carrie Chatman Catt, president of the National American Woman Suffrage Association and an activist in the peace movement in America, attended the session. Catt praised the illiteracy work as being second in importance only to the movement to prevent future wars.[29]

The conventions for the western and northern states were held during 1922, and the meeting for the South was conducted in April of the same year. Stewart was especially pleased with the northern conference, which was held in Chicago. After the gathering, Jane Addams invited her and several other delegates to Hull House, where they talked about illiteracy and other reform efforts. Stewart was an admirer of both Addams and Catt. She considered herself cut from the same bolt of cloth as these reformers, and she was proud that they were interested in her work.[30]

Although the conferences were arranged on short notice and were poorly financed, the public interest they received pleased Stewart, who noted: "I had no idea they would prove so popular, and, naturally, am gratified." The meetings were so successful that when Stewart announced that others would be held in the future, some cities offered free accommodations for the delegates in return for the right to host the gatherings.[31]

Despite the growing popularity of the movement against illiteracy, there were also complications for Stewart. Because she was such a self-motivated person, accustomed to directing her own affairs, it was inevitable that she would clash with the bureaucracy of the N.E.A. She found that the money allotted to her as chairman of the association's illiteracy committee was constantly being delayed. The organization was also reluctant to finance her conferences, and only her own personal income and her managerial ability made them possible at all. As early as November 1921, she wrote to Stiles: "Sometimes I think I was foolish to open headquarters with N.E.A., so slow and cumbersome."[32] To Stewart, the rigidity of the organization was stifling progress in the eradication of illiteracy. She realized, however, that only through its auspices could she continue her work, so she attempted to make the best of the situation.

Stewart's dissatisfaction with the N.E.A. did not keep her from seeking aid from her friends in the General Federation of Women's Clubs. At its annual meeting in Chautauqua, New York, in 1922, the organization agreed to focus its attention on illiteracy and to provide her with an appropriation for the Illiteracy Division. As with the N.E.A., she was glad for the cooperation of the Federation, but she was also impatient with what she considered to be its bureaucratic inefficiency.[33]

During 1922, Stewart's dependence on the two national organizations was greatly complicated by her hectic speaking schedule. Because of her travels, she was always behind in answering correspondence. One week she was touring the South, giving two speeches a day; then she would catch a train and rush to Iowa, Kansas or California to give an address. Her talks were much in demand, and she strove to answer all requests. During the year, she spoke before almost every type of audience imaginable, from Rotary Clubs to Indian tribes. At one point she reported enthusiastically to Stiles that she had visited the birthplace of Sitting Bull and had even danced with the Sioux Indians in North Dakota.

Because Stewart's schedule demanded that she spend much of her time on trains, she made the most of the situation. She found railroad personnel to be very cooperative, and they allowed her to set up make-shift offices in the Pullman and dining cars. So impressed was she with the cooperation of the railroad men that she wrote jokingly to her secretary: "If I ever should consider matrimony, I think I shall wed a Pullman conductor. They are so kind and gracious."[34] To help with clerical matters, Stiles forwarded her correspondence to her. In this way, she could carry on the paper work of the illiteracy movement while in transit between lectures.

Despite the cooperation of the railroad personnel, coordinating the illiteracy work while traveling around the country was at best difficult. Stewart's schedule was uncertain, and her mail was constantly being forwarded to wrong addresses. She often wrote Stiles that she needed a secretary on her end more than she needed one in Frankfort. Her strenuous speaking campaigns also took a heavy physical toll, and she was constantly plagued by fatigue and laryngitis.

Yet, Stewart retained her optimism and her belief in the righteousness of her work. She was having an impact on the people who heard her, and she was spreading the word about the problems of illiteracy in a more pervasive manner than ever before. She always kept a positive point of view, and even a sense of humor about her extensive travels. Once during an especially exhausting tour of Iowa, which was conducting its own illiteracy crusade, she wrote to Stiles, "If Iowa will fight illiteracy in the same strenuous way she is rushing me thru this state, they can have it wiped out in six months time."[35]

On the rare occasions when Stewart took a rest from her speaking engagements, she usually went to Pine Bluff, Arkansas, to visit with her brother Glenmore and her two sisters Stella and Flora. On other occasions, she would return to Morehead to visit with various members of her family. Her brothers and sisters were concerned about the rapid pace at which she lived, as well as the physical and financial strain on her. She listened to their entreaties, and she sometimes even agreed that she worked too hard, but she was never willing to give up her crusade. It was the driving force in her life, and it marked her contribution to the world. In lieu of a husband and children, she had a crusade, and the illiterates of the world were her adopted offsprings.

In September 1922, *Moonlight Schools* was released by Dutton. The public response was positive, and reviews were favorable. The book told about the origins of the Rowan County night schools, the progress of the illiteracy movement in other states, and the methods employed to teach illiterates. Her friends congratulated Stewart on the success of her book; she was happy with the response to *Moonlight Schools* and was already planning another book. She told Lela Mae that one volume would help sell the other.

By the end of November 1922, Stewart decided to rest from her speaking schedule and to begin work in earnest on her second book. Wanting a warm climate during the winter months, she chose Tucson, Arizona, where she stayed until the end of December. She fell in love with the city and greatly enjoyed her stay. She walked in the parks, read under the moonlight, and met many new friends. Two of these new friends were a young couple known to us only by their first names—Oswald and Ruth. The two young people had recently married, and Stewart grew fond of them during her stay. In her diary, she noted that they were "such a wholesome couple—a love affair so pure and refreshing. Blessings on them. It has been a great joy to find a young couple so guileless and so fraught in their devotion to each other. It restores one's faith in young people, in young love, and in the world."[36]

Despite all the personal sorrow she had known in her marital relationships, Stewart was not embittered; she still held a romantic view of love between a man and a woman. The relationship of Oswald and Ruth exemplified many of the characteristics of true love she had learned from her mother and for which she had hoped in her own personal life. The attributes she admired in the two young people were the same she had sought in her own life. She noted that Oswald "is a true gentleman, born in Louisville. He has exquisite taste, lovely manners, and many fine sentiments." Ruth, she noted, "is pure and good and unselfish."[37]

During her time in Tucson, Stewart also paused to take stock of the previous year, observing: "I have no quarrel with the year 1922. I shall remember it always with joy and gratitude as one of the best and brightest years of my life."[38] She listed the many things for which she was grateful. These included many new friends, a noble cause, a gracious heavenly father, a savior's tender love, good health, an expanding opportunity, employment that helped to meet her debts, delightful places to travel, changing seasons, and "the perfect love that casteth out fear."[39]

An assessment of accomplishments during the previous twelve months was a habit that Stewart had begun a few years earlier. She always started her review by expressing her faith in God and her thankfulness for a mission in life. She usually listed the names of new friends that she had made, and she always noted progress made in the crusade against illiteracy.

Stewart not only reviewed the events of the past year, she set out several resolutions for the new year. For 1923 her resolutions included the following: read and record something from the Bible every day; keep the Ten Commandments; observe the cardinal virtues of temperance, honesty, truthfulness, kindness, patience, punctuality, industry, diligence, and unselfishness; write something every day; read some every day from sources other than the Bible; reduce her weight to 150 pounds; improve her personal appearance; and pay off her debts as much as possible.

These goals were ambitious, but the recording of them reflected an order-liness and devotion to planning that characterized Stewart. No casual maker of New Year's resolutions, she took hers seriously; she may not have been able to keep all of them, but she constantly worked toward them. Her resolutions also revealed the personal characteristics she valued the most; she tried mightily to exemplify these attributes in her life. They were personal traits that she had learned in her childhood, and they were an integral part of her personality.

Cora Wilson Stewart ended 1922 full of confidence and hope for the future. She summarized her thoughts in a letter to Stiles: "We are further on our way this year than we were last, and facing the best year we have ever had."[40]

Despite her growing national acclaim, Stewart still had not forgotten her defeat at the hands of the Kentucky Republicans in 1920. Once, when she found that Governor Morrow had spoken out against adult illiteracy, she was moved to anger and told Lela Mae:

> What a farce, and what cowards they all are not to recognize us by a word or by a line when they talk about eradicating illiteracy from Kentucky. Sometimes I get so mad I feel like it is meant that we should grit our teeth, role [sic] up our sleeves and wade into the fight and lick everyone of them out of Kentucky and re-establish our work if we have to do it over their dead bodies—politically speaking I guess I must say.[41]

The national progress Stewart made helped ameliorate her anger with the politicians of her home state, however. Her talks were much in demand, and she was reaching far beyond the boundaries of Kentucky. Despite frustrations with the politicians in her home state, her attention drifted further from the Bluegrass state as the rest of the world acclaimed the "Moonlight School Lady."

10

ꟻAME AND ꟻRUSTRATION

Cora Wilson Stewart began the new year refreshed and ready for additional challenges. On January 1, she wrote to Lela Mae, "1923 is going to be a good year. Let's buckle on the armor and get the illiterates out of the trenches; most of them before Christmas."[1] After leaving Tucson, she briefly visited with her family in Pine Bluff. She used this time to write and correspond with friends active in illiteracy crusades across the country. She heard from her old friend Superintendent R. H. Wilson that the Oklahoma illiteracy crusade had stalled. Hoping to encourage her friend, she shared with him her assessment of the political climate: "Just at this time there is a spirit of reaction abroad in the land. It was apparent in the repudiation of Woodrow Wilson and has cropped out in several states, but just wait a few years and the people will come to their senses and will want the very best men to lead and guide them."[2]

The political change that Stewart saw paralleled her philosophical differences with educators who did not accept the call for a new crusade to eradicate adult illiteracy. Many educators wanted to use limited educational resources on children instead of teaching adults. Stewart's Kentucky nemesis, George Colvin, voiced this position in a letter to Georgia school superintendent M. L. Brittain. In assessing the Kentucky illiteracy crusade, Colvin described Stewart as a "wonderfully brilliant woman" but noted that the Kentucky legislature had eventually voted to abandon her illiteracy crusade. He gave the following opinion regarding contemporary educational priorities in the Bluegrass State:

> We have concluded that the surest way to eradicate illiteracy is to stop making illiterates. To that end, we enacted and are enforcing a dramatic attendance law compelling the attendance of all children who are mentally and physically fit between the ages of seven and sixteen, inclusive. All illiterates in our state are illiterate from choice, as native born illiterates are elsewhere. It is a compliment to our generous emotions to give adult illiterates that which they were unwilling to receive in their youth; it probably contravenes a fundamental law of nature, however. One may not sin away his day of opportunity and hope to have it back again. Besides, there is a vast difference between ignorance and illiteracy. Our greatest curse is not illiteracy, but ignorance. We are merely perpetuating the experience of Don Quixote with the windmill, when we imagine

that we can overcome the deliberate neglect of years with an hour's mis-directed enthusiasm.[3]

Stewart did not accept Colvin's analogy with Don Quixote, nor did she share his view that the state owed nothing to adults who wanted a chance to escape from illiteracy. To her, it did not matter when people recognized their need for an education; schooling should be available to meet such needs. The variance in opinion rested on her fundamental view of human nature and her faith in the power of education. To Cora Wilson Stewart, men were capable of great deeds if they were given the proper schooling, and she believed that education had redemptive qualities comparable to religious salvation. Public denial of such training was tantamount to a moral wrong. Even if illiterates did not initially accept the offering, help should be provided to them until they saw the light.

Educators who shared George Colvin's view took a more pragmatic approach to schooling. For them, the best way to stop illiteracy was to start at the bottom by making sure children attended school. Colvin and his fellows also saw a certain justice in denying illiterates opportunities because they believed that such adults had ignored their chances when they were young. Therefore, even if there was a chance of educational "salvation" for these adults, they did not deserve such an opportunity. Ironically, Colvin was to cap his career as an educator by becoming the president of the University of Louisville, an institution of higher learning. Educators like Colvin were better schooled than Kentucky's Senator Pleasant Hogue, who convinced the state legislature to defeat Stewart's adult education bill, but they basically shared the same opinion on education for adult illiterates.

The correctness of these two viewpoints was not settled in the days of the Kentucky illiteracy crusade, and varying opinions of a similar nature still exist today. Cora Wilson Stewart's views gave her, however, the enthusiasm and hope to carry on her crusade. Like Don Quixote, she engaged in a romantic quest. Yet, unlike Cervantes's knight, she could measure her success by concrete evidence: the notes she received from teachers telling her of their experiences in Moonlight Schools, newspaper reports of the impact of her crusade, and the letters she received from newly redeemed illiterates. Such evidence inspired her romantic quest and persuaded her to continue her struggle on behalf of uneducated adults despite the changing times.

Stewart successfully organized two illiteracy conferences during the first half of 1923. The first meeting, for the Southern states, was held in Little Rock, Arkansas, April 10 and 11. The second conference was held for the Northern and Eastern states in Detroit, Michigan, on May 1 and 2. Both conferences strongly endorsed the Sterling-Towner Bill, and they also supported a more precise definition of illiteracy.[4]

Although she was glad to see the two conferences take a stand on important issues, Stewart was still concerned about the desire of some people to combine the illiteracy work with Americanization. She forcefully expressed her reservations on this subject to her friend Governor R. A. Nestos of North Dakota: "The Americanization movement deals solely with the foreign-born who cannot read or write English. Our crusade has a definite objective and a time limit, while Americanization continues long after we have taught the adult illiterates to read and write. Ours is a campaign; the Americanization work is a program of centuries. The assistance we need is immediate assistance; they need continuous help and are not so hurried."[5] She also wanted to keep the two lines of work separate because such an approach would provide more money in the Sterling-Towner legislation. Each line, Americanization and the illiteracy campaign, had separate appropriations under the provisions of the bill.[6]

Another important element of Stewart's philosophy at this point in her career was her belief in the need to help illiterates, regardless of their race, creed, or color. She had little patience with people who made excuses for the large number of uneducated adults in their states. To this point, she wrote: "Some [states] say that it is the Indians, some the Negroes, some the foreign-born and some have others on whom they lay their illiteracy—but, after all, they are all human beings and deserve their chance. When other countries see that we have five million illiterates they do not stop to see what color they are."[7]

Stewart's convictions were based on her strong Christian faith. She believed that all people were capable and deserving of redemption. While religion helped the community by saving souls, education was needed by the body-politic to save minds. It is true that she was a product of her time, and she shared many of the same prejudices as her contemporaries. She was, after all, human and was capable of the same intolerance as her fellows. In the matter of illiteracy, however, she was color-blind, and she believed that all of God's children needed redemption.

Following the two regional conferences, Stewart addressed the annual meeting of the General Federation of Women's Clubs in Atlanta, Georgia, on May 9. Because of the Federation's emphasis on the illiteracy work, she was given a longer time for her address than any other speaker.[8] At the meeting, she called on the club women to become more actively involved in the campaign against illiteracy. "The opening of a school where illiterates may throw off their shackles and may get their first real taste of freedom is as much an occasion for waving flags, blowing bugles, and beating drums as any battle for freedom ever fought with bayonets and guns," she told them.[9]

Following her speech to the Federation, Stewart conceived the idea of a national illiteracy conference to be held in Washington, D.C., during early 1924. She envisioned this event as a combined venture among the General Federation of Women's Clubs, the National Education Association, and the U.S. Bureau of Education. She was confident about coordinating this gathering because she was the chair of the illiteracy committees of both the G.F.W.C. and the N.E.A. In addition, the current commissioner of education, John J. Tigert, had been a professor of psychology at the University of Kentucky when she was directing the crusade against illiteracy in her home state. She approached the leaders of these organizations and found that they were very willing to sponsor such an event. At the suggestion of Dr. Tigert, she also asked the American Legion to participate.

At the same time she began planning the national conference, Stewart was asked to chair the illiteracy section of the World Conference of Education held in San Francisco, June 29 through July 3. The World Conference grew out of the Hague Peace Conference and other peace overtures of the time. In the United States, the event was carried out under the leadership of the Executive Committee of the N.E.A. At the same time the World Conference was being conducted, the annual meeting of the N.E.A. was held across the San Francisco Bay in Oakland.

Stewart attended both of these meetings, and she was very pleased with the results. At the World Conference, she met people active in illiteracy campaigns in countries all over the planet. After meeting delegates from Honduras, Italy, India, China, and Canada, she wrote to Lela Mae Stiles: "The World Conference was the most wonderful thing in history and our program went through in the main, and it thrills me to know that the first resolution passed was the one to remove illiteracy from all nations. Ours was considered an outstanding piece of work."[10]

In her remarks to the assembly, Stewart inspired the audience with her description of the illiteracy campaign. "This is more than a fight for literacy, it is a fight on crime, disease, war and other enemies of mankind which illiteracy brings and the removal of adult illiteracy is one of the most important problems we have to face," she told the group. Few people in the international audience had ever heard a woman speak with such passion and authority. They were moved by her eloquence, and she was chosen to head the committee when it met again in two years.

For her part, Stewart hoped to get the conference to endorse a plan to eradicate illiteracy from the world by 1935. Because she was forced to divide her time between the N.E.A. conference and the World Conference, however, she was not able to be present when the world assembly debated this proposal. Instead, each country was left to decide for itself when it would eliminate illiteracy. She regretted this result, but she was pleased that the topic of illiteracy was so highly placed on the agendas of the nations present.

Stewart's success also carried over to the N.E.A. meeting, where she was elected to the Executive Committee. This powerful group directed the work of the national organization, and she saw her election as a stepping stone to higher office within the N.E.A. In a moment of joy, she wrote to Stiles, "My candidacy for the presidency [of the N.E.A.] two years hence was launched at Oakland, and is a definite plan, so this means to change some plans and work toward that end with all possible dignified energy. Good work, diligence, and organization will accomplish it and then the status of the illiteracy work will be fixed for all time and our pathway more rosy."[11]

Although exhausted from attending the two meetings, Stewart left the Bay Area in high spirits. The California meetings even inspired her to hope for the resumption of the work in Kentucky. While in San Francisco, she talked with representatives from India and Italy about coming to Kentucky for a whirlwind tour to ignite interest in the illiteracy campaign again. She wistfully said of her home state, "If the people knew what was doing in the world, they would want the work to start without delay."[12]

Still relishing her West Coast success, Stewart returned to Frankfort to organize her office, complete a report for the N.E.A. Illiteracy Commission, and make preparations for the national conference in early 1924. During the previous year, she had become concerned with the lack of communications with her office while she traveled. Having delegated office work to the capable Stiles, she decided to put aside her writing for the time being and to concentrate on preparations for the national conference.

At this point in her life, Cora Wilson Stewart was, in effect, an entrepreneur with illiteracy as her business. She did not have the security of other educators in the N.E.A., who held positions on the public payroll as administrators or teachers, and she did not have a spouse to support her like most members of the General Federation of Women's Clubs. Instead, she supported herself through speeches, book sales, and magazine articles. She had not held any position with a regular salary since leaving her job as superintendent of Rowan County Schools more than ten years earlier. While other officials in organizations with which she dealt had clerical support staffs, she had only the loyal Lela Mae Stiles. Stewart was constantly traveling to support herself and to spread the word of the illiteracy crusade. As a result of these conditions, she often delayed preparing the reports required by the N.E.A. and the G.F.W.C. Accustomed to acting independently, she often felt stifled by the paperwork requirements of the two national organizations. She was also constantly in need of money, and the two associations were slow to send her their illiteracy committee appropriations.

Although Stewart maintained a headquarters in Frankfort, she regularly left the state to speak. At the behest of her friend Dr. A. O. Thomas, Stewart went to Maine during the fall to serve as the key speaker for that state's illiteracy campaign. Other states, including Texas, Oklahoma, and Nebraska, also called her to come help their campaigns.

While Stewart traveled to meet her speaking obligations, events in her home state offered her hope for the resumption of the Kentucky illiteracy campaign. Kentucky was scheduled to elect a new governor in 1923, and the chief Democratic candidate was U.S. Congressman J. Campbell Cantrill. In early September, Cantrill died, and the party turned to Congressman William J. Fields. A native of eastern Kentucky known as "Honest Bill from Olive Hill," Fields was the representative from Stewart's home district and a close friend. A Methodist and prohibitionist, Fields was selected by the party to run for the governorship on September 9, 1923.

Once the public heard that Fields was the candidate for governor, some of Stewart's friends tried to persuade her to run for his congressional post. Although Fields had refused to give up his congressional seat to run for governor, this did not stop some of Stewart's allies. They encouraged her to seek the office, even if she would have to contest the seat with the congressman should he lose his bid to become Kentucky's chief executive. They noted that she was the logical candidate for the office and said that she could carry 95% of the women in the district.[13]

Stewart was delighted with the selection of Fields, and she had no intentions of running for the U.S. Congress. Because of her relationship with the Democratic candidate, she was convinced that he would resume the Kentucky crusade against illiteracy. To show her support, she agreed to participate in his campaign and to speak for him throughout Kentucky.[14] At the same time she was rejoicing over Fields's nomination, she was also organizing the national illiteracy conference scheduled for January 11 through 14, 1924, in Washington, D.C. She met with leaders of the organizations involved, and she promoted the meeting as a joint effort among the four groups—the General Federation of Woman's Clubs, the National Education Association, the U.S. Bureau of Education, and the American Legion. Since the event was her idea and she was coordinating it, she began preparing publicity for the session. She naturally assumed that she would lead the event as she had the regional conferences during the previous four years.

When Stewart first envisioned the event, she did not realize that there was possible friction among the sponsoring organizations. The American Legion was not enthusiastic about the conference, and their leaders expected few Legionnaires to attend. Stewart had included the Legion only at the suggestion of Dr. John J. Tigert. The other groups had their own hopes for the meeting, while Stewart assumed that all of them would work in harmony for the good of America's illiterate adults. She was about to receive a harsh lesson in organizational politics.

Problems first surfaced when Stewart announced to the press that the conference would be jointly sponsored by the four organizations. Bureau of Education officials were immediately angry with her because they were not given the lead role. Secretary Tigert was not interested in jointly sponsoring this work; he wanted to run it. The primary reason for his concern was that the N.E.A. and the G.F.W.C. strongly favored the Sterling-Reed Bill. (The Sterling-Towner Bill had evolved into the Sterling-Reed Bill.) The Coolidge administration was decidedly against this legislation. The federal government did not want to participate in a conference in which this bill might be endorsed, as it surely would be, considering Stewart's public advocacy of it. Dr. Tigert arranged a meeting with Stewart and chastised her for releasing press statements that the conference was being sponsored equally by the four groups. He said the Bureau of Education would not participate in the meeting unless it was the lead organization. At this point, the N.E.A., in the person of President Olive Jones, superintendent of the New York City Schools, was most interested in keeping a positive relationship with the Bureau of Education and Secretary Tigert. Jones also voiced her own displeasure with Stewart for putting the Bureau and the N.E.A. in opposing positions.

For her part, Stewart was surprised by the negative reaction from Jones and Tigert. She had simply assumed that the conference was for the benefit of the nation's illiterates. As the leading public figure on adult illiteracy and the chair of the illiteracy committees of the N.E.A. and the General Federation, she expected to coordinate the conference with equal participation among all of the organizations. She considered other issues to be petty differences among the four groups, and she was not interested in the jockeying for position that was occurring.

The leaders of the four organizations finally agreed that the U.S. Bureau of Education would sponsor the national conference. This decision was made without consulting Stewart, and she was deeply hurt. She took it as a personal affront that she was forced to play a subordinate role to officials in the Bureau of Education. Prior to one meeting of the leaders of the four groups, she expressed her disappointment to Lela Mae Stiles:

> I cannot see that I have much chance with three having combined, with all playing for prestige and power, and the N.E.A. wishing to conciliate and hold the good will of the Federation. These two days have been the most bitter ones I have spent. It seems that I must stay for a week and have this second meeting and then it will develop whether I am to work up this conference or whether I am to retire and hand it to Mrs. Cook [Tigert's assistant, chosen to coordinate the conference]. In the meantime, I am not authorized to do anything and am suspended. I feel like starting for Kentucky tonight. Wouldn't you?[15]

Stewart's problems with the national conference were somewhat relieved by developments in her home state, where the Fields campaign was picking up momentum. Committed to work for Fields, she rushed home from a lecture tour in Maine during late October and spent the last ten days before the election making two speeches per day on behalf of her friend. She urged the women of the state to vote for Fields, and she drew enthusiastic audiences wherever she appeared. She predicted that Fields would, in her words, "clean house" in Frankfort and provide the needed moral leadership for the state. For the first time in her life, she openly campaigned for a candidate for the state capital. She was so confident that Fields would resume the Kentucky crusade that she willingly stepped away from her usual stance of public neutrality. She even canceled speaking engagements in Texas, Nebraska, and Oklahoma and drove herself to near exhaustion speaking for the Democratic candidate.

Stewart was delighted when Fields won against the Republican challenger, Charles I. Dawson, 356,035 to 306,277. In a letter to Governor Henry J. Allen of Kansas, she said: "I participated actively during the last ten days and was delighted with the results. The new governor is one of my warmest personal friends and my home congressman."[16] In preparation for the new initiative against illiteracy, she asked Kentucky Federation of Women's Club lobbyist Mrs. J. C. Layne to meet with Fields to express the Federation's support for a revival of the illiteracy campaign. Mrs. Layne arranged a meeting but reported disappointing results. She told Stewart that Fields kept saying he was for education but that the state was not ready for a resumption of an illiteracy campaign. When the Federation lobbyist told the governor-elect that Kentucky was a leader among other states in this work, he said he did not care what other states thought about Kentucky. He told her, however, that he would be glad to confer with Stewart from time to time regarding educational matters. Mrs. Layne ended her report to Stewart with the sardonic observation, "Coolidge hasn't anything on our new governor."[17]

Incredulous about Fields's reported attitude, Stewart arranged a meeting with him in early December. As in his conversation with Mrs. Layne, the governor-elect was hesitant to talk about resuming the illiteracy campaign. After saying there was a need to build up interest in the work for a year or two, he expressed reservations because the two previous governors had opposed the illiteracy crusade. When Stewart reminded him that Governor McCreary had supported the work, he said that McCreary had her to help him. When she offered to help him also, Fields replied that it would not be fair to ask her to make that sacrifice because she had moved on to the national level. Referring to this statement, Stewart acidly noted to Stiles, "So considerate—they never think it unfair when they want me to withdraw and help them get elected to office."[18]

Stewart was crushed by Fields's attitude, and she told her secretary: "Of course, my ideal was a governor who would hold up the banner and say 'this is right. I stood for it in my public utterances and I stand for it in my official capacity.' Instead of coming to Kentucky to stand with him and fight for this, I shall have to come and feel always that the fight is on my shoulders, and when it fails then it will be, 'I told you so.'"[19] She went on to describe how she had hoped to bring Indian and Italian educational leaders from the World Conference on Education into Kentucky to help with a renewed crusade. She speculated that it would have been better to have brought in these educators and campaigned against illiteracy in Kentucky instead of helping Fields get elected. In exasperation, she wrote: "Lela Mae, there is but one way to get these politicians, and that is to nail them to a platform, and so far as women are concerned, they have not realized that we are on earth."[20]

Fields was not totally aware of the depth of Stewart's disappointment, but he soon would be. He wrote to her before taking office and asked for her suggestions on an educational program for the state. She made several recommendations, including resumption of the illiteracy crusade. When Fields again expressed reservations about an illiteracy campaign, she wrote to him: "How you could ever assume that I would draft one [an educational program] and leave out the illiterates is more than I can understand. I shall desist from any effort to thrust the banner into unwilling hands. My presence at your inaugural, I judge, will not be necessary."[21]

For his part, Governor Fields was more concerned with other matters. He was preparing a $75 million highway bond issue, which occupied much of his time after taking office. He had hopes of developing the normal schools in Morehead and Murray, and he favored a three cents per gallon gasoline tax. Ultimately, he never pushed Cora Wilson Stewart's illiteracy program, and his bond initiative failed also. For her part, it would be a long time before she forgave "Honest Bill from Olive Hill" for disappointing her.

Stewart's frustration on the state level was matched by her problems on the national level. The conference for which she had worked so hard was taken out of her hands and placed clearly under the control of the Bureau of Education. The American Legion was actively courting the Coolidge administration in hopes that it would help World War I veterans. The leader of the General Federation of Women's Clubs, Mrs. Thomas G. Winter, hoped to parlay the conference into greater recognition for the G.F.W.C. and a possible political appointment for herself.[22] Stewart's hopes of using her position with the N.E.A. to get the support of that organization were dashed when Olive Jones told her that she would not support any introduction of the Sterling-Reed Bill at the gathering because it might anger the Coolidge administration. Jones threatened to oppose every conference resolution that mentioned the education bill.

The anger Stewart felt about the political maneuvering of the four groups was increased by the frustration she felt from not being allowed to take the leadership role in the conference. Instead, she was reduced to working behind the scenes for the event. At one point she expressed her disappointment to Winter: "It is extremely embarrassing to me to have Dr. Tigert and Garland Powell [head of the Americanization Division of the American Legion] passing on the question of whether I shall or shall not speak on the Illiteracy Conference as they are passing on all speakers suggested."[23]

As a freelance illiteracy crusader, Stewart also felt hampered by having to work through the federal bureaucracy. At one point, she wrote to her friend Wil Lou Gray, head of adult education for the state of South Carolina, "The problem of handling the conference is different from any I ever attempted before and there is a great deal of red tape in anything which the Bureau of Education has a part in."[24] After years of working on her own, Stewart was not accustomed to being required to have the approval of bureaucracies in the illiteracy work. She normally made unilateral decisions regarding adult illiteracy, and she chafed at the thought of giving way to others who did not have her familiarity with the work. As was her habit, she accused the leaders of the four organizations of playing politics. "I seem to be the only one who has played no politics and all the others are trying to save their faces and work for their own personal advantages and for the advantage of their organizations. It grows more discouraging," she told Stiles as the conference approached.[25]

It is true that each organization had its own agenda for the meeting and was unwilling to let Stewart lead the conference. Furthermore, they knew that Cora Wilson Stewart was a freelancer they could not control. She never considered that the four groups might have objectives for the conference other than illiteracy; instead, she focused only on her vision for the illiteracy work. The illiteracy crusade needed the Sterling-Reed Bill because it would give $7,500,00 to the states for illiteracy work; this was all that mattered to her.

As was her custom, Stewart withdrew to the high ground and claimed that only she had pure motives. Convinced of the righteousness of her view, she was unwilling to compromise. She had pioneered the crusade in the United States, and she resented efforts to sidetrack it. Equally as important, she was hurt by the unwillingness of the four organizations to acknowledge her vision and to follow her in planning the meeting.

All the machinations behind the scenes were unknown to the public. The press hailed the upcoming conference, and every state except Idaho and Nevada sent delegates. The group convened at the Department of the Interior building on January 11, and Secretary of the Interior Hubert Work offered opening remarks. Stewart presented the keynote address, and it was one of her usual splendid oratorical performances. After the general session, group meetings were held on such topics as "Organization, Management, and Financing of Movements for the Eradication of Illiteracy," "The Teaching Staff," and "Courses of Study and Methods of Instruction."[26]

In its final report, the conference made ten recommendations. All of these dealt with possible actions by the states and required no federal commitment. In fact, the final report noted that the four groups had agreed that "the discussion of the Conference shall be limited to the agenda, which deals with the educational and not the political phases of the question, and which, by mutual agreement of the four agencies, exclude discussion of Federal Legislation affecting the Bureau of Education."[27] This statement was a direct reference to the Sterling-Reed Bill.

Friends later told Stewart that the conference was outstanding and offered their congratulations to her for planning the meeting. In reflecting on the event, Stewart was glad that it was over. She was appreciative of the plaudits given her, and she reported to her friend A. H. Chamberlain, editor of the *Sierra Educational News*: "We were hampered at many points during the arrangement of the conference and many were doubtful if the four agencies could ever be brought to work in co-operation. It was done, but only after much sacrifice on my part."[28] An important outcome of the conference was an agreement that the four organizations would not produce a committee to oversee the resolutions adopted at the meeting. For her part, Stewart was happy with this decision; she was tired of working with the four organizations, and she had no desire to be part of a joint committee.

Because of the problems she had encountered in planning the national conference, Stewart began to reconsider her relationship with the General Federation of Women's Clubs and the N.E.A. She came to realize that being chair of the illiteracy committees of these two groups was actually a hindrance to her. The organizations provided national prestige and even a modest amount of money, but they had many levels of bureaucracy that hindered her. The two groups were also constantly requiring her to write reports describing the work of the illiteracy committees. She was always late in preparing these assessments because she was consumed with the necessity of traveling and lecturing on various aspects of the illiteracy crusade.

When one considers the nature of her work, it easy to understand how Stewart lost patience with the organizations she counted on to help her. She had been a freelancer since 1913, when she left the superintendency of the Rowan County Schools. Since that time, she had not held a regular paying job. Instead, she had supported herself through her talks, institute instruction, and sales of her writings. Such a life had made her a very self-reliant person. For personal strength, she drew on her devout religious beliefs. By now, she believed that God had called her to crusade for the elimination of adult illiteracy. She had proven that she could make a living in this manner, but her lifestyle inevitably caused her to be intolerant of bureaucracies.

Stewart's approach to the illiteracy crusade was in direct contrast to the growing specialization in the education field. The teaching profession was becoming more structured and was coming into the hands of an establishment led by highly educated people with advanced degrees. These individuals held governmentally funded positions that offered security. Such leaders were able to take a systematic, deliberate approach to issues because there was no need to produce immediate results. By contrast, Stewart was the exact opposite of this group of bureaucratic educators. She was a crusader, a campaigner, and a reformer who did not have the same security as public school teachers and administrators with salaried positions. For its part, the educational establishment was coming to view her as too independent. She owed no debts to any organization; she served only her cause. In the view of the people working within organized education, she seemed to be too free and too much of a loose cannon; this conflict would intensify in the coming years.

Stewart's personal finances were also a constant source of trouble because she used much of her personal income to support her work. Like any small business person, she plowed back into her business much of the "profits" that she earned. The result was a growing level of public awareness about adult illiteracy, but an uncertain level of prosperity for her. She was helped financially by family members, who provided her with some money. As she had helped her brothers and sisters when they were young, they now turned to help their older sister.

Realizing that the illiteracy crusade must have financial support, Stewart sealed her fate with the N.E.A. soon after the January conference: she decided to testify before the Congress on behalf of the Sterling-Reed Bill. She wrote to Lela Mae Stiles soon after the national conference, "I am making a sudden decision to go and appear before the Senate Committee for the bill—Sterling-Towner [Sterling-Reed] is the biggest thing the N.E.A. has and the biggest aid to the illiterates."[29] She knew that her testimony would in essence kill any chance she had of becoming the president of the N.E.A. Under the leadership of Olive Jones, the N.E.A. was courting Bureau of Education chief Tigert, and he was opposed to the education bill, as was the Coolidge administration. By testifying in support of the legislation, Stewart risked the wrath of the Bureau of Education and the N.E.A. At this point, however, she did not care. She believed that the bill was the nation's best hope for the adult illiteracy work, and after attending the national conference, she questioned her ability to function within the constraints of an organization such as the N.E.A.

Stewart appeared before the Senate Committee on Education and Labor in late January and before the corresponding House committee in February. She presented all the arguments in favor of the bill. She cited the needs of the illiterates and pointed to all the good that such a bill would provide in the states. Dr. James H. Ryan, executive secretary of the National Catholic Welfare Conference, presented the negative side of the bill. He charged that the bill would produce federal control of education, weaken education efforts in the states, increase the federal bureaucracy, and increase taxes. He finished by noting that the states had not called for this federal assistance.[30]

Leaving Washington after her testimony, Stewart began making plans to distance herself from the G.F.W.C. and the N.E.A. She asked the G.F.W.C. to find a new chair for the organization's Illiteracy Division. Surprised by the request, Mrs. John D. Sherman of the Federation asked her to remain as leader of the department until she found a successor. Stewart reluctantly consented and continued to head the Illiteracy Division until early 1925.[31] Next she began to separate herself from the leadership of the N.E.A., an action she was reluctant to take because the organization had helped her for many years. She was also giving up possible advancement within this influential organization. Stewart had been disappointed, however, by the actions of the N.E.A. during the January conference, and she had alienated some of its most powerful leaders.

Stewart lost more enthusiasm for the N.E.A. because of its continued support for Americanization and its successor, Adult Education. In 1924 the N.E.A. changed its Department of Immigrant Education to the Department of Adult Education. Mrs. Stewart viewed this change as a lack of commitment to adult illiterates. In the past, she was insistent that the illiteracy crusade not be mixed with Americanization; she had the same concerns about the Department of Adult Education. She feared that this new division would overshadow the work with native-born illiterates, and she was not willing to let this happen.

Since 1924 was a presidential election year, it might be expected that Stewart would again try to get federal support for her work. In contrast to her work in the 1920 presidential election, however, she decided not to campaign for the 1924 Democratic candidate, John W. Davis. She had lost her enthusiasm for the political leaders of the day, even though she privately supported Davis. The

Democratic party tried to get her to travel and speak on behalf of their candidate and even advertised her as a speaker, but her experience with Governor Fields had soured her on the effectiveness of politics. Late in 1924 she wrote to her old friend General Sears: "I am sorry that I was advertised as a speaker in the Democratic National Campaign. It does not help my work to have such announcements go out. I was one of Governor Fields's champions in his race for Governor. It was the first time I had ever participated in state politics. He has disappointed me so bitterly as a friend and as an official that I am not on visiting terms with him at all."[32]

Thus 1924, which had begun with such high hopes for Stewart, ended with frustration and more mountains to climb. She was moving away from the two groups that had sponsored her movement for the preceding four years. Hampered by their bureaucratic structures, she resented being dependent on them. Stewart also saw a growing commitment to Americanization and its successor, adult education, instead of concentration on adult illiterates. Because of these events, she concluded that she must establish her own national organization if the illiterates were to avoid getting lost in the educational shuffle.

Although it was a difficult year for her, Stewart had many accomplishments. She spoke to large groups of people throughout the country on the subject of adult illiteracy, and she was constantly traveling to different states to help local illiteracy campaigns. Money was always a problem, but she entered the new year with resolve. She was committed to creating an entirely new national organization that would focus on adult illiteracy, and this was her goal for 1925.

11

$\mathcal{P}$LANNING A
$\mathcal{N}$ATIONAL $\mathcal{C}$RUSADE

Cora Wilson Stewart knew that organizing a movement to coordinate illiteracy campaigns would not be easy. As modest as the financial appropriations of the General Federation of Women's Clubs and the N.E.A. were, the organizations' prestige as established national associations brought credibility that any new group would have to earn. Stewart knew that before beginning a national organization, she must first stabilize her own finances. This meant that she needed income to pay off her personal debts. To this end, she accepted several speaking engagements, beginning with a conference of the World Association of Daily Bible Schools in Washington, D.C. Soon after this conference, she traveled to Texas to speak before the state legislature in support of a bill to help the illiteracy campaign in that state. The bill passed as a result of her remarks.[1]

In early March, Stewart met with her old friend Dr. A. E. Winship in Lexington, Kentucky, to discuss her plans for a new illiteracy organization. At first, Dr. Winship was taken aback by the idea of a national organization and the difficulties in forming such a group. He knew that the N.E.A. had formed its own adult education division, and he wondered how the members of that section would react to a separate organization. Stewart explained her concerns with the N.E.A.'s broadening focus on adult education, and Dr. Winship concurred with her assessment. He finally agreed to help her form a national organization; together they made a list of influential men and women whose endorsements would be useful in implementing Stewart's plan.

In compiling this list, Stewart and Winship called on their past associations with reformers and Progressives. Once the list was complete, Stewart began making the rounds to get the necessary endorsements. One of the first people she visited was Jane Addams. Stewart deeply admired the Chicago reformer, whom she often referred to as "Saint Jane." Addams invited her to dinner at Hull House. When Stewart described her plans, Addams told her it would take someone who was willing to work very hard if a national association dedicated to eliminating adult illiteracy was to be established. After Stewart assured her that she was that person, Addams suggested several potential supporters and agreed to serve on the board of directors of the new organization.[2]

One of the next people Stewart contacted was William Allen White, the influential editor of the Emporia, Kansas, *Gazette*. Stewart had first met White at the 1920 Democratic convention, and she was now ready to build on this acquaintance. She approached White while he was eating breakfast in the dining room of the National Arts Club in New York. Moving over to his table, she said, "Let me eat with you." He answered that he would be delighted, and they began a conversation. When told of her plans, White made several suggestions about prospective board members. He was so deeply interested that when she asked him to join the organization, he accepted.

By the end of the year, Stewart had received pledges of help from more than twenty-five prestigious individuals. These included her friend Governor Henry J. Allen of Kansas, Governor R. A. Nestos of North Dakota, novelist Ida Tarbell, sculptor Lorado Taft, John H. Finley, associate editor of the *New York Times*, *Century* magazine editor Glenn Frank, and medical reformer Sally Lucas Jean. She also sought and received the endorsement of her old Morehead friend Dr. F. C. Button and several educators who had supported her in the past.

Of all the people Stewart wanted to enlist, none was more important to her than Carrie Chatman Catt. She was a great admirer of Catt as well as Jane Addams. In comparing the two women, Stewart once noted, "She [Catt] is a great woman—a great American—frank-honest and fearless—not afraid to speak her opinion. I found no woman with the child-like simplicity of Jane Addams—I believe she is the most Christ-like woman in America while Mrs. Catt is more like a female Moses."[3]

The former women's suffrage advocate was now active in the world peace and child labor movement, and Stewart was not sure that she would join the illiteracy crusade. Stewart tried to meet with her in July, but their schedules could not be coordinated. She finally met with Catt on New Year's Eve. The two women discussed various matters, and Stewart described her plans for a national illiteracy organization. Catt expressed reluctance about joining any new organizations, although she said the removal of illiteracy was second in importance to mankind only to the peace movement. Stewart reminded her that four years earlier Catt had encouraged her to expand her work to a national level. Stewart told Catt that she had taken this advice seriously. She said if Catt did not help, it would weaken the illiteracy cause and would deeply discourage her. Catt replied: "Oh well, I won't desert you. Will it help any to have my name?" Stewart assured her that such an endorsement would be invaluable, and Catt agreed to serve on her board. Catt also agreed to counsel with her periodically, noting that advice was the one thing she had the most to give.[4]

When she was not contacting prospective members of the board for her national organization, Stewart was giving speeches throughout the nation. She was completing her term as chair of the Illiteracy Division of the N.E.A. and this position allowed her to work for her cause across the country. One of her speaking tours included a trip to the Northeast, where she spoke at Vassar College. Here she was disappointed with her performance, noting that either she was "too sick or the girls too thoughtless to be effective."[5]

In the spring, Stewart made a tour of the South. She was especially impressed with a state illiteracy conference conducted in Alabama, where she was the keynote speaker. Held under the auspices of the University of Alabama, the meeting was praised by Stewart, who observed how nice it was to see such a conference sponsored by a university. She remembered that in the early days of her work, academicians had claimed that adult illiterates could not be taught to read and write. Following the Alabama meeting, she went to Florida, where she held three meetings for illiterate Negroes and lectured at Florida A & M College. She noted that enthusiasm for the illiteracy crusade was great in Florida, especially among the black population, and she applauded the work of President J.R.E. Lee of Florida A & M. The state teachers' association liked her lectures so much that they asked her to make another tour of the state in the fall. Stewart praised the Florida educators because they had taken a census of their illiterates and had the names of these adults on record for future reference.

Returning from Florida, Stewart passed through South Carolina, where she addressed the teachers of adults at Winthrop College in Rock Hill. During her stay, she took time to travel thirty-five miles into the country to visit Lucy Ann Bolen, a seventy-five-year-old woman who had recently learned to read and write. Stewart praised the work of her friend Wil Lou Gray, who was in charge of the adult education work in South Carolina. She noted that Columbia University was sending a psychologist to South Carolina to study the effort in that state and to issue a report on the psychology of teaching adult illiterates and near-illiterates. Further expressing her opinion of academicians, she wryly noted, "We have gained something when, instead of disputing our claim and declaring that adults could not learn to read and write, the experts have come to find the movement worthy of study and scientific report."[6]

While on her Southern tour, Stewart visited the Georgia State Penitentiary, where she found that 1,100 of the 3,000 prisoners were illiterate and that no efforts were being made to instruct them. Appalled at this condition, she went to the head of the Georgia State Prison Board and persuaded him to start reading and writing classes for the inmates. She next visited the federal prison in Atlanta, where she found that only a few people were receiving instruction and that they were using children's readers. The use of children's books for adults always angered her and this was no exception. She insisted that the inmates be given adult readers, and she eventually prepared a text for this purpose entitled *The Prisoner's First Book*.[7]

Illiterate inmates had always been a favorite concern of Stewart's. She thought that the prisoner behind bars in jail was analogous to the person who was shackled by illiteracy. Her Georgia findings inspired her to conduct a survey of all federal and state penitentiaries to determine the number of illiterate

A Moonlight School in Alabama.

inmates. From her study, she learned that there was an unusually large number of illiterates in prisons across the nation. In her opinion, this was further proof that illiteracy and crime fed on each other; if inmates could read and write, they could get meaningful jobs and they would not have to turn to crime to support themselves.

On the basis of her survey, Stewart began to agitate for the teaching of all inmates. She called for each federal prison to hire an educational superintendent to coordinate the teaching of illiterates. She argued that people who left prison without an education were ill-fitted for the outside world. They could not earn a decent living, and they would inevitably turn to crime and end up in jail again.[8] Her concern for prisoners eventually led her to advocate that illiterate inmates not be released until they had learned to read and write. She forcefully stated her position in a letter to Washington State legislator H. E. Goldsworthy:

> I think the attempt to eliminate illiteracy and to improve the educational status of inmates of the penitentiary can be justified on economic grounds, pure and simple, entirely apart from any moral or sentimental considerations. The illiterate is a burden on society; he can not defend himself from imposition, and is easily led into evil ways because of his incapacity to understand his fellows. To allow the illiterates to return to civic life is foolish and wasteful, for they are sure to return sooner or later to the penal institutions from which they were sent out as defenseless as when they first entered it. I look upon education as a means of preparing men for self-supporting citizenship, and think that the improvement of the education of illiterates in the penitentiaries can be abundantly

justified in dollars and cents. I do not expect such education to make them over ... but I would try to remove, so far as possible, the great handicap under which they labor.[9]

In discussing illiterate prisoners, Stewart also pointed out another area in which she disagreed with the educational establishment:

One of the principal difficulties that we met in the introduction of this work is that some leaders, state superintendents and others are inclined to talk about them [illiterate prisoners] being morons and impossible to teach without their giving them any sort of test or chance. I do not know that a large number of them would be found of subnormal mentality. I doubt if very many could be found that were not able to master the elementary branches.[10]

By the middle of the year, Stewart had to turn away from the prison work to focus on the upcoming N.E.A. conference in Indianapolis, Indiana. This meeting marked her last session as chair of the Illiteracy Commission of the Association. It was also an important conference because she planned to use it as an opportunity to solicit the help of fellow members for her national organization. At the suggestion of her friends, she had remained silent about her plans before the N.E.A. meeting. Stewart had found it difficult to keep quiet because the N.E.A. had failed to support the illiteracy crusade in a manner that she thought best. At one point, she had even drafted a letter to the organization outlining her objections to the N.E.A.'s lack of support for her work, writing: "The work is not getting on as effectively and extensively as such a great cause merits and is not being financed adequately by the Association. As a matter of fact, the N.E.A. either has not the financial ability to carry on this great work of emancipating the illiterates or else is not sufficiently interested to make the vigorous attack on illiteracy I had hoped."[11] She thought twice about the letter, however, and decided not to mail it.

In essence, Stewart was correct. The N.E.A. had chosen to take a broader approach to the educational needs of adults. It had transformed its Division of Immigrant Education into a Department of Adult Education in 1924. There was a movement underway to systematize, study, and better organize the educational training of adult learners. Many of the proponents of this view came from the universities of the Northeast, and they wanted to move away from the crusading methods of an earlier day. The systematic approach of the adult educators was anathema to Stewart, however. She also did not think the adult educators had her commitment to relieving adult illiteracy; she believed the N.E.A. approach would result in adult illiterates being lost among a myriad of other educational needs. To her mind, this would take the illiteracy movement back to where it was before the inception of the Moonlight Schools.

At the N.E.A. meeting, Stewart made the final report of the Illiteracy Commission. She presented a summary of the history of the committee and told of its accomplishment since 1918, when it was first established. The report was impressive, noting progress in developing illiteracy campaigns in 26 of the 48 states over the life of the committee. As planned, Stewart also used her time at the conference to get several of her N.E.A. friends to agree to serve on the board of her new organization. This was to be the last N.E.A. conference in which she would play a significant role. She had served on the powerful executive committee of the Association, and she could have become even more influential if she had remained in the inner circle of the group. If she was driven solely by personal ambition, she could have modified her position and risen through the executive committee of the organization perhaps even becoming president. She was committed to her cause, however, and she saw that the N.E.A. was not willing to pursue this mission with the vigor she thought necessary. For her, involvement with the N.E.A. was always a way to further the illiteracy crusade. When the Association moved away from her goals, she took her program elsewhere.

In the short run, Stewart took it to the world level. As soon as she left the N.E.A. meeting, she rushed off to Edinburgh, Scotland, for the World Conference on Education. As chairman of the Illiteracy Section of the gathering, she conducted the proceedings with the same distinction she had exhibited two years earlier. The conference met July 20 through July 28. Stewart's good friend Augustus O. Thomas, superintendent of schools in Maine, was the president of the World Federation of Educational Associations, which sponsored the event. Dr. Thomas agreed to become a member of Stewart's soon-to-be-formed illiteracy group, and he often counseled with her regarding educational matters. Stewart greatly enjoyed the opportunity to compare notes with individuals involved in educating illiterates around the world. She admired the advancements made in China, and Chinese illiteracy crusader Jimmy Yen encouraged her to visit his country when she had an opportunity. Her visit to Edinburgh was reported in the U.S. press, which praised her world vision of the need to teach illiterates.

In reporting on the conference, the *Christian Science Monitor* quoted Stewart's views on the work with adults. This report included her growing conviction that the illiteracy movement must remain a crusade and not become a stale academic exercise. According to the *Monitor*, she said, "I just hope teachers of illiterates will remember that every individual is important and worthy not merely of the best educational help but of the best human help. The reaction must be that of brother to brother. If we lose that, we lose the motive of the crusade, no matter how much else we have in numbers or official support or money to put into it."[12] Stewart's concern for the human element in the illiteracy work was to often resurface as she developed her national organization. She feared that professional educators were stifling the enthusiasm and passion of the illiteracy crusade, emotions she believed were a necessary part of any successful work with adult illiterates.

Following the World Conference on Education, Stewart traveled throughout Europe for the next two months. Wherever she went, Paris, Milan, Geneva, or Monte Carlo, she spent much of her time researching illiteracy. She wrote to members of her family and to Lela Mae Stiles describing her travels. At this point, Stiles began looking for another job. Since Stewart no longer had the financial backing of the G.F.W.C. and the N.E.A., she did not have funds to continue paying her secretary. By September, Stiles had started working part-time at another clerical position. She told Stewart, "Do not forget that you are the one who I consider still the 'boss' and that no allegiance of mine will ever waver elsewhere." Stewart was not happy that her faithful secretary had to look for employment elsewhere, but she had no choice. The two women remained close friends despite Stiles's departure.[13]

When she returned home from, Europe, Stewart learned that she had received the *Pictorial Review* magazine's award as the woman who had made the greatest contribution to American life for the year 1924. The award originated the year before, and Stewart had been a strong contender for the initial prize. Her friends in Kentucky, especially former Cumberland County school superintendent Cora S. Payne, mounted a drive to win her the award. Stewart was aware of the nomination, and she was delighted that she had been chosen to be the second recipient of the prize. The award carried with it a $5000 cash award, which made it especially beneficial.[14]

The national press wrote about the honor and recounted Stewart's work on the state, national, and international levels. More than 600 people were nominated for the award, and a ceremony in honor of Stewart was planned for November in New York. Stewart had little time to savor the *Pictorial Review* award, however, since she was scheduled to make a western speaking tour. While on the tour, she began plans to call the first session of the group she was forming to combat illiteracy on a national level. She told William Allen White that she wanted to have the first meeting in Washington, D.C., on November 30. In that way, the group could open its office by December 1 and make a public announcement of its formation by Christmas.[15]

Stewart's western tour included Oregon and Washington, where she worked with her friend Superintendent of Schools Josephine Preston. While in the West, she visited the Northwest Indian Conference during November. Educators and Indian agents from four northwestern states attended the three-day meeting. She developed a book for the illiterate Indians, similar to *The Soldier's First Book*, and persuaded the conference attendees to make eradicating illiteracy a top priority. She was proud of the book she developed for the Indians because she always believed that each group of adults should have a text pertinent to its own needs. She wrote to her friend Sally Lucas Jean during the conference about her thoughts on this subject: "I have always said that each group of illiterates should have a text book that applied to their own conditions and interests, and through this we could lead them out into the broader fields."[16]

American Indians always held a special attraction for Stewart. Like the mountaineers of eastern Kentucky, the Indians represented to her an unspoiled body of people. They were natural and close to the earth. They were uncorrupted by civilization, and there were a large number of illiterates among them. She continued her interest in Indians, and the native Americans returned her affection. Finishing her western tour, Mrs. Stewart came back east to make final plans for the national organization to combat illiteracy. Her hopes to open the office in November were delayed by speaking engagements, so she decided to wait for the new year to call the first meeting of the board. During December, the N.E.A.'s Adult Education Committee invited her to attend a meeting. By this time, she was distancing herself from the N.E.A., and she refused to attend the meeting of the adult educators. Her differences with the N.E.A.'s adult education approach were philosophical. She believed that the illiteracy movement required the total commitment of the people involved with it and feared that adult education, a more broadly based movement, would divert the energies of the illiteracy crusaders. She expressed her concerns in a letter to Robert C. Deming, president of the N.E.A. Department of Adult Education. Deming had invited her to attend a conference on adult education sponsored by the U.S. Bureau of Education. In her reply to the invitation, she said:

> I am sure you know of my sincere interest in adult education. I feel sympathetic toward the work of your department, of course, but the friends of the illiteracy crusade, at least those who have been with it from the beginning, are unwilling to dissipate their energies in the various phases of adult education and at the present stage of the campaign I feel that the work to which I have given my life for so many years has a right to all my energies.[17]

Stewart further expressed her concerns to her old friend Dr. Winship in mid–December:

> You see the need of making it clear about illiteracy and adult education. Some folks are about to confuse the issues and are involving our illiteracy leaders in places in a more extensive program than they have funds or energy to carry on, which means that the illiterates will be neglected just as much as they were before the illiteracy crusade began. The illiteracy crusade deals with all over ten years of age who cannot read or write. Since it takes in those in the teen ages and tries to lead them into the day schools, it can hardly be consistently called adult education. In Europe adult education is carried on through universities and designed to give educated people college courses. I have made a hard fight to keep the illiteracy crusade from being confused with immigrant education and other things. We have a definite proposition: It is simply to teach five million people to read and write and to do it in a given time. This opens up the way for them to go through school and through college, and they will benefit from the adult education movement as others are now doing.[18]

For their part, the adult educators were puzzled by Stewart's response because they saw no conflict between their objectives and hers. Robert C. Deming expressed these views in his response to her rejection of his invitation to

Cora Wilson Stewart during the 1920s.

attend the adult education conference sponsored by the U.S. Bureau of Education.

> This speedy reply is prompted by a state of mind in which astonishment predominates. Do you know that this department is engaged in work of the elementary education of native and foreign-born adults only? Our job too is to remove illiteracy and to obtain a citizenry that reads and writes the American language. The secondary and specialized forms of adult education have not entered our field as yet. Your job is our job, we are covering the same fields and our rosters are all the heads of state depart-

ments in the south and elsewhere doing the same work which you are engaged. Our problems are common problems in method and purpose— e pluibus [sic] unum. By all means, as you say, give all your time and energy to your chosen life work, but in so doing give it so that every minute and ounce will count to the uttermost through the inspiration and help you give others and they can give you for concerted attack.[19]

The adult educators were sincere in their offer of cooperation, but they did not have Cora Wilson Stewart's "institutional memory" of the early days of the illiteracy crusade. They had not struggled to get college professors and other specialists to admit that adult illiterates were even capable of learning. They had not suffered the same lack of funds, and they had not seen their movement preempted by other educational establishments. Stewart's unpleasant experience organizing the national illiteracy conference during 1924 convinced her that large national organizations such as the N.E.A. had agendas that went far beyond adult illiteracy; such organizations would use the illiteracy movement to advance other goals. She also knew that the illiteracy crusade required a tremendous amount of energy. She gave the movement her total physical and emotional being all the time. In her view, the crusade needed a public that was excited about the prospects of helping less fortunate citizens; it required a spirit similar to that found in religious revivals. She thought that adult education was not such a focused movement, and she feared that it would take away energy needed to eradicate illiteracy.

Stewart had worked hard to develop a group of supporters who would focus on illiteracy itself; to lose these workers to a more broadly based effort was unthinkable. After fighting for so long to keep the illiteracy crusade on course, she was not prepared to surrender it to the proponents of adult education.

12

ℬIRTH OF THE *N.I.C*

As was her yearly custom, Cora Wilson Stewart closed 1925 by taking stock of the events of the past twelve months. While composing her summary of the preceding year, she was staying at the National Arts Club, 15 Grammercy Park, Manhattan, New York. Not only was the club a favorite of hers, it was a popular meeting place for many prominent people. In her diary, she noted, "I feel so privileged to be in this Club—such a pleasant environment."[1]

Stewart was satisfied with the advances made during the previous year. "The year 1925 was one of my best and happiest—but 1926 will have its privileges and blessings," she wrote.[2] Her diary detailed her contacts with prospective members of the planned national organization, and she gave lengthy reports on her interviews with Carrie Chatman Catt and William Allen White. She had made great progress in developing a board of directors for her new organization, but she knew that the upcoming year would require her to concentrate even more completely on her goal if the organization was to become a reality.

Her diary revealed Stewart's ability to focus on the illiteracy work to the exclusion of other matters. Her January 1, 1926, entry described events of the previous night when New Year's Eve parties brought groups of revelers to the club after an evening out "on the town." "The gaiety disturbed me not a bit," she wrote. "I was content to give thanks for the wonderful year that was going out and to prepare my spirit for the one that was entering in."[3] Later the same night, while she was recording her plans for the upcoming year, another group of celebrants came into the writing room of the club. Dressed in a variety of costumes for an upcoming masquerade party, members of the noisy group invited her to join them. She courteously declined the invitation, noting in her journal: "I left the gay throng but did not return. The quiet suited me better for meditation and planning."[4]

Stewart's concentration on the task ahead was also evident when Lela Mae Stiles visited her early in 1926. Stewart noted that her former secretary was more interested in the sights and events of New York life than in the plans for the illiteracy crusade. In her diary, she matter of factly observed, "With my struggle here to lay a new foundation under a national organization—one would suppose she would be deeply interested and would be devoting some time to it. But her mind runs to the beaux—the shows—the clothes—so I must get a more serious-minded secretary and one who will share the load."[5]

In making resolutions for the new year, Stewart also reaffirmed her dedication to the crusade, writing: "I consecrate myself anew to the task of wiping out illiteracy. It means more humility, more system, a balance between work and play, the elimination of all false trappings in mind and dress—the simple life but the busy one. This is the day's great adventure—a vow to live and be and act after the spirit and more for the cause."[6] The same diary entry outlined her planned readings for the upcoming year. Biblical selections included the Old Testament books of Isaiah, Esther, Ruth, Job, and the Psalms. Poets for the new year were Dante, Shakespeare, and Goethe. Fiction included Mark Twain and Tolstoy. Philosophy by Aristotle was part of the program, and her choice of biography was Ida Tarbell's *In the Footsteps of Lincoln*. Earlier in 1925, Tarbell had agreed to serve on the board for the new illiteracy organization, and Stewart had become an admirer of the writer.

Stewart drew great strength from reading Tarbell's story of Lincoln; during the next several weeks, she repeatedly expressed her admiration for the sixteenth president in her diary. Her observations usually assumed a personal tone. In one entry she wrote: "Mrs. Tarbell has dignified Lincoln's family—a thing that needs to be done for all Ky. mountaineers. She removes the grotesque from his love affair and the melancholy that followed it—Hurrah for Ida Tarbell and her journeying to find the truth about Lincoln."[7]

At one point, Stewart evaluated Lincoln's life, noting both his strengths and weaknesses. Her assessment clearly reflected the similarities she saw between herself and the sixteenth president:

> He suffered humiliation. He was a man of grief (sorrow at ten for his mother, sorrow for his affianced, Ann Rutlege). He was impractical in the sense that the world thinks of a practical man—He had no money sense. He helped his father and mother. He had weaknesses—In his youth he wrote foolish "almost risque," things and was affected by some atheistic literature, but in manhood, he attended church, read his Bible and finally believed he was one instructed of God. He grew out of his weaknesses became strong, became tolerant and sad. He was fit to be martyred.[8]

While Stewart admired the sixteenth president, she still acknowledged that he was not perfect. At one point she observed, "Lincoln and Isaiah, there's only one way to advance beyond them—Jesus and perhaps Woodrow Wilson. I believe Lincoln was a devout man but Wilson stood up for Jesus by a church relationship. I wish Lincoln had done so."[9]

Her reading about Lincoln also caused Stewart to think about her own family situation. "Tonight, I was thinking of my childhood," she wistfully reflected. "Reading a story reminded me that it was sad for one to love no home that could not be pleasantly remembered. I can remember a loving mother but no house now stands that I can go into or wander around."[10] Cora Wilson Stewart's diary entries at this time in her life also reflect her admiration for Jane Addams and Carrie Chatman Catt. Each served as a model for her—Catt the female Moses, Addams the Christ-like figure.

By the 1920s, however, the major accomplishments of both Catt and Addams had passed, and they were no longer the favored public figures they had been twenty years earlier. Jane Addams had gained national notoriety by opposing American entry in World War I, while Catt's support of the world peace movement was suspiciously viewed by many citizens. Tarbell had also known her greatest success during the first decade of the twentieth century. To Cora Wilson Stewart, however, such issues were not important; these women were crusaders just like her and that was what mattered.

To her elite list Stewart added Abraham Lincoln, the backwoods politician, who became president and, ultimately, a martyr. Like her, Lincoln had known great sorrow and disappointments; a fellow Kentuckian, he had risen above many challenges to achieve success. In freeing the slaves, Lincoln had found a cause similar to Stewart's; the new year gave her a chance to again commit herself to her cause of freeing the illiterates. It was a cause that allowed her to shield herself from the personal tragedies she had known in her private life. With total dedication to eradicating illiteracy, she could face middle age without a husband and children. Her cause gave her life meaning as she entered her fifty-first year, and she nourished it as carefully as any mother ever nurtured a child.

Stewart's personal life was not without family connections, however. She drew closer to her brothers and sisters and their children as she grew older. These family ties gave her great comfort. She loved her nieces and nephews and took joy in celebrating the stages of their lives. As a fifty-one-year-old woman, she would never know the personal emotions and loves of a mother, wife, and grandmother, but she could enjoy her brothers and sisters, her nieces and nephews.

During her time at the National Arts Club, Stewart planned the initial meeting of her national organization. She sent telegrams to prospective board members and hoped to arrange a Washington, D.C., meeting on February 12—appropriately enough, Abraham Lincoln's birthday. Since many prospective board members planned to be in the nation's capital during the next week for the N.E.A. national conference, however, she could not use Lincoln's birthday for the first meeting. Determined to attach extra significance to the first session, she changed the meeting to Washington's birthday, February 22. On that date, the group convened at 10 A.M. in the Williard Hotel.

The participants adopted the name "National Illiteracy Crusade" (N.I.C.) and set a goal of wiping out illiteracy from the United States by 1930. They selected William Allen White, who was unable to attend the session, president of the organization. Besides White, Jane Addams was elected vice president, along with Glenn Frank, president of The University of Wisconsin. Stewart was chosen as director of the organization, and a total of 35 men and women formed the initial board. Many of these individuals were educators who had long been supporters of Stewart's work, such as Josephine C. Preston, A. O. Thomas, Charl Williams, and A. E. Winship. Other board members included social reformers, three governors, and one artist—Lorado Taft.

The press reported the beginnings of the National Illiteracy Crusade and applauded the organization's objective of eradicating illiteracy by 1930. Besides setting a goal, the group decided to establish a committee of 100 people to assist the original board of directors. Stewart planned to choose these people from the school superintendents of the country. A modest budget of $10,000 was adopted for the first year. The American Red Cross provided headquarters for the new organization in its building in Washington and arranged for the Crusade to bank free of charge at the Washington Loan and Trust Company.[11]

The Crusade also set as its mission the publicizing of illiteracy conditions in the United States, and it resolved to send out free readers to individuals working with uneducated adults. Plans were made to conduct illiteracy conferences similar to the ones Stewart had organized while working with the N.E.A. Finally, the names of illiterates were to be collected from the Census Bureau and forwarded to local illiteracy campaigns.

William Allen White was surprised to learn of his election as leader of the group. He tried to defer from the job, but Stewart reminded him of his earlier interest in the work. After her appeal, he wrote back: "All right, sorry you chose me and because I can't wiggle out I have got to serve and do my best. I will do everything but go around and make speeches or stay at home and write articles. Don't ask that. Otherwise, I am yours."[12]

Despite White's less than enthusiastic response, Stewart was pleased to have the noted journalist as president of the N.I.C. "You have lighted a thousand candles in my heart and what is far more important insured the illiterates their chance by your acceptance," she wrote to him.[13] White's acceptance of the Crusade presidency marked the beginning of a meaningful and mutually respectful relationship with Stewart. She often sought his advice, and he was always willing to help her in her role as executive of the organization. Remembering her unpleasant experience with the leaders of the four groups sponsoring the 1924 national conference on illiteracy, she was also careful to keep White informed about the work of the Crusade. She regularly sought his consent before taking any unusual or innovative actions.

Within two weeks of organizing the National Illiteracy Crusade, Stewart received a letter from President Calvin Coolidge. Coolidge noted that he had watched with "considerable interest the growth of the movement to eradicate illiteracy and am glad to learn that it has recently crystallized in the organization of the National Illiteracy Crusade, which has for its purpose the wiping out of illiteracy by 1930."[14] Coolidge went on to applaud the organization and to encourage its work, but he did not mention the possibility of federal support.

The presidential endorsement pleased Stewart, and she even met with the

Bureau of Education secretary, John J. Tigert, to discuss possible cooperation. Remembering Tigert's attitude during the 1924 conference, however, Stewart was skeptical about the Bureau's help. In a letter to Sally Lucas Jean, she expressed her fear that the Bureau would, in her words, "anesthetize" the work:

> It is a big problem to decide just how they can help in the Bureau, and yet not make the matter so mechanical that it will kill the spirit of the whole thing—I am going to do my best to show them in time. There is a group, you know that wants to work by courses of study, by training teachers, and other processes of a complete system. The trouble is that they want to do this in places where there is not a campaign being carried on. This method, to me, is like that of putting electric fixtures in places where there is no power house and where the torch has not even been carried.[15]

Stewart continued her faith in the whirlwind campaign methods of the earlier decades. She believed there must be a revival before an institutionalized church could be established. Her views were diametrically opposed to those of the bureaucratic educators in the federal government as well as the growing adult education community. For the moment, however, Cora Wilson Stewart was more concerned with the financial future of the N.I.C. than with philosophical differences among educators. Following the first meeting of the Crusade board, she spent the next three months traveling across the country talking with financiers about the needs of the N.I.C. She met with little success and had to rely on *Pictorial Review* prize money for many of her expenses.

Her difficulties in raising money did not lessen Stewart's hopes for the movement. She wrote to White in mid–April, "My letter to you yesterday did not convey all of the hope and encouragement that I feel. We have no finances as yet, but have one very fine prospect and also have a contribution offered that has not been accepted for reasons that I will tell you when I see you."[16] The prospect to which she referred was provided by the Woodrow Wilson Foundation. The Foundation had used a fund-raiser named Burr Price to successfully raise $35,000. Stewart explored the possibility of Price working for the N.I.C., and the Crusade board agreed to hire him on a commission basis.[17]

Contented to leave the thorny issue of financing to someone else, Stewart went back to the life of campaigning that she preferred. Working the Chautauqua circuits, she scheduled numerous engagements for the summer months. While preparing to leave for one speaking tour, she received a copy of an editorial published in the Grand Rapids *Press*. The editorial challenged Stewart's claims about the number of illiterates in Michigan and asserted that most of the state's illiterates were immigrants. The editor opined, "If persons cannot be reached by an educational system like ours, then it is a crime to go about crusading in their name." Adding insult to injury, the editor finished by stating that he detested "paid directors" and charged that Stewart should first clear up illiteracy in the South before she moved into Michigan.[18]

After reading the Grand Rapids editorial, Stewart wrote to White, noting with a sigh, "A Grand Rapids (Mich.) editor says that my quoting Michigan's illiteracy figures to a Michigan audience was sensational and bizarre, and that I should work in my own illiterate South. He hates 'these paid directors.' It might comfort him to know that I am starting South now to swelter for the cause at the decrease of several hundred dollars in my rapidly waning fortunes."[19]

Stewart's efforts to develop support for the N.I.C. also produced some bizarre moments. Seeking the endorsement of other national organizations, she contacted the Daughters of the American Revolution early in June. Soon afterwards, she was visited at Crusade headquarters by Mrs. Anthony Wayne Cook, the president general of the D.A.R. When the D.A.R. leader learned that Jane Addams was a member of the N.I.C. board, she began verbally attacking the Hull House reformer in front of Stewart. Suspicious of the Crusade, Cook took a copy of the organization's letterhead with her for closer scrutiny of its board members.

The next day, Stewart was invited to D.A.R. Washington headquarters, where, in her words:

> I found six lusty defenders of the flag who branded five members of our board as Reds: Jane Addams, Glenn Frank, C. C. Catt, Ida Clyde Clark, and Ida Tarbell—and who advised that we should ask these people to resign. There was a grilling fire of questions as to why we had started out to fight illiteracy, who we were anyway to attempt it, who authorized it and why we undertook it without their advice, approval, or consent. They demanded to know if I was an "internationalist." My particular inquisitor was John Thomas Taylor, of the American Legion, of offensive manner.[20]

In describing the incident to White, Stewart speculated how melodramatic it would have been if at the end of her inquisition, she had suddenly taken out her little Bible with the flag on the inside that she carried everywhere. She warned White that he should be especially aware of one of the interrogators, a colonel from the War Department, who claimed White was "an unsavory character." In the final words of her letter to the Kansas editor, she noted:

> To leave the absurdity of it now, I want to say that, being guileless, I went to the D.A.R as to a group of women of patriotism, loyalty and idealism, and I found arrogance, suspicion, and intrigue. The serious aspect of it is the lack of D.A.R. and, they say, American Legion cooperation for the time being. Perhaps, though, they may start their own private campaign and we should at least provoke them to good works.[21]

White was not surprised by Mrs. Stewart's experience with the D.A.R. because he had had his own problems with the organization, as he wrote to her: "I was interested and amused at the sport you had with the Hate-Peddlers down at the D.A.R. They are a funny bunch—people who are Ku Kluxers at heart and just have too much money to put on a sheet and pillow case."[22] The attitude displayed by the American Legion and the D.A.R was typical of many patriotic organizations at the time. The movement for world peace and the unsuccessful effort to have the United States join the League of Nations left many people suspicious of individuals who appeared to favor international cooperation among nations. Reformers like Catt and Addams were dubbed "Reds" by these superpatriots, and anyone who favored American involvement in world affairs had their loyalty questioned. Popularly referred to as One-Hundred Per-centers, members of these groups distrusted most reformers, and their attitudes typified the nativism that pervaded America in the 1920s.

For her part, Stewart feared that her new organization might be branded with negative publicity. At this early stage, the N.I.C. needed all the help it could muster, but she would not desert her friends on the N.I.C. board of directors. There was no doubt about her patriotism, and she had no patience with groups who labeled her friends and supporters "Reds." Unfortunately, her 1926 meeting with the D.A.R. and the American Legion was not Stewart's last contact with the superpatriots.

There was little time for Stewart to consider her D.A.R. experience as she headed South for a speaking tour. She spoke before another statewide illiteracy conference sponsored by the University of Alabama and praised the University for supporting such a gathering. She wrote to White: "I can look back a few short years to the time when university people felt it their sacred duty to dispute our claims that grown men and women had learned to read and write. This work was in their eyes non-professional and unessential."[23]

Stewart was gratified that the university played such a prominent role in sponsoring the illiteracy conference. The Alabama experience raised her hopes that the academic community might catch the crusading spirit. The growing awareness of the illiteracy crusade also helped moderate her concern over the N.I.C.'s financial problems. Ever the optimist, she wrote to White in late June:

> We have everything but money—we have the best cause on earth, wonderful friends, many volunteers, excellent publicity, and, oh, yes, we have our first money too. We made our first deposit today. Mr. William Montgomery, President, Acadia Mutual Life Association volunteered $500. He has sent $200 of it. All of this struggle is an old story to me. The Kentucky work was financed on a shoestring. I have financed the work here thus far from the Pictorial Review, all of it that was left after I had paid old illiteracy debts, with interest on them.[24]

After touring the southern states, Stewart headed north, where she lectured in Michigan, Illinois, Iowa, and the Dakotas. She was able to further her interest in illiteracy among the Indians on this trip, and in July she traveled to Spokane, Washington, and met with a committee of U.S. Indian agents. She had prepared a draft of her reader for Native Americans, and she shared it with the assembly. Following her conference with the agents, she went to Glacier Park and spent a week on the Blackfoot Indian Reservation. She counseled with local educators to determine the best way to teach the illiterates on the reservation. Based on her visits, she concluded that Indian illiteracy was among the most difficult problems she had yet faced. She also learned that the Northwest Indian Congress believed illiteracy was the greatest obstacle to progress for the tribes. With the aid of her friend Josephine Corliss Preston, she persuaded the Congress to take a stand for the removal of illiteracy as the first step in a program of Indian welfare and development.

Always popular among the tribes, Stewart made many friends on her travels to the reservations. She was intrigued by Indian names, and she collected and shared them with relatives when she returned south. She also developed a correspondence with some of the tribe members. As the Indians learned to read and write, they wrote letters to her displaying their new literacy skills. She treasured these rough notes from Native Americans and kept them throughout her life.[25]

The travels in the West were not easy for Stewart. She often developed a sore throat from her speeches, and she was usually fatigued from traveling by train. She was over fifty years old, and her hectic schedule took a heavier physical toll each year. She was happy to be in the campaign, however. Near the end of a western tour, she joyously wrote to her friend Mary Elliott Flannery, "I am so much like a soldier in the trenches most of the time that it is difficult to reach me; I spend about two or three weeks in Washington and then am on the battlefield."[26]

On her return from the Northwest, Stewart stopped by the University of Wisconsin, where N.I.C. boardmember Glenn Frank was president. She spoke to the American Association of University Women assembled at the institution. After hearing her, the group passed a resolution calling for the eradication of illiteracy in the United States.[27] Unfortunately, when Stewart arrived back in the nation's capital, she found that Price had not raised any money for the Crusade. She explained the situation in a letter to White: "Mr. Price of New York did not raise one penny and the task has fallen on me again. I have great hopes that the end of the next sixty days will see us in better shape financially."[28]

The finances of the Crusade continued to occupy Stewart during the latter part of 1926. Following a suggestion from White, she tried to get philanthropist Julius Rosenwald to join the N.I.C. board, and she traveled to Florida to talk with J. C. Penney, as well as other wealthy businessmen. Most of her attempts were in vain, but she was not deterred. Whenever a possible source of funding was suggested by a board member, she followed the lead. On one such visit to Louisville, she received the largest contribution of the N.I.C.'s first year from Theodore Ahrens, president of the American Radiator Corporation.[29]

When not dealing with funding problems, Stewart focused her attention on the conditions of illiterates in state penitentiaries. She corresponded with wardens in Kentucky and made personal visits to prisons in Florida and Virginia. At Richmond, she observed six classes being offered for illiterates. She praised the Virginia prison system, noting: "Virginia has taken steps forward.

She requires all illiterates in the penitentiary to learn and has a full-time Educational Director for the institution. This is what we want to secure in every state."[30]

For Cora Wilson Stewart, the financial and operational aspects of the N.I.C. were not the only issues she faced. New problems appeared on the horizon when her earlier fears about the development of the adult education movement were confirmed; in 1926 the American Association of Adult Education was founded. The possibility of such an organization forming had been growing for several years; in 1924, Nicholas Murray Butler, president of Columbia University, had given expression to the need for such a movement when he said: "The continuing education of the adult is suffering from a lack of organization, from imperfect administration, and from no emphasis at all."[31]

During 1924 and 1925, interested individuals met, and several regional conferences were held on the subject of adult education. It was one of these meetings that Stewart had refused to attend in 1925, although she had been invited by the N.E.A.'s Robert Deming. Finally, on October 16 and 17, 1925, various adult educators came together and agreed to establish a national association, underwritten by a grant from the Carnegie Foundation.[32] From its beginning, Stewart was leery of cooperating with adult educators, despite their overtures toward her. She feared that the new movement would detract from the illiteracy crusade. To her, its focus was too general and took away from the concentrated drive needed to eliminate illiteracy. Since her earliest days in the Moonlight Schools, she had focused on redeeming adult illiterates. Advocates of adult education, on the other hand, believed that training should be "pointed less toward righting an educational wrong, less toward securing for the underprivileged that which has been withheld, and more toward providing an ideal of continuing education throughout life for all types of adult individuals."[33]

For her part, Stewart continued to champion the need for crusades to excite the public and to help the illiterates, whom she pictured as lost souls in need of redemption. She held to her opinions about the important role of lay people in the crusade against illiteracy as well. To her friend Julia Harris, she wrote:

> As to the University wiping out illiteracy, the leadership should be in a State Illiteracy Commission for the time at least. The problem needs concentration, and it also needs to be dramatized. This neither a State Department of Education, nor a State University will do. After the teaching of illiterates has become an accepted custom and a public demand, the work might then be made a division of the State Department of Education, but it is not so well to pioneer it under that agency.[34]

Stewart feared that if the work with illiterates was abandoned to the adult educators, it would be studied, analyzed, and ultimately "anesthetized." She had many friends in the educational field and had been a school superintendent, but she believed that bureaucratization of education was taking much of the heart and soul out of teaching.

Another issue was that the leaders of the adult education movement had been trained in the universities of the Northeast; many had Ph.D and Ed.D degrees and many were men. In the past, such academics had been her most persistent detractors. In the earlier days, they had challenged her claims that older adults could learn. Now academicians were questioning her revivalist methods of arousing public attention about the illiteracy movement. They sought to organize, to institutionalize, and to take a "scientific" approach to the problem of illiteracy. Such leaders looked suspiciously at reformers of an earlier time, calling them "propagandists" and charging that crusades were not really "education."[35] They were beginning to put Cora Wilson Stewart in this category.

Other academicians differed philosophically with Stewart's approach of eliminating illiteracy by helping adults as well as children. For example, University of Georgia professor Joseph S. Stewart wrote to her upon learning that she had persuaded the Georgia state superintendent of schools to call an illiteracy conference for the state. He said, "I think your position that the best way to stop child illiteracy is to educate the parents is unsound." He also noted that many adult illiterates were eager to send their children to school to better themselves. Like many other educators, he thought the best way to eliminate illiteracy was to teach children.[36]

Stewart's debate with the educational establishment would intensify during the upcoming year, but as 1926 drew to a close, she had at least accomplished the establishment of the N.I.C. The financial status of the organization was fragile, but this was nothing new for her. She ended the old year with hope and a healthy amount of enthusiasm for 1927.

13

GROWING PAINS

At the end of 1926, Stewart was in Decatur, Illinois. She went to Abraham Lincoln's home and even visited his gravesite at Springfield Oak Ridge Cemetery, where she knelt and offered a prayer. By this time, she had finished her study of Lincoln, and her admiration for the sixteenth president was high indeed, as she compared him to her mother: "He [Lincoln] was so human, so elemental. My mother had his spirit. She was a woman of sorrows but she laughed, and jested, told jokes and stories. She was benevolent, forgiving, sympathetic and tolerant. She used choice English."[1]

New Year's Eve of 1926 was quite different from that of the previous year. Although Stewart was not at her favored National Arts Club, she still expressed the same dedication and conviction as the previous year. Her diary entries also show her deepening religious faith. She wrote in her daily journal: "God grant that I may make a real stroke for the illiterates this day. This is God's message of assurance to me for this day."[2]

During 1926, Stewart had experienced the challenge of establishing the N.I.C. She had made great strides, but she knew that the success of the organization would require even greater commitment. Seeking help, she drew on her strong religious convictions. In her diary, she wrote, "My prayer is that I may be led daily, hourly, that I may be pure and may be a shining light to the illiterates, blazing with the truth of men's need and men's call."[3] Her resolutions for the new year revealed the characteristics she thought most important in the continuing crusade. These personal traits were "Concentration—no swerving aside from the task—a firm no to those who seek me for other programs. Courage—no fear to ask people to help wipe out the country's illiteracy—a task that all should share. Joyousness—as a habit, count your blessings. Faith—trust in God, all things will come right with vigilance and energy to bring them about. Economy—as far as possible."[4]

Because of the daunting task ahead, Stewart used her religious faith like a shield against troubles that might darken her spirits. Early in the year, she cheerfully noted in her diary: "These days are wonderful. I am living in glory. The love of God consumes me and his goodness enriches and perfects my life. I have never been so happy, so hopeful, or so grateful. God be praised. I ought to achieve more for I am in the spirit to do his work. Life is so full of a number of things that we all should be as happy as kings."[5] Much of Stewart's success in 1927 and 1928 resulted from her ability to work through other organizations to further the aims of the N.I.C. The national Parents Teachers Association (PTA) supported the N.I.C. by holding special drives with local chapters opening Moonlight Schools for illiterates. Despite Stewart's withdrawal as leader of its Illiteracy Division, the General Federation of Women's Clubs, continued to draw heavily on her counsel. During 1927, the Federation planned to take an illiteracy census of one county in each state and to teach all illiterates in that area.[6]

The U.S. Bureau of the Census was by now also a close working partner with the N.I.C. The agency promptly provided the names of illiterates to local illiteracy campaigns when requested by Stewart. Her work with prisoners was also an important part of the N.I.C. effort, and she continuously lobbied prison officials to offer schooling for illiterate inmates. Her efforts were not in vain: in Alabama, for instance, a special director was hired to head the work with inmates after Governor Bibb Graves declared that illiteracy must be eradicated from the state's prisons.[7]

The one dark spot on the horizon was money; the N.I.C.'s financial situation during 1927 and 1928 did not brighten, despite the best efforts of Stewart and others to interest national financiers in the Crusade. The financial report of the organization showed that during the first year of its existence, it spent $7375. Much of this was provided personally by Stewart. When one considers that the projected budget for the first year was only $10,000, however, this modest amount does not seem so disappointing.[8] As in her days with the Kentucky Illiteracy Commission, Stewart received no salary for her work with the Crusade and relied on her lectures for income. To this end, she traveled throughout the country on the Chautauqua circuits. Billed as the "Moonlight School Lady," she journeyed from state to state telling the story of the early days of the Rowan County work. Combining current needs with her lectures about past accomplishments, she described the efforts of the N.I.C. and challenged localities to join in the crusade against illiteracy. At this point in her life, Stewart was acclaimed as one of the best lecturers in the country, and years later people would remember having heard her talk. Her talks were always an event, and each oratorical performance drew heavily on her physically and mentally. Often the throbbing nerve condition for which she had been hospitalized nine years earlier recurred. For inspiration, she developed a routine of kneeling in prayer before each talk, asking God for strength and guidance.

Stewart's endurance was based on her deepening conviction that God had called her to the cause of eradicating illiteracy. In her diary she wrote: "I believe that our heavenly father has called me to a mission. To speak and write and work on behalf of all illiterate men and women whose eyes are blind to his word and whose lives are limited and darkened by ignorance."[9] Stewart's work on behalf of the Crusade was also helped by her positive working relationship with

William Allen White. The newspaper editor was always willing to offer advice and even provided incentives for local school teachers who taught Moonlight Schools. He gave free copies of his biography of Woodrow Wilson to the top teachers in various sections of the country. Stewart was grateful for his assistance, and she kept up a lively correspondence with him; he reciprocated her admiration. Early in 1927, he wrote to her: "Your letter is most cheerful and it has brought me joy. I was glad if I could be of any help to you in Washington, and I want you always to call on me when I can help you."[10]

Like White, other N.I.C. board members were available to help, and Stewart relied on their moral support. For this reason, she was distressed by the continued attacks of the American Legion and the D.A.R. on White, Jane Addams, Carrie Chatman Catt, and Ida Tarbell. In 1927 the D.A.R. drew up a blacklist of prominent Americans who were considered "REDS." White answered these charges in the newspaper, igniting a war of words with the patriotic women. The Kansas editor did not relish the fight, but he could not stand being labeled an enemy of the United States by the Daughters.

Stewart applauded the response of her Kansas friend and denounced the charges made against the members of her board. She even thought of publicizing her 1926 Washington meeting with the D.A.R. and the American Legion. This meeting weighed heavily on her mind, and she repeatedly described it in letters to friends. The charges against Jane Addams, whom she regarded as a Christ-like figure, were especially irritating. In relating the details of her 1926 visit to a friend, she told how her inquisitors had feared that Jane Addams might spread pacifist ideas in teaching illiterates. Stewart speculated that the men asking the questions were representative of munitions concerns. She cheekily observed, "If I had been asking the D.A.R. to help me teach the illiterates how to shoot, these would have been the very fellows to have called in; but I only wanted help in teaching them to read and write." She went on to note that she did not belong to any peace society, so she could not be called a pacifist, "though the name has no odium in my opinion," she added.[11]

In a letter to White, Stewart reported on another visit she made to the D.A.R. Washington headquarters in early 1927. Sent to the headquarters by the Red Cross Central Committee chairman, Colonel John Barton Payne, she was shown writings that the Daughters thought represented Communist propaganda. "I was closely watched and I was not even allowed to read and judge it for myself, but under strict supervision my eyes were directed to words, sentences and passages marked in red ink," she noted. "The Bible read in this manner could be made to appear a vile book."[12]

The D.A.R. conflict weighed heavily on Stewart. Two years earlier she had considered joining the organization, but she did not like its tactics. She wrote to her friend Sally Lucas Jean, "I believe I have a better way of being patriotic than the system that they seem to be following."[13] In another letter to a Georgia friend, Julia Harris, Stewart said that her experience with the D.A.R would probably not be her last: "I feel sure it is only the beginning. We have not yet been checkmated in any of the states by the group who set the stage here, but some such effort may be made at any time."[14]

Despite Stewart's support for her board members, the prejudices of patriotic organizations eventually did influence her. In 1927 she was asked to visit and study Russian illiteracy along with a committee of American educators planning to travel to the Soviet Union. Upon receiving the invitation, she enthusiastically replied to the organizer, Dr. K. E. Richter: "I have been tremendously interested in Russia for many years because of the high percentage of illiteracy there, and nothing would delight me more than to go with such a commission as yours to investigate the illiteracy situation there first hand. I am going to try and brush everything out of the way to accept the invitation."[15] She cleared her calendar and canceled speaking engagements so she could go to Russia. Upon hearing of her plans to travel to the Soviet Union, her friend Sally Lucas Jean advised her to check with Colonel John Baron Payne of the Red Cross before finalizing her arrangements. Jean wrote, "This will save any complications which may arise from the 'patriotic' Americans who find cause for criticism in any assistance given the so-called Reds."[16]

Her friend's advice prompted Stewart to have second thoughts about the advisability of the trip because she knew that she needed support throughout the country if the illiteracy crusade was to continue to grow. She was willing to stand up for her friends on the N.I.C. board, but she did not want to risk being branded a "Red" herself. In one letter about the trip, she wrote, "Our work [the illiteracy crusade] is of such nature that I have to be very particular about any connections I may form or any committees I may join, so I have to take much pains to go into this matter thoroughly."[17]

Fortunately, her decision-making process was eased because the Chinese illiteracy campaigner Jimmy Yen was scheduled to come to the United States at the time the committee was to travel to Russia. She used the Yen visit as a way to get out of the trip to the Soviet Union, writing to one of the committee organizers: "I regret the loss of the wonderful trip to Russia. Between the opportunity of helping illiterates in Russia or in China I would have no choice, but when I can aid those in China and through them help our own, my duty is clear."[18]

In reality, Stewart was intimidated by the possibility of being blacklisted like her fellow reformers. Having avoided such attacks over the years, she was unwilling to risk the negative publicity that the Russian visit might produce. The Jimmy Yen visit was a convenient excuse, but a disingenuous one. She had known of his visit when she first expressed interest in the Russian trip, and it was not a deterrent then. It was only after her friends encouraged her to reconsider her plans that she used the visit of the Chinese illiteracy crusader as a reason for not traveling abroad. She was not prepared to risk her work for the chance to go to Russia.

Stewart's decision also reflects the threatening nature of the times. If a personality as strong as Cora Wilson Stewart could be influenced by the "Red

Scare" of the 1920s, it must have been indeed strong. She continued to support her friends Addams, White, Catt, Tarbell, and Frank against the bigotry of the 1920s, but she never publicly risked her own reputation. For their part, her friends did not ask her to speak openly on their behalf, and they never questioned her courage. They were appreciative of her personal notes of support. They knew that she was dedicated to eliminating adult illiteracy, and this cause was her only focus. It is intriguing to speculate about what Stewart might have accomplished if she had visited the Soviet Union. With her reputation and knowledge of adult illiteracy, she might have been able to benefit the uneducated in the Soviet Union. She might also have brought back a better understanding of conditions in that country for people in the United States.

After the cancellation of the Russian trip, Stewart left her speaking tours to attend the biennial meeting of the World Conference on Education, in Toronto, Canada. The session was held August 7–13, 1927, under the direction of her old friend Dr. A. O. Thomas. For the third time, Stewart presided over the Illiteracy Section of the meeting. She conducted her part of the meeting successfully and was chosen to chair the next meeting two years later in Geneva, Switzerland.[19]

During this time, Stewart continued her efforts to provide appropriate reading material for illiterates. Her desire to create such a primer led her to write *Mother's First Book*. Released in 1928, the volume provided lessons for illiterate mothers on how to bathe, feed, and generally care for their babies. It also contained lessons pertaining to home, family, school, and community. The nutrition lessons were taken from the Red Cross course, and Sally Lucas Jean consulted with her on the health portion of the book. The Association of American Soap and Glycerine producers contributed $1000 to the production and distribution of the book, which was sponsored by the Association's Cleanliness Institute.[20] The introduction to the book noted that it was designed for home use, and mothers were encouraged to keep personal copies as a reference resource. The lessons "aim not only at teaching women to read and write, but at leading them to better home practices and higher ideals in their home and community life."[21]

Stewart claimed that she was prompted to write the book because she had seen many bookless homes in the southern mountains. After talking with a Red Cross worker, she found that no similar book existed, and she decided to create such a work. She called the book "our machine-gun in the battle to free illiterate mothers."[22] Using the *Mother's First Book*, a drive to teach illiterate mothers was launched on Mother's Day, May 12, 1928. The wife of Secretary of Labor James J. Davis, herself the mother of five children, accompanied her husband to the Red Cross building in Washington and taught the first lesson to an illiterate mother. The books were distributed free through state illiteracy commissions for home use by new readers.[23]

Following the release of the book, Stewart proudly told of how many sons and daughters in far-away states received unexpected letters from their mothers who could now read and write. Considering her close relationship with her own mother, her sense of accomplishment in being able to help women in this manner must have brought her extra satisfaction. Conversely, because of Cora Wilson Stewart's turbulent marital life and the tragic death of her own child, her creation of the *Mother's First Book* seems ironic. She never gave any evidence, however, that her personal life prompted her to write the book. In her mind, the volume was simply another tool to help eliminate illiteracy.

Mothers were not the only group to receive special attention during 1927 and 1928; Stewart took a special interest in black illiterates. Since the days of the Kentucky campaign, she had noted the high level of illiteracy among African-Americans and their positive response to the Moonlight Schools. Her study of Abraham Lincoln also reminded her of the needs of uneducated blacks. She observed that Lincoln had freed the Negroes from slavery but that many of them still endured the shackles of illiteracy.

In 1927, on a tour of the South, Stewart wrote to Roscoe Edlund of the Cleanliness Institute: "The cause flourishes in many places and seed being sown in others that will bear fruit sooner or later. I had an especially profitable tour of the southern states to reach our mass of Negro illiterates and had a marvelous response."[24] Her commitment to relieving black illiteracy caused her to make it one of the primary focuses of the N.I.C. during 1927, along with projects for the Indian and prison populations. She planned to hire a field worker to work specifically with the black population. Only the lack of funds kept her from realizing this goal.

Stewart's southern tour and her focus on black illiteracy took her to Louisiana, where she wrote to a friend that she had a chance to "stir things up." She knew that Louisiana had the highest level of illiteracy in the South, and over the years, she had regularly encouraged Superintendent of Schools T. H. Harris to conduct an illiteracy campaign. To date, Harris had resisted her entreaties, but a new governor, Huey Long, would soon enter office and help her cause.

In the meantime, Stewart concentrated on the work of maintaining the N.I.C. office in Washington, sending out readers, answering requests for illiteracy statistics, and conducting speaking tours. As usual, she was again spreading herself very thin, but she was able to accomplish a great deal. She traveled throughout the country, making talks, encouraging local campaigns, and helping with illiteracy conferences. Whenever she needed rest, she visited her relatives in Kentucky, Florida, and Arkansas. These family visits gave her a chance to relax from her hectic pace. She treasured the time with her family and watched with joy the development of her nieces and nephews.

In addition to coordinating the N.I.C. work, Stewart pursued funding opportunities whenever possible. During 1927 and 1928, she approached John D. Rockefeller as well as other financiers without any real success. As she noted in a letter to her friend Governor Henry J. Allen of Kansas, "I am constantly on the job, never at any time on vacation—Yet I realize I am hampered for the lack of funds which limits our operations."[25] Lacking money, she again turned to outside organizations to help the N.I.C. During 1927 and 1928, she talked with representatives of the N.E.A. and the Eastern Star, and she spoke at the annual meeting of the American Farm Bureau. In all of these contacts, she used the opportunity to spread the word of the N.I.C. and solicited the organizations' assistance in the crusade against illiteracy.[26]

The years 1927 and 1928 also represent a time in which the differences between the N.I.C. and the adult educators of the country were becoming more pronounced. Stewart outlined these variances in the report of the Illiteracy Committee of the National Council on Education in 1928. This forceful document laid down the battle lines between the two camps:

> The movement [to eradicate illiteracy among adults] has now attained nation-wide and even world-wide proportion, and where no method was being proposed, today various methods are being suggested and many doctors are appearing with remedies that would apply. Two distinct methods, or schools of thought, have developed in this new field of education. One group, despising the day of small things, says, "away with these crude pioneer methods with their spectacular and vociferous campaigning. We want no volunteer teaching. System and money are the things. We will have no schools for illiterates save those with paid teachers especially trained for teaching adults." They claim for their method stability and thoroughness. They would quickly standardize and set their institutions. They would turn out fewer products through longer periods of school attendance, who would, according to their theory, be better trained. This group of educators would be professional rather than pioneers.
>
> The other school of methods speaks and says, "Until we have enlightened and enlisted the educated public to come to the aid of the illiterates, there is need of beating the drum, hence a vociferous outcry against illiteracy and a spectacular campaign to bring everybody to the rescue is essential. We welcome trained teachers and are glad to see them paid, but we claim that it is the right of others to help a brother out of the ditch if they can reach him first. We regard the illiteracy movement as the Red Cross work of education. We agree that it is good to be thorough and well to systematize, but we say you must build your house before you can set up equipment and begin to keep books. We ask how are you to get the money for a system of schools for the people and paid trained teachers until you have aroused the public sufficiently to bring the state to appropriate funds, and where are you to get teachers trained to teach adults save in the school of experience in teaching adult illiterates. We believe in efficiency, but not in too much fixation at this stage of the game."[27]

Of course, Stewart came down clearly on the side of the latter philosophy and held to the methods that had proven successful for her in Rowan County. To her, the campaign against illiteracy was not the sole province of educators. She asked in her report: "Did the day schools wait for trained teachers and money to lengthen their term? No, they started with the preacher, the doctor, the peddler, and the blacksmith as teachers and ran for a two or three month session. By these crude efforts education was popularized until a longer term with teachers better trained was secured."[28]

Cora Wilson Stewart was clearly outside the growing tide of education that emphasized study, organization, and a dispassionate approach to schooling. The new social sciences were influencing the educational establishment, and the holders of advanced degrees who controlled the reins of organized education tried to distance themselves from the type of campaigns that Cora Wilson Stewart championed. She wanted an active, vital crusade that appealed to the human spirit and excited the public. She feared that the movement to eliminate illiteracy would lose its soul if the adult educators won; for their part, the growing crop of Ed.Ds and Ph.Ds wanted a scientific, logical approach to the education of adults. They looked down on the amateurish illiteracy campaigns as mostly "propaganda."

While Stewart's views on education might not have changed, her political partners in the campaign against illiteracy were encompassing a wider spectrum. During her years with the N.I.C., Stewart came to work with many former Progressives. Many of these men and women were Republicans like Henry J. Allen and R. A. Nestos. Like many of her Progressive friends, including White, Jane Addams, and Henry J. Allen, she was also a supporter of Herbert Hoover. Hoover had been especially helpful in getting the Census Bureau to provide information on illiterates when he was secretary of commerce, and he was an admirer of Woodrow Wilson. A lifelong Democrat, Stewart could not come out and publicly support Hoover's 1928 candidacy for president, but she offered her private endorsement. Stewart's attraction to the Iowan was partly based on her dislike for the Democratic candidate, Alfred Smith of New York. Smith was an avowed opponent of prohibition, so this alone was enough to sour Stewart on him. Her objections went beyond the liquor issue, however; she disliked the city brashness of the New Yorker. In May 1928 she wrote to Governor Allen concerning Smith: "It seems that even eight years as Governor of New York has not worn off the crudeness of the East Side."[29]

When Hoover won the election, Stewart was delighted. She knew that the N.I.C. would have a friend in the White House. Her happiness over Hoover's election, however, was tempered by a letter from William Allen White saying that he was forced to resign as president of the N.I.C. because of health reasons. Deeply disappointed by White's letter, she convinced him to remain as leader until a successor could be named at the annual board meeting in February 1929.[30]

Stewart ended the year 1928 much as she had started 1927. She was optimistic about the future and focused on spreading the work of the N.I.C. The financial situation of the organization had improved little, but small contributions were beginning to filter in. The new presidency of Herbert Hoover also offered her hope. Her dedication to her cause never wavered, and she expressed this clearly in a letter to her Washington secretary, Evelyn Williams. In denying

Evelyn's request for time off during the Christmas holidays, Stewart said: "You know that I do not think of our work as business ever, but as purely a missionary one and a rescue work. I can think of nothing that will give me as much joy Christmas as to be able to go out and start one person on the road to learning. I did have that privilege one Christmas when I was visiting my brother, Mr. Wilson. In fact, I started two."[31]

When the new year began, Cora Wilson Stewart did not know it but 1929 was to be a seminal year in her work against illiteracy. For nine years she had worked on the national level to make the country aware of the issue of adult illiteracy, and she had struggled for three years to develop the N.I.C. During the last year of the 1920s, her efforts on the national level would begin to pay off. Unfortunately, these opportunities came at the same time the U.S. economy dove into the greatest depression in its history.

As usual, Stewart started the new year by listing her resolutions for the upcoming twelve months. Sounding the familiar themes of dedication and hard work, her resolutions included "1) trust and love God; 2) conserve health by rest and regularity; 3) complete unfinished tasks; 4) Do fewer tasks and every one as well as possible; 5) Enrich mind by study."[32] She resolved to accept fewer speaking engagements so that she could make a better impact. Feeling somewhat stale from presenting her familiar address on the Chautauqua circuit, she pledged to prepare better for each speech. She also made a commitment to study the geography and history of each county to be visited during the year.[33]

One of the first issues that Stewart had to deal with at the beginning of the year was finding a new president for the N.I.C. When the board convened its third annual meeting in February, the members selected Dr. John H. Finley, associate editor of the *New York Times* to serve as their leader. A former commissioner of education for New York State, Finley had known Stewart since the days of the Kentucky campaign. Stewart was very happy with the selection; Finley was her personal choice to lead the N.I.C. At the same meeting, the board also voted to wage a special campaign to reach and teach as many illiterate mothers as possible before Mother's Day. As she wrote to White, the board believed this campaign "would dramatize the work anew and aid in vitalizing a general campaign."[34]

Even more important than the Mother's Day program to Stewart was the work begun in Louisiana, where a new governor, Huey P. Long, had been elected in November 1928. Known as the "Kingfish," Long would do much to stir up national politics before his eventual assassination in 1935. In the late 1920s, however, he was just beginning to establish his reputation. One of the efforts he supported was a crusade against illiteracy. Such a program was desperately needed because the 1920 census showed Louisiana had the highest illiteracy rate in the nation—21.9 per cent. In early 1929, the state began a massive illiteracy campaign that Stewart called, "One of the most dramatic efforts to wipe illiteracy out that the world has ever seen."[35] Following the established Moonlight School pattern, Louisiana committed $100,000 to the program.

Scholars have given credit to Huey Long for the Louisiana illiteracy campaign. His most reliable biographer wrote: "This [adult illiteracy] was a problem that the state would have to attack by a new method of instruction, he [Long] decided. Working with [Superintendent of Public Instruction] Harris, he devised a plan to set up throughout the state a number of night schools that would offer illiterates the rudiments of education."[36]

Of course, the system credited to Long was the Moonlight Schools that Cora Wilson Stewart had pioneered eighteen years earlier. Long was the catalyst for the Louisiana program, and the impetus he gave the crusade should not be ignored. He did not originate the idea for the campaign, however, nor did he spark the idea in T. H. Harris, superintendent of schools. As Harris noted at the time:

> Mrs. Stewart is largely responsible for the movement. She has been hammering at me for years to induce me to head a movement of this kind in Louisiana, but until recently I have steadfastly held out against her overtures, taking the position that effort and money should be concentrated on the children and let death take care of the adults. I finally decided that she was right about the matter and so we organized the drive against adult illiteracy.[37]

A long-time associate of Stewart, Harris called her to Louisiana several times during early 1929 to speak to and counsel with educators about the illiteracy work. The N.I.C. gave 2500 free books for the campaign, and Stewart's joy at the success of the Louisiana crusade was obvious. She wrote to N.I.C. president John Finley:

> I spent some days there [in Louisiana] recently with Dr. M. S. Robertson, of the State Department of Education, who is in direct charge of the adult schools, and never have I seen such bright, eager faces as I saw in those classes. The State has spent $100,000 on these schools this spring, the entire amount appropriated. Mr. T. H. Harris, State Superintendent of Education, supposed that amount would be ample. He had no idea that so many would enroll. They have surprised him indeed. The whites have thrown aside their pride and stepped boldly out, declaring their illiteracy and seeking to throw off their bondage. The Negroes are even more eager and are simply stampeding the schools.[38]

The response in Louisiana was so great that the state needed more money for its work. Harris asked Stewart if the N.I.C. could secure enough funds to complete the campaign. He estimated that another $100,000 would be needed. She was excited about the prospects in Louisiana and promised Harris to help. The state planned to have a special session during the summer especially for Negroes, as well as extending the effort to the prison population. She wrote to Finley of the Louisiana request, "Surely there is some noble citizen who will be proud to write a check for $100,000 to help the State Department of Education carry on this great work."[39]

In Stewart's opinion, the Louisiana crusade was an excellent example of what could be accomplished when all elements of a state worked together to eradicate illiteracy; she did not want to lose the opportunity to showcase the campaign. With this hope in mind, she set herself to the task of raising the needed funds. She approached a variety of financiers and foundations, with little success. For his part, Dr. Finley wrote an editorial in the *New York Times* about the Louisiana campaign and contacted several potential contributors.

Other N.I.C. boardmembers became involved as well. Finally during the summer of 1929, help for the illiteracy crusade was found. Julius Rosenwald, the American philanthropist, was a guest at the White House at the same time President Hoover was considering a program of social welfare. When Rosenwald expressed his willingness to finance some of these needs, French Strother, administrative assistant to President Hoover, suggested that he help the National Illiteracy Crusade. Strother was a former staff writer for *World's Work* magazine, which was edited by Herbert Houston, a member of the N.I.C. board. Through these connections, Strother was familiar with Stewart's work.

Soon after this meeting, Alfred K. Stern, director of the Julius Rosenwald Fund, wrote to Stewart and asked to meet her in Chicago. They arranged a meeting at Hull House, where Jane Addams presided. Edwin Embree, president of the Julius Rosenwald Fund, was also present at this meeting. After discussing the N.I.C. needs, the Rosenwald Fund officials agreed to provide $235,000 for the campaign against illiteracy, $50,000 of which was allotted directly to the Louisiana effort. The Fund agreed to provide smaller grants to individual states who could match the money dollar for dollar.[40]

In this way, Stewart was able to help the Louisiana campaign. She was proud of the progress in Louisiana, and her faith was to prove well founded; the 1930 census showed a dramatic decrease in adult illiteracy in the Pelican State. Among whites, the rate of illiteracy fell from 10% in 1920 to 7% in 1930. Among blacks, the rate of illiteracy fell from 38% to 23%. To Stewart, this campaign was further verification of her work; it proved what could be accomplished when politicians and educators worked together to adequately fund and conduct an illiteracy crusade.

The Louisiana campaign and the Rosenwald funding were not the only N.I.C. accomplishments during 1929, however. Early in the year, Stewart contacted Harley Fiske, president of Metropolitan Life Insurance Company, asking that his company send out a message encouraging the elimination of adult illiteracy. She had gotten the idea from certain magazine advertisements in which the company had presented public service announcements regarding the need to vote and other civic topics. J.E.D. Benedict, advertising manager of the company, answered Stewart's letter. Benedict stated that Fiske was interested in Stewart's suggestion, but he noted that the company president thought it was outside Metropolitan's scope of work, which dealt with health. Undeterred, Stewart tried to persuade the Metropolitan leaders that illiteracy was directly related to health. To Benedict's initial letter, she responded:

There has been no extensive research on the subject, but enough has been revealed to determine that [health and illiteracy are related]. Doctors and nurses have repeatedly declared that the unsanitary conditions in illiterate homes blocked their best efforts to check disease. During the influenza epidemic [of World War I] this was especially noted. Iowa, the state that ranks first in literacy, leads in the health of school children. Among the twenty million policy holders of the Metropolitan Life Insurance Company, there are probably a million illiterates. All we may do for them in the way of education, will aid in protecting their lives. Moreover, we are trying to aid such people to read literature which comes to their homes from your and other concerns.[41]

The Metropolitan executives were finally convinced by Stewart's arguments. On a corporate level, the company committed itself to a $50,000 advertising campaign in twenty-eight national magazines. The ads encouraged people to reach and teach individual illiterates with whom they were familiar. Art work for the campaign was developed by James Montgomery Flagg, the originator of the Uncle Sam ads during the First World War.

The company also agreed to send to prospective tutors grooved writing pads and appropriate readers. An immediate public response followed the appearance of the ads, and the N.I.C. received six thousand letters asking for the special material for teaching illiterates. Requests came from all 48 states, and 396 of the inquiries came from 11 different foreign countries. The combination of the Louisiana crusade and the Metropolitan life promotion meant a rising demand for the *Country Life Reader* series. Sale of the books had risen during 1928. In the first half of 1929, sales reached 69,851, the largest number since World War I. The sale of these readers meant that B. F. Johnson was able to provide a royalty check to Stewart for $602.29.[42]

With the Metropolitan Life campaign underway, Stewart left the United States to attend the World Federation of Education Associations meeting in Geneva, Switzerland, July 25 through August 4. She was again selected to lead the Illiteracy Section of the conference. Topics of the meeting included "The Need for a World Definition of Illiteracy," "Illiteracy in Relation to Other World Problems," and "In Relation to World Peace and International Good Will."

While at the conference, Stewart exchanged ideas with many illiteracy workers from around the world. She told them of the work of the N.I.C. and recounted the recent successes in the United States. The representatives passed a resolution calling on all governments to offer educational opportunities for illiterates as a way to promote international goodwill. They also urged her to get the U.S. government involved in the crusade as an example to the rest of the world. Stewart took all of these suggestions under consideration and began formulating a plan to accomplish this goal when she returned home from her trip. As she had done four years earlier in 1925, she traveled throughout Europe after the world conference. During this time, she wrote back regularly to friends and relatives and kept in close contact with her secretary, Evelyn Williams, concerning the development of the Metropolitan Life project.[43]

When Stewart returned to the United States in September, she was ready to ask the Hoover administration to establish a federal illiteracy commission to lead campaigns similar to the Louisiana crusade. While passing through New York, she visited with N.I.C. boardmembers Herbert Houston, now president of Cosmos Broadcasting Syndicate, Dr. Finley, and Ida Tarbell. All four individuals agreed that the federal government should appoint a national illiteracy commission. Their decision was influenced by recent news stories of President Hoover's meeting with a fourteen-year-old illiterate boy in the Virginia mountains. The press had praised the president for establishing a school for the boys and girls near where the youngster had been found.

Stewart next talked with Senator Henry J. Allen, who had moved to the U.S. Senate after recently serving as Kansas governor. She asked the senator to accompany her to the White House for a meeting with Hoover to ask for federal support for the crusade against illiteracy. Allen advised her to first gain the support of Secretary of the Interior Lyman J. Wilbur, a former president of Stanford University and Hoover's chief adviser on educational matters. Stewart was eager to move ahead with the program, but Allen, a close friend of Wilbur, persuaded her to lay the necessary groundwork first. Hence she met four times with Wilbur and Allen and explained to the secretary the status of illiteracy in the country as well as the efforts of the N.I.C. and the resolution passed by the World Conference of Educational Associations.

From the meetings, Stewart gathered that the secretary was interested in the illiteracy crusade, but she was concerned about his approach to federal involvement, as she wrote to Senator Allen:

> The one difficulty that I foresee is that the Secretary may lean toward the view of Dr. Mann [an Adult Education specialist in the Bureau of Education], who favors studying illiteracy. It is well to study, but such an announced purpose would start the commission off as a research body, which would not appeal to the imagination of the country at all. We do not wish to slow down the present enthusiastic effort that is going on in so many places at this time. One of the essential things, as I see it, is to strengthen the present movement and interest people everywhere.[44]

Stewart wanted the new commission to get actively involved in sponsoring campaigns such as the one being pursued in Louisiana. Always ready to move forward, she feared that the momentum gained in recent months would be lost. She suspected that the federal government was unwilling to take part in a crusade and that the adult education specialists in the Bureau of Education were as cautious as they had been in the past.

Unbeknownst to Stewart, economic circumstances were about to have a devastating impact on the illiteracy movement and the entire nation. While the negotiations with Wilbur were underway, events were culminating that produced the stock market crash on October 24, 1929. This occurrence signaled the beginning of the Great Depression, which would eventually bring the economy of the country to a near standstill. Unaware of the economic events about to happen, Stewart was happy when Wilbur wrote a letter to President Hoover suggesting the establishment of the National Advisory Committee on Illiteracy (N.A.C.I.). Stewart argued that the president should appoint the commission. In her mind, such an act would give momentum to the big drive needed to educate illiterates before the 1930 census. Hoover agreed that the commission should be established, but he decided to let Wilbur appoint the committee members.[45]

The events of the Great Depression would soon occupy the attention of the president and the nation. Unfortunately for Stewart, who had worked so diligently to bring the illiteracy crusade to such a high point, the depression would limit the effectiveness of her plans; just at the moment of her greatest triumphs on the national scene, the economy was about to short-circuit her efforts.

In any event, the members of the committee were appointed in November, and the committee was organized in December 1929. Dr. Wilbur was elected chairman, and Dr. William John Cooper, U.S. commissioner of education, was elected vice chairman. Cooper, a recent Ed.D. graduate of the University of Southern California, represented the cautious type of professional educator with whom Stewart often disagreed. An executive committee was named composed of Secretary Wilbur, Cooper, Herbert Houston, former North Dakota governor R. A. Nestos, Florida Congresswoman Ruth Bryan Owen, daughter of William Jennings Bryan, Senator Henry J. Allen, John H. Finley, Jr., Louisiana school superintendent T. H. Harris, Rufus W. Weaver, and Stewart. Stewart was chosen to chair the executive committee.

The makeup of the committee overlapped purposely with the board of the N.I.C., and Stewart's influence in the selection process was obvious. She was hopeful that the committee could give impetus to the crusade already in progress, but she wondered about the role the N.I.C. should play regarding the committee. In mid–November, she expressed her concern to Houston:

> I hope we can have it [the N.A.C.I.] take some active steps that will be helpful just now rather than go entirely into the class of a study or research group, as certain persons seem to favor. We shall want to guide it if possible in the best way. Our N.I.C. will need to determine its policy in connection with the committee, whether it will march ahead or fall in behind. If our organization should have funds to operate vigorously that might determine the policy. We have prospects just now that will be finally decided on the 16th. Frankly, it had been my thought that if President Hoover formed a strong Illiteracy Committee, we would probably strengthen the cause by operating through it. Since this was not done, our course would seem to be to strengthen our organization as well as aid in the work of the Advisory Committee.[46]

The "prospects" Stewart referred to on the sixteenth involved a request to the Rosenwald Fund to appropriate money for the N.I.C. On that date, the Fund approved a grant to cover the cost of the Crusade budget for the upcoming year. With this accomplished, Stewart saw that the N.I.C. work could still continue. Having lost the opportunity to get the president directly involved, she still wanted the N.A.C.I. to have a big initial impact. On November 14, she wrote to Houston again about her wishes for the committee: "I should like to see its every stroke a big, broad, effective one and let this country and others, as well, feel that which it speaks with authority."[47]

Stewart's concerns were based on her suspicion of the adult education specialists in the Bureau of Education. She wanted a crusade, and she hoped that the national government would provide the funds and leadership necessary to match the Rosenwald money for the states. Determined to see that the crusade did not falter, she contacted state superintendents of education concerning the matching Rosenwald money. At one point she talked with the Virginia superintendent of public instruction about hiring someone to lead the illiteracy program in Virginia. According to Stewart, "He said he could secure somebody and spoke of sending them to Columbia University for training. I was silent. I would have said, 'send him to Louisiana' had I said anything."[48] She was convinced that the nation's universities and colleges were not the best places to train people for the battle against adult illiteracy. The "laboratory" of Louisiana would be a much better teaching ground. She wanted to keep up the momentum of the crusade; in her mind the best way to learn the basics of the illiteracy crusade was in the field, not in the classroom.

As the N.A.C.I. prepared for its first meeting in December, Stewart began laying the foundation so that the committee would not turn into a study commission. She wrote to Louisiana superintendent Harris concerning the role she thought the N.A.C.I. should play. She wanted the federal government to provide money to match the Rosenwald funds, which were expended through the state boards of education "without too many restrictions."

Stewart also wanted the Census Bureau to send a list of illiterates to each state superintendent. At this time, the Census Bureau was still sending out upon request the names of illiterates in each county. The N.I.C. had been very effective in getting these lists for local campaigns. Stewart wanted to expand the practice; she did not know that the Census Bureau was about to stop providing the names of illiterates altogether. In finishing her letter, she told Harris of her fear that the N.A.C.I. would lose its momentum. As she said, "That [not providing support for local efforts] to my mind would slow down rather than speed up action in the communities and states now engaged in a campaign against illiteracy. A vigorous start by our group would be of value to their morale just now."[49] Stewart was not aware of the impact of the economic crisis in the nation. Ironically, at the time that the movement she had labored to nurture on the national level was gaining financial support, the economic system of the country was beginning a decline that would stifle her initiatives.

The N.A.C.I. held its first official meeting in December at the Department of the Interior. There was unanimous agreement on the goals of the program and a great deal of enthusiasm among the members, but there was no promise of federal money to match the Rosenwald money. The Rosenwald Fund gave the committee $25,000, which Stewart thought totally inadequate for the task at hand. She did not openly express her disappointment at the meeting, but she confided to Superintendent Harris, "Needless to say that $25,000 for all the work of this National Committee does not look very big to me."[50] She was pleased, however, that the group authorized the formation of illiteracy committees in each state, and they turned over this task to her.

Stewart's disappointment at not getting more money for the work was genuine. After so many difficult years, she had hoped that this time the money from the Rosenwald Fund would spark the federal government to take an active role in the illiteracy crusade. She wrote of her disappointment to Governor Nestos: "It seems unfortunate that we cannot get vast sums of money just now to aid the states in their warfare on illiteracy for as some of us realize this is a psychological moment."[51]

It truly was a psychological moment as Cora Wilson Stewart indicated. The Rosenwald Fund offered incentives that were previously unknown, and the formation of the N.A.C.I. marked the first time illiteracy had ever received commission status within the federal government. The Louisiana campaign served as a shining example of what could be achieved if a state truly supported Stewart's methods. The Metropolitan Life project was evidence of the business community's growing interest in illiteracy and what could be done when the corporate sector of the nation became involved in the work. Unfortunately, it was also a psychological moment of a darker hue. The economic clouds of the depression were breaking with a storm that would carry all before it. The state and the national governments would struggle to deal with the immediate needs of the people and the crusade against illiteracy would lose its newfound momentum. The economic turmoil would sap the strength of the nation for voluntary crusades such as Stewart championed.

Stewart did not recognize the rising tide in December 1929, nor did she know of the ultimate fate of her illiteracy crusade. She still had her strength, and she was prepared to battle all odds to further her cause. In the face of harsh economic times, she prepared for new struggles. She was used to economic challenges; soon she would also have to contend with a challenge to her leadership of the crusade. This challenge would come from her opponents in the adult education movement.

STRUGGLE FOR CONTROL

Based on events of the previous year, 1930 began as one of the most promising years in the life of Cora Wilson Stewart. There was more money than ever before at her disposal for the crusade against illiteracy, her books were selling well, the National Advisory Committee on Illiteracy had been established by the president of the United States, and successful campaigns against illiteracy were being waged in her native South.

Problems were looming, however, that would challenge Stewart's control of the illiteracy campaign. She would struggle with adult education specialists of the U.S. Bureau of Education as she had with the educational establishment that stopped her efforts in Kentucky. Professional educators with advanced degrees would label her a "propagandist" and a "crusader." As in the days of the Kentucky crusade, she would again be denied the respect she thought was hers by academicians and bureaucratic educators. To avoid what happened in the final days of the Kentucky crusade, however, she was determined not to let political maneuvering stop her program.

As the new year dawned, Stewart was in Balsam Park, Florida, preparing for a speech. Building on the authorization given her at the December N.A.C.I. meeting, she scheduled a series of public addresses to encourage an intensive drive against illiteracy before the 1930 census. During the first three months of the year, she concentrated her efforts in the South.

To increase visibility for the N.A.C.I, Stewart arranged for Fox Movietones to film short features on the work with adults in Virginia and Louisiana. She sent news stories across the nation, and as usual, the press provided excellent coverage of her efforts. Newspapers from Key West, Florida, to Santa Monica, California, carried stories and editorials praising the formation of the N.A.C.I. and challenging the nation to make a concerted drive to reduce illiteracy before the 1930 census.[1]

The print media repeatedly recounted stories of the original Moonlight Schools and traced the history of Stewart's role in the illiteracy crusade. Stewart was quoted extensively, and whenever she was asked to estimate the reduction of illiteracy since the 1920 census, she optimistically predicted decreases of fifty percent in the number of adult illiterates. In news stories, she described the methods that had been used in the Moonlight Schools since the original Rowan County campaign. To encourage participation from both teachers and illiterates, she stressed how simple it was for any educated person to teach the basics of reading and writing to an uneducated adult.

All the publicity the N.A.C.I. received was not positive, however. The American Federation of Teachers (A.F.T.) criticized the formation of the committee and sent a strong letter to Secretary Wilbur, charging that illiteracy campaigns were educationally and socially unsound. The letter asserted that the methods used were superficial and inefficient. In the eyes of the Federation leaders, the entire scheme was a political gesture that would hurt the cause of literacy more than help it. The claims of Moonlight School success made by Stewart were questioned by the organization, and the ease with which she said illiterates could be taught was not believable to the A.F.T. leaders.[2]

As workers in the front lines of education—the public schools—the members of the Federation knew how difficult it was to teach the basics of reading and writing. They resented Stewart's claims that it was so simple to teach literacy skills that any educated person could do it. They also had, however, a vested interest in seeing that teachers held the reins of the illiteracy crusade. The A.F.T. was trying to build its own sense of professionalism. By emphasizing that anyone with an education and a willingness to volunteer could participate in the illiteracy campaign, Stewart detracted from the uniqueness of teaching that the Federation was trying to establish.

For her part, Stewart was guided by the same principles she had followed for twenty years. She wanted to help the illiterates because of a moral sense of obligation to the less fortunate and a strong belief in the power of education. She had seen how volunteers, both formally trained teachers and laypersons, could help the crusade. She wanted to enlist as many people as possible in the struggle. It was a war that needed all available soldiers; she recognized the importance of the regular troops consisting of trained teachers, but she also knew that the fight needed a militia composed of civic-minded laypersons.

Despite the negative reaction of the American Federation of Teachers, the overwhelming response of the nation toward Stewart was positive. In recognition of her achievements, she was awarded in February the Ella Flagg Young Medal, given annually by the National Council of Administrative Women in Education to recognize outstanding achievement among female educators. The award was named for the former superintendent of the Chicago City Schools, Ella Flagg Young.

While Stewart focused much of her attention on the N.A.C.I., she did not forget the National Illiteracy Crusade. She saw a continuing role for the organization because the Hoover administration did not want the N.A.C.I. to get involved in organizing local campaigns. Instead, the committee seemed destined to study the problem and to provide publicity about the impact of illiteracy. To complement the N.A.C.I., the N.I.C. hired two field workers to coordinate illiteracy efforts in the states. These field agents traveled throughout the country organizing the work made possible by the Rosenwald Fund. They also spoke before local, state, and national organizations about the illiteracy campaigns. In this way, Stewart was able to use the N.I.C. to take an activist approach in local crusades.[3]

With the support of the Rosenwald grants, active campaigns were conducted in Georgia, Alabama, South Carolina, and Louisiana. In Georgia, 40,848 people were enrolled in the schools.[4] Good results were also reported in Alabama, where Clutie Bloodworth, a long-time associate of Stewart, was in charge of the illiteracy campaign. In South Carolina, Wil Lou Gray continued to lead the forces fighting adult illiteracy and reported success with the lay-by and opportunity schools for uneducated adults. In Louisiana, Superintendent Harris, along with his associate Dr. M. S. Robertson, used the $50,000 Rosenwald grant to further the work already in progress. News reports indicated that 75,000 people were enrolled in the night schools in the Pelican State.[5]

Stewart personally visited several states to encourage the beginning of night schools. In Mississippi, she met with the state superintendent of schools to urge him to apply for a Rosenwald grant. She ruefully noted that the administrator claimed there were so few white illiterates in Mississippi that it was hard to rouse public attention. She was well aware, however, that the level of illiteracy in Mississippi was among the highest in the nation. In a report to her office, she sadly noted that the public was against educating Negroes and that the superintendent was not optimistic that a crusade would become popular as long as this sentiment held. Despite these obstacles, she persuaded the superintendent to name a state illiteracy commission and to ask the legislature for $25,000 to match a similar amount offered by the Rosenwald Fund.[6]

In accord with the N.A.C.I. action at the December 1929 meeting, Stewart used her network of friends to get state illiteracy chairpersons appointed in forty-four states. Following her usual practice of getting other groups involved, she also enlisted the support of twenty-three national organizations. Rotary International, whose president, Luther Hodges, would later become governor of North Carolina, was among these groups. An active supporter of the campaign, Hodges emphasized the work in local clubs and revitalized the illiteracy work in his home state.

The General Federation of Women's Clubs selected an active national Illiteracy leader, Mrs. Bibb Graves, wife of the former Alabama governor. She developed a structure of local state chairpersons to assist in the campaign. Reviving her relationship with the N.E.A., Stewart persuaded the Association to refer all inquires about illiteracy to the N.A.C.I. as well as providing exhibit space for the committee at its two 1930 conventions.

The National Congress of Parents and Teachers, long a supporter of the illiteracy movement, appointed chairpersons in each state to assist the work. Stewart even enlisted the help of the American Automobile Association (AAA), which was asked to determine the impact of illiteracy on the sale of automobiles. Drawing on her experience with the Metropolitan Life Insurance Company,

Brooks Bridge Moonlight School students, Chambers County, Georgia.

Stewart hoped to attract the help of the automobile industry by showing industry leaders the negative influence of illiteracy on their sales.[7]

While the momentum created in early 1930 pleased Stewart, the adult education specialists in the Bureau of Education continued to frustrate her. She resented the need to clear publicity through the Bureau and constantly complained to friends of the "red tape" that was required before the N.A.C.I. could take any action. She also complained about "conflicting ideas" that the bureaucrats were putting forth.

In fairness to all parties, Stewart was accustomed to working on her own, acting unilaterally about matters of adult illiteracy; as a result, she felt cramped by the requirements of the federal bureaucracy. Also, as with the 1924 National Conference on Illiteracy in Washington, she thought that the administrators in the Bureau should defer to her experience and expertise in such matters. She resented being required to clear details with people who had little knowledge of the work with adult illiterates. For their part, the officials in the Department of Interior were merely trying to perform the duties assigned to them. It is doubtful that these men had ever worked with a woman who had the strength of will of Cora Wilson Stewart when it came to matters of adult illiteracy. They were often perplexed by her attitude.

Yet the conflict went beyond matters of operational procedures to issues of philosophy. The adult education specialists took a conservative view of how to best pursue the work. These differences appeared soon after the start of the new year when a publicist hired to help the N.A.C.I. objected to the Fox Movietone film featuring the campaigns in Virginia and Louisiana. Unimpressed with the mass medium of film, he claimed that the short movie was an inefficient form of publicity. His charges angered Stewart, who had arranged the feature.[8]

There was also a distinct difference of opinion about who should control the illiteracy campaigns in the states. The trained educators of the Bureau of Education thought that leadership should be invested in the educational bureaucracies of each state. They also resented the activity of the N.I.C., which they thought was in competition with the N.A.C.I. For her part, Stewart, along with N.A.C.I. members R. A. Nestos, Herbert Houston, Henry J. Allen, and Ruth Bryan Owen, wanted participation by citizen-volunteers.

Regarding the need for forces outside the educational bureaucracies, Stewart wrote to Nestos in early March: "Of course we will need volunteer agencies for a long time to come. Some of the states are afraid of Federal control and have refused to cooperate with the National Advisory Committee on Illiteracy for that reason."[9] Nestos shared her opinion as well as her suspicion of the adult educators and wrote to her:

> I personally feel that for the next couple of years at least, and as much longer as it will take the various states to enact the required laws and to improve the mental attitude of the educational forces in combating the problem of adult illiteracy, we must continue our volunteer organization and be prepared to give most of the direction, supervision and inspiration through the volunteer channels. Only when a state has organized effectively should the national volunteer workers be withdrawn.[10]

The volunteer work was important to the members of the N.I.C. because they had invested much time and effort mobilizing forces in the states. They were suspicious of the formally trained adult educators who came to the movement after the groundwork had been laid. They had also seen that local educational forces were slow to take action, while volunteer groups, ranging from the P.T.A. to local business associations, were supporting the crusade. Stewart and her N.I.C. board members were unwilling to give up the help of these useful groups until the formal education structures of the states proved they were capable of taking over.

To Stewart, the N.I.C. was essential because it was becoming apparent that the N.A.C.I. was interested in providing information, not action, in the illiteracy campaign. In her mind, there was a need for an activist group to help on the local level, and the N.A.C.I. was obviously not going to fill that role. She especially distrusted Dr. Rufus W. Weaver, a member of the N.A.C.I. board and an adult education specialist in the Bureau of Education. She wrote to Houston, "Dr. Weaver has been ponderous and pessimistic in his discussion with me and has turned to the committee with his views. Busy people have no time to be drawn into such discussions. Action is what we need."[11] In a letter to Nestos, she further outlined her objections to Weaver: "In the history of our crusade, I have met the type of mind several times that wanted to define the problem, state a policy and face the difficulties. Such persons are more likely to engage people in argument than to inspire action. Dr. Weaver would like to be the employed secretary of our committee. His recent actions and expressed views have not convinced me that our cause would flourish under his guidance."[12]

In another letter, Stewart noted that Weaver wanted to clear a radio address she was planning. She wrote: "To me that seems a sort of 'red tape' procedure, which somewhat 'out tapes' the long time officials. You know how they get very much tangled up and have to submit everything and ask for approval before taking a step."[13] Stewart's suspicions about Dr. Weaver were typical of her attitude toward other adult education specialists in the Bureau of Education. She thought that such individuals failed to recognize that the cause was what mattered most. She forcefully stated this view to Nestos in early April: "The program of the past few months has developed ambition in some quarters that needs to be curbed and jealousy in others that must be met and dealt with. We need to brush these things out of the way and go forward. It will take strong and valiant souls to do it—souls that are not bound by loyalties to their interests or other personalities, but by one loyalty, and that, to the best interest of our cause."[14]

Stewart planned to use her influence to see that the N.A.C.I. had the proper leadership. She told Nestos, "The all important question for us to decide at the May meeting [N.A.C.I. executive committee meeting] will be one of leadership." She speculated that the adult education forces were prepared to capture the movement from her and the lay members of the committee; she was determined to keep this from happening.

To keep control of the movement, Stewart contacted Louisiana State Superintendent T. H. Harris and convinced him to talk Dr. M. S. Robertson, the coordinator of the Louisiana illiteracy campaign, into coming to Washington as director of the N.A.C.I. Familiar with Robertson's work, she thought he would champion her goals. She made sure that her supporters were present at the May N.A.C.I. board meeting, so that Robertson would be selected. With Harris's assistance, Robertson was persuaded to come to Washington, and the committee chose him as executive director.[15] Stewart warmly welcomed Robertson to his new position and immediately began sharing her vision of the work with him.

Aware of the conflicts that had been growing in his department and intent on avoiding future squabbles, Secretary Wilbur asked to meet with Stewart concerning her role as head of the executive committee of the N.A.C.I. At this meeting, Wilbur told her she could give advice to Robertson but she was not to give him orders. In a letter to Herbert Houston, she described her reaction to Wilbur's remarks:

> I asked him [Wilbur] about guidance, and he said he would be glad to have me give him [Robertson] guidance on the general aspects of the work, but not on the educational. It is not necessary to tell you, or is it necessary to tell the nation, that I have spent my whole life in educational work. It would seem a little strange if one who has guided other nations on their illiteracy problems in four world conferences would not be expected to guide a new Director of our Committee on educational matters. I write this without the least bit of feeling, but with just a little amazement.[16]

Stewart did not believe that her role as a board member should exclude her from the operational features of the work. Always involved in the day-to-day working of the various illiteracy programs, she was not willing to separate herself from the functional side of the crusade. During the following two months, Stewart's frustrations grew. She regularly provided Robertson with ideas about the N.A.C.I., while working as a hands-on administrator for the N.I.C. She grew increasingly disenchanted with the new director, who drew closer to the views of the adult education specialists in the Bureau of Education. For his part, Robertson was perplexed and depressed by Stewart's attitude. He wrote to Harris: "Stewart feels that I should do whatever she suggests regardless of what I think of its effect on the work of the National Advisory Committee. I hope Stewart will decide to cooperate with me enthusiastically in planning and executing the program for the year." He went on to express his willingness to work with her but noted, "My only problem is that I cannot afford to do a thing that doesn't square to my ideal of duties that have been reposed to me."[17]

The rift between Stewart and Robertson widened over a manual for teachers of adult illiterates to be published by the Bureau. Written by Dr. William Scott Gray, an adult educator, the plan called for 192 hours of instruction instead of the traditional 96 hours that Stewart had always said was needed for new adult learners. Stewart disliked this proposal because, in her words, "this puts our committee into adult education."[18] Having for so long touted the Moonlight Schools as a brief, intense program of study that focused on the immediate needs of illiterates, she feared that Gray's manual required a more extensive commitment than states and localities could or would make.

In a letter to Governor Nestos, Stewart further stated her objection:

> Our Committee [the N.A.C.I.] has set up state committees with the idea that an emergency exists—lined up for a campaign against illiteracy, not to open and develop a system of adult education. This [the Gray manual] encroaches and overlaps the work of other agencies which can carry on adult education work and for which our committee and its work is the forerunner. We are the John The Baptist movement that must go before and make straight the way for adult education so far as the millions of illiterates are concerned. But we have not the means or the time to do the whole system and scheme of adult education, neither is it desirable that we should undertake it.[19]

As usual, Stewart focused on the basic needs of the most needy illiterates. She rewrote the first eight chapters of the manual to reflect her views and then sent it back to Gray for further work.[20]

For his part, Dr. Robertson supported the idea of more extensive training, thus earning the growing displeasure of Stewart. He also resented the apparent conflict between the N.I.C. and the N.A.C.I. Hoping to set Robertson straight, she turned for assistance to his mentor, Harris. In August, she wrote to him: "It grieves me to say that instead of bringing to us the constructive plans and the enthusiasm of the Louisiana campaign, Dr. Robertson has concerned himself with raising absurd issues, such as the supposed rivalry between our committee and the N.I.C. and to assume rivalry between the authority of Secretary Wilbur and myself."[21]

Stewart went on to assure Harris that such ideas existed only in Robertson's mind and that there was no rivalry between her and Wilbur. After asserting this fact, however, she did concede:

> Naturally, after all these years of waiting and working for some participation in the illiteracy movement by the government, I would seek above everything else now to make that participation effective. I have given Dr. Robertson freely of my time and thoughts since he has been here and have made every effort to insure his success. I am sorely puzzled over his attitude and lack of real cooperation. It is something that in almost twenty years of experience, I have never had to cope with before, in those associated with me in this work.[22]

Later Stewart explained to Harris her views about the teacher's manual which Robertson now supported. Noting the increased number of hours required of new learners, she said, "This, I think, may put our committee into the field of adult education. Should we not concentrate on our task and first get the millions of illiterates taught to read and write?"[23]

For his part, Robertson grew increasingly pessimistic about the prospects for continuing the illiteracy campaign. Not only was Stewart trying to dominate him, but the sickening economy was drying up state funds needed for the work. In late August he wrote to Harris: "I do not know of any good prospects of getting much money to spend on illiteracy on a national scale during the next year. So many of the states are so hard up for money to maintain their regular schools that it will be difficult to get them to spend much on illiteracy. However, I still have hope."[24]

In the rural South, where illiteracy campaigns were most needed, public schools had suffered for many years. The depression made this condition worse. Legislators were quick to blame educational leaders for extravagance, and the struggle to keep the day schools afloat absorbed the energies of local school administrators. This left little time, talent, or resources for the illiteracy crusade.[25] In part, Stewart shared Robertson's view about short-term funding, but she was already making plans to get other national foundations to supplement the Rosenwald money. No stranger to funding problems, she was better prepared to cope with the financial crisis than Robertson, who was accustomed to receiving public funds for education.[26]

The conflict between Robertson and Stewart came to a climax in early September, when the Techniques Committee of the N.A.C.I. met to consider the manual prepared by Dr. Gray. In preparation for the committee meeting, she wrote to her old friend Governor Nestos:

> I hope the Committee on Techniques will not feel arrogant and will not resent the fact that interested friends of the cause who have sacrificed much for it are ready to present their earnest views. I think that we should welcome opinions and suggestions from both laymen and educators, and especially from the members of our National Committee. After all, is not the task one that must be performed by united effort of both groups?[27]

At this meeting, Stewart's call for a shorter period of instruction was considered along with the longer period advocated by Dr. Gray. The Techniques Committee, dominated by the adult education specialists in the Bureau of Education, was clearly at odds with Stewart on this issue. Whatever hopes she had for the committee meeting were lost when Dr. Robertson supported the technical experts on the committee. The group chose the longer period of instruction. Disgusted, Stewart told Herbert Houston that Robertson never once spoke in her behalf, and she added that he "was a pitiful figure in the meeting. It was a complete desertion."[28]

With this event, Cora Wilson Stewart decided that she must get rid of Robertson as the executive director of the N.A.C.I. She asked Harris to lure Robertson back to Louisiana with a job offer. When the Louisiana school superintendent replied that he had neither money nor a job to offer, Stewart proposed to pay Robertson's salary if Harris would create a job and persuade the N.A.C.I. executive director to return home. Harris acceded to her request and agreed to provide Robertson with a job if Stewart paid his salary.

In early October, Robertson resigned his position and moved back to Louisiana. Stewart wrote to Harris, "am informed by Secretary Wilbur Dr. Robertson has offered his resignation to take effect immediately and it has been accepted. Am sure this is best all around. While I am sorrowful over the necessity of this step I am deeply grateful for the fine understanding which you have shown and for your effort to clear up the situation."[29]

The next day, Stewart tried further to relieve any misgivings that Harris might feel. "His [Robertson's] resignation was brought about in such a way that not even a member of our executive committee excepting yourself and Secretary Wilbur had to be made acquainted with the situation," she wrote. "Dr. Robertson said to me that you had done what you had agreed with me to do [urge him to resign]. I reminded him that all of the influences in this world could not move you to advise him to do something that was not for his own best interest as well as for the good of our cause. I am sorry that he feels bitter against me. My desire to promote and exalt him was an overweening one."[30]

For his part, Harris wanted to end the unpleasant situation quickly. Regarding financial arrangements, he wrote to Stewart, "I think perhaps the best way to handle the matter would be for you to send remittance direct to me and I will pay Mr. Robertson with office checks. I may or may not tell him the source of his salary and expenses."[31]

The incident with Dr. Robertson shows the extent to which Stewart identified with her movement. She had worked so hard and so long to create the illiteracy movement as she knew it that she was willing to pay to have a job created for Robertson to be rid of him. It is important to note that she never asked Harris to hide from Robertson the source of his income; this was the Louisiana superintendent's decision. Yet the entire affair shows that the illiteracy crusade was such an integral part of Stewart's life that she was willing to take extraordinary steps to maintain control.

In her own mind, Stewart easily justified her actions. In a letter to Harris, she wrote, "He [Dr. Robertson] had a glorious opportunity and lost it here when he might have made a great success by a little team work. In the last weeks of his stay, he joined deliberately with those who sought to turn our movement from a direct, simple, inexpensive program into a long, tedious one of adult education which would cost the states millions of dollars and would educate only the few comparatively."[32] In another letter a week later, she told Houston: "I wish Dr. Robertson might be saved from embarrassment, but as between his personal feelings and our cause, I think he can best afford to suffer for we have a responsibility here that is tremendous."[33]

Stewart's opposition to Dr. Robertson and the adult educators of the Bureau of Education was based on her philosophical view of the work as well as her personal investment in it. Wanting to keep the crusade focused on the most needy illiterates, she refused to risk the expansion of the movement into areas beyond the most elementary level. Such an expansion, in her mind, would divert resources away from the immediate purpose, thus decreasing the chances of eradicating illiteracy. She clung to the idea that illiteracy was a blight that must be "cured." It required radical surgery, not the protracted treatment advocated by the adult educators. Furthermore, the campaign needed the help of all people, not just the organized educational forces in the states. To this end, it had to capture the imagination of the public and "humanize" the people in need.

Stewart's views were further expressed to Rotary International president Luther H. Hodges. Stating her objections to the manual created by the N.A.C.I. Techniques Committee, she told the future North Carolina governor:

> This whole program is set up from the educator's point of view without sufficient thought of the laymen or the public. It is mechanical and, in my opinion, will not inspire people to cooperate as they might do with something that is stated in more human terms. We must have something

that will appeal to the imagination of the public and will make them think about the illiterates as human beings. If they think in terms of training courses, censuses, and survey, it will be difficult to secure hearty cooperation.[34]

The objections Stewart raised were also based on what she perceived as a lack of respect given her by urban educators with advanced degrees. Such people, nearly all of whom were males, often looked down on her and her techniques. She resented such treatment, for she knew that illiteracy in urban areas was a major problem, as it was in rural areas. Once in a letter to Houston she said:

In national conventions and illiteracy conferences school men from New York have tried to overawe me and to take the leadership, asserting boldly that they were doing better in New York than elsewhere. I have known this was not the case. The whole matter of educating the illiterates in urban centers is one for us to attack vigorously now. They have all the facilities in these places and plenty of money and yet they have lagged behind rural districts in their efforts to eliminate illiteracy.[35]

If the problem with Robertson occupied much of Stewart's time in mid–1930, it was not the only frustration she faced. For more than fifteen years, the U.S. Census Bureau had provided the names of illiterates to localities engaged in campaigns. With the arrival of the depression and the enrollment for the 1930 census, the agency changed its position; it refused to deliver names of illiterates from the new census. When the change in policy was questioned, the U.S. Attorney General's Office agreed with the Bureau's action. This action meant that local illiteracy campaigners could not get the names of illiterates from the 1930 census lists. This blow was devastating; even the supportive Nestos was distressed by its implications and wrote to Stewart: "We might as well turn the task over to the Adult Education group, and the educational forces alone because of the difficulty of distinguishing readily between sheer illiterates and near illiterates."[36]

For her part, Stewart thought the Census Bureau approach might offer an opportunity to carry the matter to the U.S. Congress, where new attention could be focused on the crusade. To this end, she had a bill introduced in Congress instructing the Census Bureau to provide the names of illiterates to the N.A.C.I.[37] Unfortunately for her, the bill never passed, and never again would the U.S. Census release the names of uneducated adults for an illiteracy crusade.

In addition to the Census Bureau's action, Stewart was still occupied with the impact of Dr. Robertson's departure. She prepared for a showdown with the adult education forces at the December 1930 meeting of the N.A.C.I. Executive Committee. Convinced that this meeting would determine the future of the Committee, she wrote to Nestos, "I wish to say to you that the next meeting of the Executive Committee will perhaps decide our fate. Those who put us into the Technique question so deeply are moving heaven and earth to capture our headquarters and to put one of their Adult Education men in charge."[38]

Stewart's fears about the fate of the N.A.C.I. were well grounded. Various adult educators, notably members of the American Council of Education, tried to convince Secretary Wilbur that Stewart should not lead the Committee. Aware of the growing sentiment among the adult educators, she turned again to Senator Allen, a close friend of Wilbur, for support. She asked him to speak to the secretary on her behalf. Prior to the executive committee, she wrote to Allen:

> The die will be cast on December 15, when the executive committee meets. My conference with Secretary Wilbur yesterday convinces me that influences are at work with him to force me into the background. He is a higher institution man, which naturally puts him in sympathy with the people of that type and their ideas. He has much to overcome in order to realize my value to this work. He told me himself that the group who desire to control consider me a "propagandist" and a "crusader" instead of an educator. I feel sure that your interest in the work and your loyalty to me would prompt it [speaking to Wilbur on her behalf] but there is an additional matter. We have set up forty-four state committees with governors, American Legion commanders and other state leaders on them, and I feel it would be breaking faith to turn the organization over to something else than the cause for which they were organized.[39]

In accord with Stewart's request, Allen spoke to Wilbur and convinced him of her importance to the N.A.C.I. For her part, she worked diligently to see that a majority was present to support her at the executive committee meeting. She was successful; the committee remained in the hands of forces sympathetic to her.

With Dr. Robertson out of the way, Stewart took charge of the N.A.C.I. offices. In correspondence with Houston, she asserted that the Census Bureau's refusal to release names of illiterates was not catastrophic. Ever the optimist, she said that the states could conduct their own illiteracy census, and she outlined a variety of ways in which the work could continue. She enlarged the role of the N.A.C.I. office and sent out 20,000 pieces of mail to the various illiteracy campaigns during October and November. She boasted to Houston that this number compared to only 1000 pieces of information that were sent out while Dr. Robertson was in the role of executive director.[40]

Thus at the end of 1930, Stewart remained in control of the N.A.C.I. She had for the moment held off the adult education forces. Her short-term success was a Pyrrhic victory, however. The depression was drying up the money and energy necessary for a successful nationwide campaign against adult illiteracy. During the next two years, it would be a challenge to keep both the N.I.C. and the N.A.C.I. afloat.

For Stewart personally, the year had been a financial success. Her publisher, B. F. Johnson, renewed the contracts for her texts and produced a revised edition of the first *Country Life Reader*. During the first half of the year, Stewart earned royalties of $865.45 on the sale of 28,731 books. Considering her usual financial situation, this was a substantial amount of income.[41] She was aware, however, of the price she had paid during the previous year; her observations about 1930 lacked her usual cheerfulness. She confided in her diary that 1930 "has been a very eventful year, full and interesting and victorious, but not without its trials." Despite her mixed review of the year, she ended her observations on a note of satisfaction. She had held on to the cause she cherished, and had not compromised, despite significant odds. No longer the political novice she had been in 1920, she had, for the moment at least, avoided the loss of control she experienced in Kentucky. With an air of contentment, she summarized the year: "My Lord has brought me through turbulent times to victory and peace with health and hope always uppermost."[42]

15

THE GREAT DEPRESSION AND MORAL REARMAMENT

The Census Bureau's refusal to release the names of illiterates was a severe blow to the work of the illiteracy crusade. Stewart actively worked during 1931 and 1932 to get legislation passed that would direct the agency to release the needed information. The Bureau's position remained unchanged, however, and it became much more difficult to identify illiterates in localities around the country.

Not surprisingly, Stewart blamed the adult education specialists for the position of the Census Bureau. She wrote to Nestos on March 27, 1931:

> I believe that the adult education group antagonized the Director of the Census in this matter and have hampered us there. We were getting the names of illiterates by states and counties very readily and even had a clerk from the N.I.C. sworn in to copy such lists. The men from the eastern states began to demand that a new type of illiterate census be taken. They urged that all who did not read, write and speak English be declared illiterate and so listed. Then they urged that a general test should be made and all from the "fourth grade" down be listed as illiterate. They took up so much time and asked such absurd things—not knowing their ground at all—the Census Bureau got very annoyed about the whole matter and had a law drafted, I judge, that would rid their Bureau of the entire problem.[1]

As usual, Stewart took a harsh view of the adult educators. Unfortunately for her, the Census Bureau never changed its position, and the N.A.C.I. and the N.I.C. were left to search for other means of identifying illiterate adults. While the Census Bureau refused to release the names of adult illiterates, it did issue statistics from the 1930 census. As statistics became available, they were sent to localities where illiteracy campaigns were underway. The local press received these reports and noted increases and decreases in the number of illiterates around the nation.[2] To relieve her frustration with the proposed census legislation, Stewart turned her attention to one of her favorite groups—the American Indians. From March 7 through March 22, 1931, she visited the

175

Blackfoot Reservation in Glacier Park, Montana, where she directed an intense clinic for illiterate tribesmen. In all, 235 Indians attended the classes. Brought in and housed at government expense, they attended three classes per day, covering 22 lessons. To help in the project, she developed a simple newspaper to use as a text. As usual, the classes taught the same lessons of civic responsibility, cleanliness, and moral uprightness that Stewart had incorporated in all her texts. She personally directed the classes, and, as in the past, she loved working with the Native Americans.

The Native Americans reciprocated Stewart's admiration and more than 200 learned the basics of reading and writing while at the clinic. They were so appreciative of her efforts that they adopted her into the Blackfoot tribe; they even gave her an Indian name—appropriately enough calling her "Chief Woman."[3] She wrote to relatives of her Montana experiences and sent them souvenirs from the reservation. In the years ahead, she would treasure memories of her accomplishments with the Blackfoot.[4] Because of the lack of funds at the N.I.C. and the N.A.C.I., Stewart decided to use the newly popular medium of radio to spread the word about illiteracy. She scheduled a series of five national radio broadcasts over the CBS Radio network during February, March, and April. She was aided in this effort by Herbert Houston, chairman of the N.A.C.I. Committee on Information. As president of the Cosmos Broadcasting Network, Houston was in an excellent position to facilitate the national broadcasts.

The purpose of the programs was to interest and enlist the public in the campaign to blot out illiteracy and many speakers made presentations. On February 18, Stewart broadcast over WMAl, Washington, D.C.; on February 23, Lorado Taft spoke over WBBM in Chicago; on March 9, Dr. John H. Finley broadcast from WABC in New York; on March 23, Alfred K. Stern, of the Julius Rosenwald Fund, aired his message on WBBM in Chicago; finally, on April 8, Secretary of the Interior Lyman Wilbur spoke over WMAl in Washington, D.C.

News releases describing the broadcasts were sent to the print media before the talks, and the press responded positively with editorials and news stories both before and after the programs. Personally, Stewart was not satisfied with her talk. She was just recovering from influenza, and she told Houston: "My voice shows the effects of it and since this was the second attack this winter the poor voice is just about permanently out of tune."[5] Despite reservations about the quality of her voice, she received numerous positive comments about the series. Over the next ten years, she would have several opportunities to use this new mass medium to tell the story of the illiteracy crusade.

As might be expected, funding for the N.A.C.I. and the N.I.C. continued to be a constant problem during 1931 and 1932. Stewart spent much of her time searching for money to match the Rosenwald grant. She was successful in getting a donation from the John D. Rockefeller Foundation, and this allowed the N.I.C. and the N.A.C.I. to continue operations until the end of 1932. The poor economy forced her to reduce staff, however, and to perform much of the field work on her own.

The teacher's manual created by the N.A.C.I. was popular, despite Stewart's reservations about its recommendations on the length of school terms. Eleven hundred manuals were sent out during the first month of 1931. For her part, Stewart kept up an active correspondence with local illiteracy efforts; she was never too busy to respond to local volunteers who asked for suggestions on how to conduct their illiteracy campaigns. Such efforts were becoming more difficult as the economy grew steadily worse. Alabama educator Clutie Bloodworth summarized the attitude of many on the local level when she wrote to Stewart, "The county superintendents are still decidedly at sea because of the depression and the uncertainty about legislative appropriations for another year but we are proceeding with the work of removing illiteracy the best we can under the circumstance."[6]

Ever vigilant about the influence of adult education advocates, Stewart made certain that a majority of her supporters were present at the N.A.C.I. executive board meetings. Prior to the May 1931 session, for instance, she wrote to Governor Nestos and encouraged him to attend, explaining, "I have sometimes anticipated difficulties at other meetings that did not arise, or rather did not materialize because our friends were in the majority and were alert. This meeting may be one where the unexpected will happen."[7]

No problems developed at the meeting, but the minutes of the May session do provide an interesting insight into the workings of the N.A.C.I. and Stewart's position in the group. One might expect that she would have dominated the meeting, but this was not at all the case. Secretary Wilbur presided for most of the session, and all members of the committee actively participated in the discussions and motions. The extent of knowledge of the members about N.A.C.I. operations is proof that they were no "rubber-stamp" for Stewart. She offered her point of view and the members of the group were deferential to her opinions, but she never tried to force her ideas on anyone. The group often turned to her for suggestions and reports on the work of the N.A.C.I., but the minutes make clear that each member was actively involved in the program. Much of the meeting dealt with financial difficulties and possible sources of money. Members discussed several potential fund-raising schemes, and Senator Henry J. Allen was the most vocal member.

Despite Stewart's reputation as a "propagandist," the other members of the committee seemed more interested in publicity than she. The minutes clearly show that the members wanted the committee to function as a source of information about the illiteracy crusade, and they did not want to get actively involved in any operational aspects of local campaigns. Whenever Stewart brought up the possibility of direct involvement in local crusades, the other members emphasized that the primary function of the N.A.C.I. was to publicize the problems of adult illiteracy.

One curious aspect of the meeting was the group's speculation about the use of the medium of radio. The May board meeting occurred one month after the last national radio broadcast on illiteracy; the committee discussed the powerful influence of radio and its possible impact for good and bad as a source of information. Stewart did not offer any opinions during this discussion, but several members expressed concern that the radio might be used by demagogues to mislead the public. On the positive side, Secretary Wilbur speculated about the possibility of putting radios in the homes of illiterates as a means of helping them cope with their lack of literacy skills.[8]

The May 1931 meeting provided no immediate worries for Stewart, but the longer she stayed at the N.A.C.I. the more she grew suspicious of the adult educators in the Bureau of Education. She regularly wrote to individuals working in the field about the importance of keeping the crusade aimed at the most needy individuals. In one such letter to Luther Hodges, she observed: "If we want to wipe out illiteracy, we absolutely must stick to the task and get the adult beginners taught rather than trying to do the whole job of high school and specialization. We have often indicated this to the friends who are doing this work, especially when they have decided that they can take on more than the actual campaign among illiterates."[9]

Stewart's view was being increasingly challenged by educators who saw a need for training beyond the very basic level offered by the Moonlight Schools. The world was much more complex than the one of Rowan County in 1911. The adult educators believed that a higher level of training was needed for a person to be considered literate. In addition, these educators approached adult education as a lifelong learning process, and their ideas reflected the influence of the new social sciences.

Stewart detested this technical view of education. A reformer cast in the mold of an earlier time, she wanted to generate a campaign to attack the social ill of illiteracy. The adult educators wanted a dispassionate and scientific approach that was the antithesis of her view. Her feelings toward their approach carried over into other areas of her life, as well. In response to a letter from her Kentucky friend Cora S. Payne about possible employment in the Washington Red Cross, Stewart observed: "They [the Red Cross] have a great deal of 'red tape' there now and have become as they call it 'technical.' I hate the word. It means that they expect everybody to have some special training for Red Cross work."[10]

Since Stewart often equated the illiteracy campaign with Red Cross work, her views about "technical" training transferred to education. She looked around her and saw individuals with advanced degrees who were assuming positions of power in the education field. Having come of age at a time when few women earned such advanced degrees, she had never pursued training beyond the normal school. She had no such degrees and had never had the time to earn such certification; she was too busy with the fight against illiteracy. Consequently, as the years passed, she was increasingly out of step with the network of adult educators who carried impressive academic credentials. Many of these people came from the universities of the Northeast and were academic scholars. It was no mere coincidence that most of these opponents were men.

If Stewart was out of step with the professional forces coming to dominate American education, she remained popular with the American public and served as an inspirational symbol for the American people at a time of great need. A series of magazine articles and newspaper reports painted her in a sympathetic light. All of these noted her mountain origins and told the story of the Moonlight Schools. These reports were filled with nostalgia and "human interest" that appealed to people trapped in the throes of the depression. By telling how the mountaineers of eastern Kentucky were able to rise above their backgrounds to gain knowledge in the Moonlight Schools, the reports gave hope to the people of the 1930s. The titles of the magazine pieces reveal the nature of their contents: "Education Under the Moonlight," "Moonlight Trysts For Education," "Mountaineer," and "Just to Read and Write." In all of these articles, Stewart was portrayed as either the heroic figure who helped the benighted out of their darkness or as the kindly mother figure who received letters from the newly emancipated illiterates.

A typical report, this one featured in the popular *Literary Digest*, noted: "As she read one after another [letter from redeemed illiterates], a mist came before her eyes, and one saw not the official director but the "moonlight lady" of Rowan County, who thought nothing of riding ten or fifteen miles through the mountains to visit one of the night classes—and still thinks nothing of it."[11] Another article, entitled "Mountaineer," described Stewart's background in "Bloody Rowan" and told the story of the beginnings of the Moonlight Schools. The article went on to praise the night schools' potential for eliminating illiteracy. It emphasized Stewart's early work and the strong disposition she had displayed two decades earlier. The writer of the article noted: "She zips around the country, lectures here investigates there. But when she goes back to Rowan County, she rides horseback through her mountains, and stops to talk to some of her pupils."[12]

Stewart's image in the press was carefully cultivated and clearly represented the view Stewart wanted expressed about herself. It did not totally square with the middle-age lady who enjoyed fine clothes and the company of the National Arts Club, but it represented her impression of herself. Despite her enjoyment of the finer things of life, she still viewed herself as the Rowan County pioneer who opened the Moonlight Schools in 1911. One can easily imagine how the nostalgic descriptions of the "moonlight lady" were greeted by the educators who wanted to "systematize" and "study" the issue of illiteracy. Such articles only encouraged the educational leaders of the 1930s to view her as a "crusader" and a "propagandist."

If Stewart's standing among professional educators in the United States suffered, it met no such fate on the international level. For the fourth consecutive time, Stewart presided over the Illiteracy Department of the World Federation of Education Associations biennial conference. At this meeting, held in Denver in July 1931, she introduced four former American illiterates who recounted their experiences in learning to read and write. The four included in her words, "a native born mountaineer, a foreign-born white, a Negro and an Indian."[13] Each of these individuals told of their attendance in night schools and described how they had learned the basics of reading and writing. They each expressed appreciation for the opportunity to learn to read and write and told of the importance of these skills to them.

Stewart found this World Conference particularly meaningful because it came close to the twentieth anniversary of the beginning of the Rowan County Moonlight Schools. In early September, she noted the symbolic nature of this date in a letter to Herbert Houston: "Twenty years ago today we started out in search of Rowan County's illiterates and tomorrow night will be the twentieth anniversary of its movement—the opening of the moonlight schools. Has it all been worthwhile? You would have thought so indeed if you could have heard from four former illiterates addressing the World Conference on Education in Denver July 28."[14] The next day, she expressed her continuing resolve in another letter, telling Houston: "Am starting in today with renewed zeal and courage. We shall show illiteracy no quarter."[15]

Much of Stewart's effort during 1931 and 1932 was focused on prisoners. Using N.I.C. funds, she hired Dr. J. K. Hoke of William and Mary College to visit various state prisons to help establish classes for illiterate inmates. She also carried on an active correspondence with local prison officials, gathering information on the conditions of prisoners and helping wardens and prison chaplains open classes for inmates.[16]

Besides Stewart's prison work, another set of classes was held for Indians in the Northwest. With her encouragement, five schools were established on the Shoshone Reservation in Wyoming, as well as the Blackfoot Reservation in Montana. The schools operated under the Wyoming State Department of Education and the Bureau of Indian Affairs Extension Service. Indian officials followed Stewart's recommended course of study, and the program was deemed successful by local administrators. In the words of F. C. Campbell, supervisor of extension work for the Bureau of Indian Affairs: "There is no question in my mind as to the value of these adult illiteracy schools."[17]

During 1931 and 1932, the economic pall of the Great Depression slowly smothered the N.A.C.I. and the N.I.C. Stewart constantly followed leads on possible funding sources, but to no avail. By mid–1932, lack of funds made it nearly impossible for her office to answer requests for materials needed in local campaigns. Conditions were so bad that the executive committee of the N.A.C.I. could not hold its regularly scheduled meeting in May 1932. Despite all these troubles, Stewart encouraged local efforts by stressing the work with prisoners. She wrote to her Alabama associate Clutie Bloodworth in mid–May, "It [the prison work] is a work that can be done without expense to the State Committee or Department of Education. If a good piece of work is done in the prisons, it should strengthen your program outside."[18]

Yet, Stewart knew the strain that the economic conditions were causing on the local level. In the same letter to Bloodworth, she said: "Your fate, I suppose, at this time is the common fate of all. It is a considerable struggle to keep the work going."[19] In a later letter to Bloodworth, she offered the following observations: "These are times of great stress with us just as they are with our friends in the states, and we have been compelled to curtail expenses and, also, to concentrate on some things already at hand."[20] She noted with some sarcasm that the American Association of Adult Education was claiming credit for work being conducted by Wil Lou Gray in South Carolina. After reading a bulletin from the Association, Stewart observed: "This is very good propaganda for adult education but very poor assistance to the campaign against illiteracy."[21]

The coming election in 1932 revived Stewart's interest in national politics. She knew that there was a move underway to repeal the eighteenth amendment, which instituted prohibition. She was dead set against the repeal and observed, "I heartily approve of the plans to organize and campaign for the election of Senators and Representatives who are against repeal and re-establishment of the old liquor traffic."[22] Her admiration for Herbert Hoover was undiminished, despite the public criticism that most people heaped on him for the national economic crisis. Upon hearing of Hoover's renomination, she wrote to the president's administrative assistant, French Strother: "While I was not one of those who rushed in to congratulate President Hoover on his acceptance speech, I rejoiced nonetheless as I heard it over the radio and realized that it was the speech of the century. Not only did the address delight all citizens who are interested in the welfare and advancement of our nation, but even the stars in the heavens rejoiced that night."[23]

Despite her enthusiasm for Hoover, Stewart was still unwilling to take a public stand on behalf of the president. When asked to cooperate with the Republican National Committee, she declined, saying:

> Daily I am using my influence in a quiet way to strengthen him [Hoover]. But our illiteracy work is identically on the same basis as the Red Cross. We must depend on the members of all parties for support—both for services and funds. If I should become publicly active in politics, it would undermine the movement which I have pioneered and to which I am devoting my life. You know I regard the cause as my first and most sacred responsibility.[24]

Stewart offered a similar response to the Democratic party when asked to join the Committee of Business and Professional Women for Franklin Delano Roosevelt.[25] Despite her reservations about publicly endorsing either candidate, she clearly favored Hoover. She admired Franklin Roosevelt and had spoken highly of him when he ran for vice president in 1920, but in a letter to Governor Nestos, she observed, "[Roosevelt] is fervent, but not mature and convincing."[26]

Ironically, Stewart, who met her greatest opposition from the Republican party in Kentucky, developed her closest relationships on the national level with members of the G.O.P. Both Governor Nestos and Senator Allen were Republicans, and she had risen to head the executive board of the N.A.C.I. under the Hoover administration. Her success resulted from her ability to maintain the illiteracy crusade as a neutral cause. By avoiding partisan politics, she was able to deal with Democrats on the state and local level, while gaining national support from Republicans during the 1920s.

Stewart's interest in national politics did not deter her from trying to find money to keep the N.A.C.I. and the N.I.C. afloat. Right up to election day, she continued to search for funding to help in local crusades. She also continued to hold to her views on adult education. In mid–October, she wrote to Clutie Bloodworth: "I see more and more an effort to divert people who started out seriously to stamp out illiteracy. Indeed, we in the South where illiteracy is so prevalent cannot afford to devote our efforts to educating adults who already have enough education to go on. I believe in education from the cradle to the grave and from kindergarten to the university, but I know how tremendous is our task and how limited the funds for it."[27]

With the election of Franklin D. Roosevelt, the time of the N.A.C.I. had passed. Secretary Wilbur told Stewart to prepare to close the office on January 1, 1933. The correspondence and other matters dealing with the office were passed on to the N.I.C., where Stewart planned to carry on the work of both groups.

In a letter of thanks to supporters of the committee, Secretary Wilbur applauded the efforts of the N.A.C.I.:

> We feel that the Committee has realized a number of its major objectives. It was created at the psychological moment when the Federal Census was just far enough ahead to make possible the stimulation of States and local communities to do their utmost to immediately improve their illiteracy records. To make the public "illiteracy conscious" has been the main aim of the National Advisory Committee on Illiteracy, and to create at the same time a sense of responsibility in the local community for the education of illiterate adults.[28]

The demise of the N.A.C.I. was a milestone in the life of Cora Wilson Stewart; she never again held any official capacity in the federal government regarding illiteracy. She did not know it at the time, but the policies of the New Deal were to affect the nation in many ways, and new leaders were preparing to come to Washington with the Roosevelt administration. In matters dealing with adult illiteracy, the new administration would be clearly controlled by the proponents of adult education. These leaders would have their chance to set national policy; they would not want Cora Wilson Stewart inside the federal government. Despite this apparent loss of authority, Stewart did not believe that her role as a participant in the work with uneducated adults had crested; she ended 1932 ready to continue her crusade against illiteracy by concentrating on the N.I.C.

Stewart watched with interest as the Roosevelt administration assumed power. She was pleased when the new president announced his intention to appoint a woman to his cabinet. She wanted her friend Ruth Bryan Owen to be selected, but Roosevelt chose Frances Perkins, former chairman of the New York State Industrial Board, to be secretary of labor. Later the same year, Roosevelt appointed Owen ambassador to Denmark, the first woman to represent the United States in a foreign country.

The new president's inaugural address also impressed Stewart. She noted that he went to church before that talk, and she praised his closing of the address with an appeal for the presence of God. She wrote to Frank Button concerning this act, "He [Roosevelt] is valiant and sincere."[29] Stewart did not wait to see what action the Roosevelt administration would take regarding adult illiteracy. Shortly after the closing of the N.A.C.I, she traveled to Kentucky in search of sponsors for the N.I.C. She was not successful, however, and the Crusade would never again be able to send workers into the field as it had in the late 1920s.

By the second half of 1933, the New Deal was beginning its own work with illiterates. The first effort came when Federal Emergency Relief Administration (F.E.R.A.) director Harry Hopkins learned that 40,000 teachers were on relief. On August 19, he authorized part of the agency's funds to be used to hire these teachers to instruct illiterates. Hopkins assigned Dr. Lewis Raymond Alderman, a former superintendent of schools in Oregon and a specialist in adult education in the U.S. Bureau of Education, to direct the work.

Stewart knew Alderman from her days on the N.A.C.I.; her assessment of him was less than enthusiastic. In a letter to a friend, she acidly observed: "I know his methods. He is a politician and full of guile."[30] Her displeasure grew when Alderman announced that anyone with less than a sixth grade education could enroll in F.E.R.A. literacy classes. Relaxing in Christiansburg, Virginia, when Alderman's policy was announced, Stewart soon made known her opposition to the federal approach to illiteracy. On December 10, 1933, she appeared on a national NBC Radio broadcast, attacking Alderman's sixth-grade standard of literacy. She asserted that when illiterates were taught in the same classrooms with students who had some training, attention was inevitably diverted to the more educated participants. She urged that the federal government provide separate classes for total illiterates. Stewart also pointed out that the definition of illiteracy the world over was the inability to read and write in any language. She charged that the Census Bureau did not accept Alderman's standard as a measure of illiteracy and said that such an interpretation would greatly lower the rank of the United States in literacy among the other nations of the world. As a final blast at the F.E.R.A.'s standard, she observed that such a measure "would make of our fathers and mothers illiterates." The idea that people like her mother, who was a teacher and who wrote so eloquently, should be considered illiterate simply because they did not complete an arbitrary grade level was ludicrous to Stewart.[31] Following her speech, she received dozens of letters from people all over the United States who shared her viewpoint. She responded to one correspondent: "The F.E.R.A. needs to get straightened out on this matter of what constitutes illiteracy. It seems that L. R. Alderman is responsible for that sixth grade nonsense. It is likely to limit their work among illiterates and that is why I felt it most needful to call the attention of the country to the blunder. Besides, we do not want the public confused about the problem."[32]

Stewart continued her criticism of the New Deal's approach to the illiteracy work and summarized her assessment in a letter to Luther Hodges: "The government is doing a little toward removing illiteracy, but as yet it has not developed into much of a campaign, excepting that the publicity makes it sound so. Some states have a five point education plan with illiteracy as one point. If they concentrated that one point on actual illiterates, it would help quite a bit but they accept people of fifth grade education and under and call them illiterates."[33]

Unfortunately, Stewart had no official position in the federal government, and her statements did little more than irritate the adult educators who directed the New Deal illiteracy campaign from Washington. Ironically, the federal program prompted many letters to the N.I.C. asking for assistance. Since she was the best-known illiteracy authority in the country, newly hired teachers from across the nation wrote to her asking for advice and suitable material for their new students. These teachers were unaccustomed to working with adults, and they earnestly sought her help. Unfortunately, these requests came at the time the N.I.C. was most destitute; there was no new money available to help the local initiatives.

Stewart sent out manuals and texts as long as money was available, but by 1934, even this was no longer possible. The requests grew as other government agencies, including the Civilian Conservation Corps, the Tennessee Valley Authority, and the Works Progress Administration, joined the work and spent unprecedented sums of money to hire unemployed teachers to conduct literacy classes. In a supreme irony, the federal government's campaign came at the time the N.I.C. was almost totally moribund; thus the National Illiteracy Crusade was unable to help the nation at the time its services were being most requested.

Never accepting the New Deal's sixth-grade standard for illiteracy classes, Stewart remained skeptical of the work being done. She did not realize that the federal efforts against illiteracy were really make-work programs for public school teachers. They were designed to take unemployed teachers off the public dole. In essence, the New Deal work with illiterate adults was an upside down version of Stewart's Kentucky campaign. In the second decade of the twentieth century, she persuaded teachers to teach voluntarily in Moonlight Schools so that illiterates might learn basic skills to improve their lives. By contrast, in the 1930s, the illiterates went to school so that the economic condition of teachers could be improved. If Cora Wilson Stewart felt like Alice after falling through the looking glass, one would not be surprised.

The federal programs with illiterates produced mixed results. In 1936, Harry

Hopkins estimated that 580,000 men and women had learned to read and write in the government programs. It is impossible to check the accuracy of these claims because the 1940 census used a new definition of illiteracy—anyone who had less than a fourth-grade education. This was in direct response to the recommendations of the adult education community. Interestingly, one of the major achievements of the programs, according to its proponents, was publicizing the problem of illiteracy. This same claim had earned Cora Wilson Stewart the disdain of the adult education community a decade earlier; she had been dismissed as a "propagandist" and a "crusader" for making similar assertions.

If Stewart was skeptical of the New Deal's work with adult illiterates, she was not alone. Critics charged that the programs were poorly planned and inefficiently executed. They observed that the efforts were hindered by the concentration on the teachers instead of the students. Many instructors were cullouts from the regular schools who seemed most interested in drawing their salaries and had little experience or desire to work with adult illiterates. Besides a lack of planning, numerous educators resented federal intervention in state schools. One schoolman in Oregon summarized the feelings of many when he noted: "In the beginning we learned that education and relief would not mix; next we learned that education and politics made a diabolical combination; and finally we learned that adult education, plus relief, plus politics, equals no education at all, but only, as one of our administrators expresses it, 'a devil of a mess.'"[34]

The federal programs to teach illiterates, plus the bad economic times, meant that Stewart was unable to revive the National Illiteracy Crusade. She tried several times to get funding for the organization but was unsuccessful. She still made occasional speeches about illiteracy and periodically appeared on national radio broadcasts to discuss the topic, but the N.I.C. never recovered.

For Stewart personally, times were indeed difficult. For twenty years, Stewart had supported herself with speeches on illiteracy; she had been preempted by the New Deal and her personal finances plummeted. She received help from family members during the 1930s, but times were hard for the other members of the Wilson family as well. Conditions were so bad that she could not afford to attend the World Conference of Educational Associations in the summer of 1934. The meeting was held in Dublin, Ireland, and this was the first international conference she had missed since they began in 1923. In deference to her, the Illiteracy Committee at the Dublin conference named her chairman anyway.

Her poor financial situation forced Stewart to look for other work. Surprisingly, help came to her in 1935 from an unlikely source—the Roosevelt administration. Aware of Stewart's abilities as a public speaker, the Federal Housing Administration offered her a job as a field representative at $3000 per year plus expenses. The new job required her to travel throughout the nation addressing women's groups and civic clubs about relieving unemployment in the housing industry. She gratefully accepted the position and enthusiastically began her work. Stewart was glad to help the national government and truly believed in the importance of the federal housing program. She wrote to her friend Ruth Bryan Owen: "This program needs some very earnest effort, such as I am trying to put into it. It is a most constructive program and is essential to the national recovery."[35]

Stewart found it easy to connect her work with illiterates to her new position. In a letter to another friend, she observed: "My readers for adults have contained many lessons on the improvement of the home and this may have been one of the reasons—in fact it was one of the reasons—why I was asked to make a speaking tour to interest the women's organizations of the country."[36]

Wherever she spoke, Stewart was asked to tell the story of the Moonlight Schools in addition to her assigned topic. Out of deference to her new duties, she tried to refrain from talking about her past work, but she usually relented when pressed by the audience. Even when she did talk about the Moonlight Schools, however, Stewart related her remarks to her new job. In Memphis she told a reporter: "As the people learned to read and write, they wanted better things and one of the first things they wanted was better homes. So you see, I've really been talking about better housing all of these years."[37]

With the waning of her influence in national matters dealing with illiteracy, it was only natural that Stewart would become involved in other causes. The financial difficulties of the mid–1930s caused her to seek solace in her religious faith; in late 1933 she attended a meeting of the Oxford Group with her good friend Sally Lucas Jean. The Oxford Group was a religious organization that would eventually carry her completely away from the work against illiteracy. Founded in 1921 by Dr. Frank Buchman, an ordained Lutheran minister who was secretary of the Y.M.C.A. at Pennsylvania State University, the ministry sought to arouse in each individual the self-assurance and power that purportedly came from following God's guidance.

Members of the organization believed that a person should have all of his acts directed by divine instruction. This guidance was received during "quiet time," when the individual prayed and communicated directly with God. The Oxford Group relied on a lay clergy and held "houseparties" in which members gave testimonials, confessed their sins, and discussed their faith. The organization was convinced that the problems of the world could be solved if individuals would follow God's direction, and it vigorously sought converts. Many of these new members were prominent men and women of wealth and culture. Always more popular in Europe than the United States, the group was nevertheless making clear progress in America by the 1930s.[38]

There were four principles on which the group was based: 1) absolute purity, 2) absolute unselfishness, 3) absolute honesty, and 4) absolute love. It was decidedly a middle-class and upper-middle-class movement, which aimed to improve world affairs by converting leaders around the world. Considering the characteristics of the organization, it is easy to understand how Stewart became attracted to it. Its four tenets were quite similar to the lofty qualities toward which she had striven over the years. Her personal feelings about her relationship to God also attracted her to the Oxford Group because she had felt divine direction in her work with illiterates. The international flavor of the group and the presence of many of her friends appealed to her as well.

The emphasis on a lay clergy, free of the "technical" requirements of traditional denominations, also made Stewart feel comfortable in the ministry. The group's inclusion of people of wealth and culture was another attraction for her. A person who always enjoyed the finer things in life (whether or not she could afford them), Cora Wilson Stewart delighted in the company of the people who were drawn to the Oxford Group.

Thus, when Stewart attended her first meeting at the Plaza Hotel in New York in November 1933, she was already a likely convert. The session, she observed, "Was well attended by men and women who looked prosperous."[39] She heard these people witness about their faith and tell how their personal relationships with Jesus Christ affected their lives. She was impressed by the testimonials, and she resolved to learn more about the Group.

In the spring of 1934, Stewart read a series of articles in *The Forum*, the official periodical of the Oxford Group. Written by Eleanor Roosevelt, Mary Pickford, Lady Astor, Pearl Buck, and Madame Chiang Kai-shek, wife of the Chinese president, these writings were on the topic "What My Religion Means to Me." Stewart was especially impressed with the last article by Madame Chiang because it emphasized that she had put her life under the guidance of God.

When Stewart attended another session of the Oxford Group in April, she heard young men and women tell of the difference the Group and its God-guided approach had made in their lives. These individuals gave testimonials about how they had been saved from personal tragedy and ruin by turning over their lives to God. Little did she know, but Cora Wilson Stewart was about to undergo a similar religious conversion.

In May 1934, Stewart attended another meeting at which participants challenged her to join the Group and to live her life by the four standards of the Oxford Group. When she asked how the Group defined sin, they told her that sin was anything that blocks one from God or other people. When asked by Group members if she had any resentments or felt enmity toward anyone for current or past wrongs, she did not admit much. She noted that, when challenged with the same question by the group, most other people at the meeting became quite defensive. She was proud that she had not reacted in the same manner when subjected to this line of questioning.

As she left, Stewart promised the members that she would consider joining them. During the next two days, she observed "quiet time" and found out that she would be required to give up her illiteracy work for a greater cause. These moments were a spiritual breakthrough for her. She described this time in her personal writings:

I was told to make my surrender—which means giving your life, your mistakes, your wrongs and all you are and have over to God. This was in the early morning—at six o'clock in the evening I was again ordered to go and make my surrender and now with whom I was to take this step toward God. I went and it was revealed to me that I had to surrender my work, which it seemed was the one thing I had held as a buffer to God. When I became willing to surrender it, I began to get the guidance—uniting with the church was one concern. I had been visiting churches of different denominations as a sort of unofficial observer. I obeyed and then I was guided to unite and clear up things with people I had distrusted or felt unkindly toward and to some who had felt aggrieved at me, straightening out my relationships.[40]

The requirement that Stewart give up the work with illiteracy was obviously difficult for her. Her internal struggle carried over into her prayers:

God asked me some searching questions. Would you rather carry learning to men than to carry salvation? Which is more important? If they are dear to you are they not dear to Christ who bears all our burdens? Is your life so vital to them now and has it been during the past few months that you can carry on for them fruitfully without God? Are you going to be loyal to Christ or the illiterates?[41]

Stewart's conversion from crusader against illiteracy to Oxford Group member did not take place in one blinding strike. For several months, she wrote of her divided feelings. She ultimately came to believe that she had a chance to provide more for the illiterates than education—she was to show them the guidance offered by the Oxford Movement. Stewart later wrote of her new role in life and the needs of the time:

God-guided leadership and God-guided followers is the crying need of America. My life has been to bring the adult illiterates their opportunity for education. God enlarged my field and gave it back to me and said, "Be fruitful." But I am shown that because of the urgency of the present crisis in America I am to be used in a very active way there with people of culture and persons in high places but that it is an intensive campaign temporary for me—which does not separate me from the task of seeing that the illiterates of the nation and the world are enlightened and brought to Christ.[42]

Soon Stewart learned of her opportunities with "people of culture and persons in high places." In June, while preparing to leave for the Kentucky mountains to work on a book, she received guidance to go to Banff, Canada, for a meeting of the Oxford Group. Her finances were very poor, and she could not afford the trip, but someone gave her the necessary money and she was able to go to Canada. In Banff, she received further guidance to go to Oxford, England, for a Group meeting with representatives from fifty nations. She borrowed money and made the trip. At this international meeting, she received further guidance directing her to devote her life to the Oxford Group and to carry the movement to others.

Stewart wrote to her sisters of her joy at finding the Oxford Movement:

> I am leaving the daily personal guidance of me to one greater than all the presidents and kings in the world, and that is our Heavenly Father, and through the Oxford Group I have learned how to have this guidance consciously rather than blindly hoping I will be guided. I am beginning to wake up to the realization of the desperate urgency of the world situation. Oxford has enlarged my vision—I mean the experience there, beyond any words I have to describe. I consider that I have been blest unspeakably in being at the two great meetings—Banff and Oxford, and learning the full plan and purpose of the Oxford Group. I have gained knowledge in three months that some in the Group have not had an opportunity to gain in years. It was not my plan at all, but God's guidance.[43]

Stewart's growing belief in the Oxford Group was expressed in a letter to Sally Lucas Jean: "More and more it is becoming apparent that world chaos can only be dissolved by turning to the wise creator of it all to straighten out the tangle."[44]

In the following years, Cora Wilson Stewart became an active participant in the Oxford Group. She attended houseparties around the country, traveled abroad, and developed a network of friends in the movement. She produced detailed writings of her religious feelings, emphasizing the tenets of the Group. As her focus on the Oxford Group grew, her work with adult illiterates continued to wane, although she periodically gave public speeches on the subject. Considering her involvement in the Oxford Movement, one might expect that she would have used her platform as an illiteracy crusader to launch a religious crusade on behalf of the Group, but she did not mix the two. Although she was a convert to Buchmanism, she kept her public speeches about her work with illiterates free of proselytizing.

It is unclear why Stewart did not mix the two works because she still had a public platform. She did write to friends and share her religious convictions, but her beliefs were largely personal and limited to her circle of Oxford Group friends. This focus on inner growth was typical of the Oxford Movement and may explain why she did not use her national platform to promote the group among adult illiterates.

The international influence of the Oxford Group grew during the 1930s. Frank Buchman noted in 1936: "Our aim is a social order under the dictatorship of the Spirit of God, making for better human relationships, for unselfish cooperation, for cleaner business, cleaner politics, for the elimination of political, industrial, and racial antagonism."[45] In 1938, as the world drew nearer to the brink of World War II, Buchman called for "Moral Rearmament" (MRA), an international effort to "return to those simple home truths that some of us learned at our mother's knee, and which many of us have forgotten and neglected—

honesty, purity, unselfishness and love. Moral recovery is essentially the fore-runner of economic recovery.[46] This lofty call was music to the ears of Cora Wilson Stewart. She spent much of her time praying, observing "quiet time," and waiting for heavenly direction before taking any action. Her copious religious writings tell of the peace of mind she gained from the Oxford Group. A person who had always exhibited a strong religious faith, Stewart found the Oxford Group ideally suited to her. After going through some angst about abandoning the illiteracy crusade, she accepted the reality of the times and acknowledged that she would not resurrect the National Illiteracy Crusade.

Cora Wilson Stewart took seriously the Oxford Group's requirements that she exhibit purity, honesty, love, and unselfishness. The movement allowed her to forgive the people she harbored animosity toward in the past. She wrote of overcoming her reservations about Olive Jones, the N.E.A. president who did not support her at the 1924 National Conference on Illiteracy. She did not reveal the names of others with whom she reconciled her feelings, but apparently she came to such accommodations in her own mind. Her correspondence in later years shows a total lack of acrimony toward anyone, and she gained a sense of contentment and peace through her religious experiences that allowed her to put to rest the problems of her earlier life. In its place was a serenity and sense of personal balance that was evident to her associates.

In her writings and conversations with friends and relatives, Stewart never spoke ill of people for whom she might have been expected to harbor bad feelings. As she moved away from her earlier career, she seldom, if at all, mentioned these people. Her sense of peace helped her maintain a positive attitude based firmly on religious convictions. Friends applauded her apparent sense of serenity. As one friend wrote, "You are bound to be happy to have accomplished as much as you have in this life and to feel so near your maker and so SPIRI-TUAL MINDED."[47]

While she was becoming spiritually involved in the Oxford movement, Stewart also discovered a place where she would enjoy personal contentment. In 1936 she began regularly visiting in Tryon, North Carolina, a resort community in the western mountains. Friends from the Oxford Movement also vacationed in the area, and she looked forward to her visits to the mountain retreat. While in Tryon, she met Mark Burrell, who sold flowers to local boardinghouse residents during the summer. Stewart always loved cut flowers, and she usually bought some from Burrell. When Stewart found that he had a daughter, Arpha, who was valedictorian of her high school class, she took an interest in helping the young woman further her education. She helped her get a scholarship to North Carolina Women's College in Greensboro, and she kept in contact with Arpha over the years.[48]

When she was not visiting in Tryon, Stewart traveled to see her brothers and sisters in Kentucky and in Arkansas. She took a personal interest in all of her nieces and nephews and followed with pride their accomplishments. She regularly sent them gifts and cards on special occasions such as holidays and birthdays. She was especially close to her brother Clefford's daughter Marion and exchanged letters with her for the rest of her life.

By the late 1930s, Stewart was content with her life, having reached a spiritual level of comfort within the Oxford Group. Stewart's friends admired her sense of fulfillment, and she enjoyed a growing network of associates within MRA. Despite her preoccupation with religious issues, she still made some speeches on the illiteracy movement and even appeared on "It Can Be Done" with popular poet and radio celebrity Edgar A. Guest. This national broadcast aired over NBC Radio in August 1937. On the radio show, Stewart told of her past accomplishments and of the work of the National Illiteracy Crusade. She even stated that the Crusade was looking for someone to back the movement so that her effort to teach adult illiterates could be completed. Despite these brave words, she had no hopes of resuming her work; by 1940 she was in full retirement from the work with illiteracy.

FINAL DAYS

With the onset of World War II, the limitations of the Oxford Group and Moral Rearmament in converting world leaders were painfully obvious. Hitler, Mussolini, Stalin, and Churchill were not observers of "quiet time," and they never waited patiently for God's guidance before taking action. The involvement of the United States in the war also had a chilling influence on the American followers of Moral Rearmament.

For her part, Cora Wilson Stewart never stopped adhering to the tenets of the Oxford Group, even when she no longer traveled around the country with the members of the movement. Her extensive correspondence with other Buchmanites shows her deep religious convictions. In the early 1940s, she moved to Pine Bluff, Arkansas, to be near her sisters Flora and Stella and her brother Glen. With the financial aid of relatives, especially Flora's husband Jesse Peers, Stewart settled into an apartment on Parkview Street, where she remained until 1958. Stewart's family became the major focus of her life, and she carefully followed the lives of her nieces and nephews. These relationships provided her with great comfort as she grew older without children of her own.

True to her nature, Stewart encouraged her relatives to read the Bible and to make religion a major component in their lives. Stewart continued to read and study the Bible herself and drew great comfort from its teachings. She seldom spoke of her educational accomplishments, although she did occasionally talk with relatives about the prominent people she had known. When not in Pine Bluff, she visited with family members in Kentucky and other states, if funds allowed. She continued to spend summers in Tryon, visiting with friends who vacationed in the North Carolina resort town. She kept in contact with Arpha Burrell, the young woman she had helped enter the Women's College of North Carolina at Greensboro. By now a public school teacher, Burrell assisted Stewart with clerical duties whenever the latter visited Tryon.

While Stewart's deep religious convictions gave her a sense of peace that was obvious to all who knew her, she remained a commanding presence in interactions with others. At times, she seemed too demanding to friends and relatives who did not know all the details of her earlier life, but this was simply a part of her personality. Age did little to alter this aspect of her character. Jeremiah

Wilson had jokingly called her "the General" when she was four years old; she still proved worthy of this nickname in old age.[1]

In the late 1940s, Stewart began to lose her eyesight, a condition that worsened as a result of glaucoma. During the early 1950s, she had several major operations to correct the condition. Her physical problems never caused her to despair, however, and she drew on her religious faith for strength. Following one operation in 1952, she wrote to her niece Marion McCrea, "I've come through [the eye operation] and I say it is faith in God that has made it possible for me to go through the experience. I said after I went to the Mayo Clinic alone [in 1918] that I would never do that again. I find that we cannot tell what we may do. Sometimes there are harder things in store for us, but if the Lord is with us we can meet them and come out victorious."[2]

Despite the operations, Stewart's eyesight could not be saved, and by 1953, Cora Wilson Stewart was totally blind. The pain continued to worsen so that by June 1957, her right eye had to be removed. The irony of her loss of eyesight is obvious. Stewart had often spoken of illiterates as being similar to blind people because they could not decipher the printed word. Now physical conditions had taken from her the ability to read and write and forced her into darkness.

Despite her physical condition, Cora Wilson Stewart never expected sympathy from others, nor did she indulge in self-pity. She wrote to her niece in early 1953: "You probably know that my sight finally went, but I want to tell you that I never felt defeated nor despaired. I set to work to make my adjustments, and to live my life with the use of the other senses and capabilities which I have."[3] These adjustments allowed her to continue an active correspondence. Whenever possible, she would get friends, relatives, or other acquaintances to write letters that she dictated. Stewart also continued to enjoy the printed word; she simply recruited others to read to her. Her handicap did not stop her from remembering friends and relatives on special occasions either. When necessary, she called the local pharmacy and had an employee read to her over the telephone the verses from suitable cards for a relative's birthday, anniversary, or other event. After hearing the stanzas, she chose the desired card and had it delivered to her so she could sign and mail it.[4]

Stewart always insisted on signing her own name to cards and letters. Her handwriting grew shakier in later years, and her penmanship, which had been so graceful earlier in life, was compromised, but she never lost this skill. In her work with uneducated adults, she had always said that writing one's name was the first symbol of literacy; in her declining years, she clung to it as a sign of independence.

Popular interest in the work of Cora Wilson Stewart was revived in the mid–1950s when a television program entitled "Moonlight Schools" was produced for the "Cavalcade of America" series. Starring Emily Davies as the young Rowan County school superintendent, the show also featured veteran "B" movie actors Lon Chaney, Jr., and George Nader in the story of the early days of the Kentucky crusade against illiteracy.[5]

As her health declined in the mid–1950s, Stewart became concerned with the proper placement of her voluminous personal papers. When the University of Kentucky asked that her papers be donated to the college library, the request was a shining moment for her. Remembering how university professors had challenged her claims about the abilities of adults to learn to read and write, she perceived the request as acknowledgment of her work. She agreed to donate the papers to the university, which received them in 1957. In 1958, Stewart also began corresponding with E. P. Dutton Company about renewal of the copyright to her book *Moonlight Schools*. In earlier years, she had spoken with relatives about a possible autobiography, but these plans never developed. By the late 1950s, the passage of time and physical limitations made that prospect impossible.[6]

For her part, Stewart carried on personal affairs without her eyesight, and she managed to live on a slender budget. Unable to travel, she enjoyed occasional long-distance phone conversations with friends and relatives. By this time, she was being supported mostly by her brother-in-law Jesse Peers. Realizing that her life was reaching an end, in early 1958 Stewart decided to return to Tryon. The family took her to Little Rock, where she made her first and last airplane flight. Ironically, it had been forty years since newspapers reported that she planned to buy a fleet of airplanes to take teachers into the Kentucky hills to conduct Moonlight Schools. Family members worried about her traveling to North Carolina unassisted, but she reassured them. As independent as ever, she safely landed in North Carolina, where arrangements had been made for her arrival. Her family did not know it when they helped her on the plane, but this was to be the last time they would ever see her.

Settling in at Tryon, Stewart again enjoyed the quiet of the small town and visited with her friends there. In May 1958, she suffered a heart attack and had to move from her apartment in Tryon to the Gaze Home. She was content in her new quarters and assured people with whom she corresponded that it was a "rest home" and not a "nursing home." Soon after her move, she was joined by her friend Aura Jones, a missionary to Africa. The two women had met during the heyday of the Oxford Movement and maintained a strong relationship over the years. Knowing that her condition was worsening, Stewart wanted her friend near, and the two women visited together for several weeks. Stewart did not complain to her family regarding her worsening health, nor did her letters betray any sense of self-pity. In her last letter to her niece Marion, she stated, "I cannot write many letters and I'm not too clear in my thinking."[7] From this statement, however, she moved on to ask about the condition of other family members. As always, she closed the letter by signing her own name.

The pains of old age could not diminish her spirit, and Stewart remained in control of her faculties up to the end. On December 2, 1958, she suffered a massive heart attack complicated by pneumonia, and she died at St. Luke's Hospital in nearby Columbus, North Carolina, at 11:10 A.M. True to her independent nature, she had already made her funeral arrangements, and her final burial expenses were paid by her brother-in-law E. B. McGlone. Following a simple service at McFarland Funeral Home, she was laid to rest in Tryon's Polk Memorial Gardens on December 6, 1958.[8]

Aura Jones stayed with her until the end. After attending the burial services for Stewart, she wrote the following to Marion McCrea: "We must all rejoice that this brave and gracious spirit is now with the Savior whom she loved so much and served thru a long useful life."[9] Cora Wilson Stewart would have found this a fitting testimonial.

EPILOGUE

Nearly forty years have passed since Cora Wilson Stewart's death, and it was more than eighty years ago that she started the Moonlight Schools. In the last decade of the twentieth century, her simple approach to illiteracy may seem unsophisticated and the level of training she championed inadequate by modern standards. When she began the Moonlight Schools, however, her ideas were eminently practical. She used the contemporary definition of literacy to fashion a system of teaching the basics of reading and writing to uneducated adults. It is true that she held to this measure after it was no longer adequate for the times, and she was slow to accept higher measures of literacy that were identified by proponents of adult education. Her reasons for concentrating on the most needy were based, however, on her belief that illiterates would be forgotten if included in classes with better-educated people.

The concerns Stewart felt were also founded on the negative reception given her by academicians when she first started the Moonlight Schools. Many academics had challenged her claim that adults could learn to read and write after a certain age, and she had proven them wrong; she was determined that attention would not be shifted away from the totally illiterate again.

Stewart's claims about the ease with which adults could be taught to read and write made the process appear very easy. People who have worked with adult illiterates know that the rate at which adults learn varies greatly from one person to another. It was not easy for many new adult learners to master literacy skills, and the challenging process of learning was often disillusioning for teachers and students who accepted Stewart's claims at face value. In her defense one must note that she believed that it was necessary to get the general public involved in the campaign against illiteracy, and she wanted to entice illiterate adults into at least trying to learn. If she made the process appear easy, it was because she wanted to make sure that both illiterates and teachers knew it was not an insurmountable task.

Like many reformers of her day, Stewart also had a naive faith in the power of education. She assumed that once people gained literacy skills, they would naturally become more productive and better citizens. As a result, society would become a better place. Her faith in the power of education was influenced by her parents' similar belief. Her views were also developed at a time when education was not universally available in the United States. Illiteracy was a major problem, and the relationship between ignorance, poverty, and disease was more easily identifiable. Today, when schooling is widespread, it is apparent that education is not a cure-all for society's ills; in 1911, however, when Stewart was beginning her work, it is easy to see how she might have viewed schooling as a panacea.

Stewart's *Country Life Readers* taught middle-class moralistic lessons that may appear chauvinistic to some people today. In this regard, she acted no differently than other textbook writers of her day. It was common for school text authors to include lessons of morality, cleanliness, frugality, and civic responsibility; in fact, such lessons were expected. This training was part of the educational system of the early twentieth century. Considering the current criticism of the value-free education that permeates the public schools of the 1990s, her desire to offer some instruction on morals would be acceptable to many people today.

That Stewart expected too much of volunteers also cannot be denied. She thought teachers should donate their time to instruct adult illiterates, and she believed that the problem of adult illiteracy could be eliminated by volunteers drawn from women's clubs and other civic groups. She was too optimistic in her assessment, but she came of age at a time when such sacrifice was expected of educators. Stewart required greater and greater contributions from the teachers; these demands ultimately provoked the defection that killed the Kentucky crusade. On the national level, she also had an unrealistic faith in the effectiveness of volunteers. One need only consider, however, the current work of Literacy Volunteers of America, Laubach Literacy Volunteers, and other community-based literacy programs to see that her faith was not totally misplaced.

Was she a "propagandist"? This term carried a very negative connotation at the time it was leveled against her; it implied that her claims for the Moonlight Schools were false. These accusations hurt her deeply. Regarding these claims, it cannot be denied that she publicized her work and that she tried to arouse the public to the needs of adult illiterates. If one implies, however, that a "propagandist" uses facts loosely and publishes lies to further one's cause, Stewart surely was not guilty of this charge. The letters from illiterates she received, the news reports published, the letters from teachers, and an analysis of the illiteracy rates in Kentucky in 1910 and 1920 reveal that the crusade did produce results.

It is equally important to remember that Stewart operated outside the educational mainstream most of her career. After 1913 she never held a publicly paid position until she joined the Federal Housing Program in 1934. In essence, she was an educational entrepreneur. In this role she usually had to appeal directly to the public for support. One of the prime rules of any business venture is to advertise. Looked at from this perspective, her efforts at publicity were an integral part of her business plan to increase awareness about illiteracy. Such publicity was often looked on as "propaganda," however, by educators securely employed in universities, government bureaus, and school systems around the country.

If Stewart was not a "propagandist," was she a true educator? It cannot be denied that she did not have the educational credentials held by a growing number of adult educators in the 1920s. It must remembered, however, that she went to college in the 1890s, a time when most women (and definitely women in eastern Kentucky) did not seek advanced degrees. She attained the position of superintendent of the Rowan County Schools at the early age of 26, and she was involved in the illiteracy crusade by the time she was 36. She had no time to seek advanced credentials, and it was unlikely, given where she lived, that she would have been welcomed into doctoral programs because of her sex. In addition, when she was superintendent of the Rowan County Schools, she was at least as well educated as other school administrators of her time. It was only in the 1920s that her credentials were questioned by adult educators with advanced degrees.

Furthermore, it must be remembered that when Stewart first began the Rowan County campaign, the U.S. Bureau of Education acclaimed her as a true educator. Bureau commissioner P. P. Claxton even offered her a position as an adult education specialist in his department. The membership of the National Education Association also recognized her by electing her to its executive committee. The world clearly accepted her as an educator; she was chosen to preside over the Illiteracy Section of the World Conference of Education Associations five times between 1923 and 1931.

Stewart's attack on illiteracy as a type of social evil may seem curious to many people today, but her approach was similar to that of other reformers of the late nineteenth and early twentieth centuries. Such advocates viewed social problems as ills that needed to be attacked in whirlwind campaigns similar to religious revivals. Cora Wilson Stewart was a product of this period; it was only natural that she would use the same techniques that her contemporaries employed.

Despite any reservations that one might have about Stewart's approach to the illiteracy work, her place in adult education is secure. She courageously challenged the conventional wisdom of the day that claimed older people could not learn once the "golden age of memory" had passed. She gave hope to thousands of illiterates and showed them that they could succeed. If she spoke to them in the language of the nineteenth-century religious revivalist, it was because this was a language they understood. It was also the language that she had learned at Anne Halley's knee; she perfected this style and became one of the most powerful platform speakers of her time.

Stewart was also correct in stating that illiterates needed immediate success to inspire them to further heights. The writing of one's name was the most immediate and visible sign of success; therefore it was this skill that she emphasized first. She also believed that actual proof of accomplishment, such as writing a letter, was an appropriate measure of literacy. Unlike the adult educators of the 1920s and 1930s, she did not accept mere completion of a particular grade level as proof of literacy. If the intervening years have taught us anything, it is that simply completing grades in school is no sign that a person has been freed from illiteracy.

Furthermore, Stewart made sure that the lessons taught in the Moonlight Schools were directly applicable to the lives of the students. She rejected using books designed for children because she thought such texts were demeaning to adults. Instead, she was the first person to insist that materials be developed that spoke to the concerns of adult illiterates. In this way, she presaged the idea of functional literacy.

Stewart was a true champion of the most needy, as well, and concentrated on total illiterates at a time when others wanted to turn to higher levels. It was not because she opposed schooling for educated adults; it was that she did not want the totally illiterate to be lost in the scramble for education dollars. From practical experience she knew that funds for schooling were scarce, and she wanted to make sure illiterates got their chance. Stewart humanized the condition of the illiterates in ways that may appear maudlin and melodramatic by today's standards, but she lived at a time when such displays were accepted. She used testimonials to touch the heartstrings and pursestrings of people who were able to help the illiteracy crusade, and she made no apologies for this approach. According to Stewart, a "human" element had to be maintained in the work with adults; this was part of her opposition to the professionally trained educators. She feared that in their attempt to organize the work, the professionals would lose sight of the illiterates as people.

Stewart was also among the first people to relate adult illiteracy to other social problems. She pointed out the connection between illiteracy and disease, illiteracy and poverty, illiteracy and poor farming techniques. If her faith in the power of education was too idealistic, she at least deserves credit for calling national attention to the relationship between illiteracy and other social concerns. She knew that to succeed, illiteracy programs had to be community-based, and she emphasized the necessity of involving different local groups in the teaching of adults. Her ideas for bringing in businesses, clergy, and even traveling salesmen were truly innovative and provide lessons to anyone involved in adult illiteracy work in the late twentieth century. Her effectiveness in inspiring volunteers was a positive example for the nation as well. She was able to get various segments of society, not just teachers, involved in the crusade. Stewart knew that the answer to the problem of adult illiteracy was not merely a matter of money. She saw the need for the entire public to become conscious of adult illiteracy, and she wanted people to help their less fortunate brothers and sisters as an act of human kindness, not simply as a service for which payment was rendered.

Stewart's work also crossed racial boundaries. Like most people then and now, she had her share of racial prejudices. Considering the times in which she lived, however, her prejudices were certainly mild, and when it came to the matter of adult illiteracy, she was color blind. She practiced what she preached. She spoke before groups of blacks, championed their education, and made sure they had opportunities in the illiteracy crusade. As a result, some of the most enthusiastic supporters of the Moonlight Schools were members of the black community, where education had been denied for so long. Stewart's interest in work with American Indians also stands as a tribute to her ability to cross ethnic lines. The Native Americans admired her so much that they adopted her as a member of the Blackfoot tribe in the late 1920s.

Most significantly, Stewart made the public aware of the problems of adult illiteracy. This may have earned her the charge of being a "propagandist," but she clearly raised the consciousness of the nation about the issue. She wanted to incite the public to action, as John Grant Crabbe had done in Kentucky in the educational "whirlwind campaigns" of the first decade of the twentieth century. There can be no doubt that she was a "crusader." She adopted a cause, and she made it her personal and professional life. Her choice of working to eradicate adult illiteracy as a chosen field was a result of her own private life. Stewart came from a background of educators, and she was trained to teach. She lived in an environment where illiteracy was prevalent, and she readily saw the difference between the way her parents lived and the lives of people who had no education.

Stewart's early life produced conflicting psychological demands, however. Despite her best efforts to live up to her mother's ideals, her tragic married life convinced her that she was not to enjoy the traditional life of a wife and mother. Without these touchstones, so prevalent among females in the early twentieth century, she sought and adopted a cause. It was a noble cause that was in harmony with her personality, and she made it her mission in life.

Stewart advanced through various stages in her crusade, but she eventually became out of step with the educational trends of the 1930s. When she lost her place as an educational reformer, it was natural that her devout religious faith would lead her to a higher plane of involvement. The Oxford Movement allowed her to combine her faith with her crusading zeal, buckling on the armor of her faith like the medieval crusaders, and it gave her a cause to which she could cling when the educational establishment of the 1930s preempted the illiteracy movement. At the same time, Moral Rearmament allowed Stewart to reconcile differences in her own personal life and led her to personal contentment in her later years. Her crusading spirit, combined with her religious beliefs, gave her the strength to bear difficult physical conditions in her declining years. She remained independent to the end, as she held on to the crusading spirit that marked her earlier life.

Whatever her accomplishments or failures, Stewart's attitude toward her life was shaped by her position as a woman. Like many females of the early twentieth century, she became active in public affairs and supported woman suffrage. She was able to use her affiliation with women's groups as an effective source of influence on the county, state, and national levels. This support brought her many energetic workers. Despite her reliance on female aid, Stewart was not an ardent feminist. After the passage of the nineteenth amendment to the U.S. Constitution, she did not push for more female rights. To her, the eradication of illiteracy was always most important, and it was on this single issue that she concentrated.

If Stewart's gender aided her in gaining female support, she also suffered the same limitations that society placed on women of her time. She was educated in late nineteenth-century America, when schooling was deemed less important for a woman than for a man. Thus, in the late 1920s and early 1930s, when professional training was becoming increasingly important in educational work, she lacked the accepted credentials. Instead, she was accused by critics of being a "propagandist" and a "crusader." It was no coincidence that nearly all of these detractors were men.

Equally as important, Stewart was a product of the Progressive era. After becoming a county school superintendent at a time when Kentuckians were awakening to the need for better schools, she soon developed into one of the state's most eloquent spokespersons for public education. She was influenced by Dr. J. G. Crabbe's efforts to improve schools, and she adapted his whirlwind campaign methods to her own work. Having come of age at a time when feverish efforts were used to attack social ills, she believed that a great campaign was required to arouse people, and she held to the simple faith that, once aroused, the public would support a worthy cause.

Equating her movement against illiteracy with such reforms as prohibition, Red Cross work, and female suffrage, Stewart pursued her work throughout the 1920s and early 1930s. She failed to realize that the campaign techniques used by the Progressive reformers were no longer popular. Convinced of the righteousness of her cause, she refused to change with the educational tides of the time; she remained a crusader after the day of the crusader had passed.

If Stewart eventually became out of step with the educational trends of her time, she clearly had no regrets for the way she lived her life. In a draft of remarks she prepared for a speech in the 1920s, she summarized her feelings about her life when she posed the rhetorical question, "What would I do if I could live my life over again?" In answer to her own question, she dramatically responded:

> I would begin fighting illiteracy earlier and hit harder all along the line. As a little mountain girl, I would begin crying aloud in the wilderness, "My people perish for lack of knowledge." In young womanhood, those who came to woo, I would send forth to crusade. All lovers should be made knights of the book and pen. If time would turn back thirty years for me what zeal of youth, what fire and spirit and energy I would put into the task. If the gods came bearing the brush of Raphael, the voice of Melba, the dramatic art of Sarah Bernhardt, the statesmanship of Lady Astor, the pen of Tolstoy and saying choose ye and take what ye will.

What would my answer be? All of these I reverence and admire, but only one of them would tempt me. I might steal a covetous look at the pen of Tolstoy, for I once craved to be an author with a universal message. But then I'd look back at that long line of millions whose eyes are closed to the book and say to the gods—Thanks very much—but from among the illiterate masses there may be a painting, a golden song, a piece of state-craft or a needed book that if my hand slacks might never see the light of day.[1]

NOTES

Chapter 1: Growing Up in the Rowan County War

1. Wilson Family Bible, Personal Papers of Marion McCrea. Hereinafter cited as McCrea Papers; "Genealogy of the Halley Family," Biographical File, in Cora Wilson Stewart Papers, University of Kentucky. Hereinafter cited as CWS Papers.

2. Cora Wilson Stewart to Homer Wilson, February 12, 1940, CWS Papers.

3. Diary of Anne E. Halley, pp. 14–15, Biographical File, CWS Papers.

4. Wilson Family Bible, McCrea Papers.

5. Morehead, *Rowan County News*, May 10, 1956.

6. Wilson Family Bible, McCrea Papers. There are at least two other possible birthplaces: The *Who's Who* biography for Cora Wilson Stewart lists her birthplace as Farmers, Rowan County, and she used this location in some of her other printed biographical material. A 1940 letter to her brother Homer implies that she may have been born in Powell County. There is no clear reconciliation of these various sites; I have chosen to use the family Bible citation, which is indicated above, as the final authority.

7. See Robert Ireland, *The County in Kentucky History* (Lexington: University Press of Kentucky, 1976), for a description of the development of counties in Kentucky.

8. Quoted in A. L. Lloyd, "Background of Feuding," *History Today* (July 1952): 456; Ireland, *County in Kentucky History; New York Times*, June 23, 1887; Morehead, *Rowan County News*, May 10, 1956; Meriel Daniel, "Two Famous Kentucky Feuds" (master's thesis, University of Kentucky, 1940), pp. 25–71.

9. Untitled autobiographical notes, January 17, 1924; "Information Sheet" (n.d.), both in Biographical File, CWS Papers.

10. Edward T. Moran [Cora Wilson Stewart, pseudonym], "The Rowan County War," *World Wide Magazine* (August 1902): 321–30; "The Founder of the Illiteracy Movement," CWS Papers.

11. Author's interview with Norman Welles, September 2, 1972, Morehead, Kentucky.

12. Untitled autobiographical notes, January 17, 1924; "Information Sheet" (n.d.), both in CWS Papers.

13. Interview with Virginia Williams, October 12, 1990, in "Cora Wilson Stewart and the Moonlight School Oral History Project," Morehead State University. Hereinafter cited as CWS Oral History.

14. "The Founder of the Illiteracy Movement" (Box 52); Wilson Stewart to Homer Wilson, February 12, 1940, both in CWS Papers.

15. "The Founder of the Illiteracy Movement," CWS Papers.

16. "The Founder of the Illiteracy Movement"; Cora Wilson Stewart to Homer Wilson, February 12, 1940, both in CWS Papers. Wilson Family Bible, McCrea Papers.

17. Morehead, *Rowan County News*, May 10, 1956.

18. Ibid.

19. U.S. Bureau of the Census, *Tenth Census of the United States, 1880*, vol. 1, p. 193 and *Twelfth Census of the United States 1900*, vol. 1, p. 183.

20. Diary of Cora Wilson Stewart, January 17, 1922, CWS Papers (Box 51).

21. Ibid.

22. Cora Wilson Stewart, "Autograph Books" I–II, Biographical File, CWS Papers.

23. Interview with Norma Powers, November 23, 1990, in CWS Oral History. Author's telephone conversation with Norma Powers, July 28, 1992.

24. Cora Carey vs. U. G. Carey, *Rowan Circuit Court Book #9*, June 9, 1898, pp. 345–46.

25. Author's telephone conversation with Norma Powers, July 28, 1992; Cora Carey vs. U. G. Carey, *Rowan Circuit Court Book #9*, November 5, 1896, pp. 59–60.

26. Morehead, *The Mountaineer* (n.d.), CWS Papers; Commercial College of Kentucky University, Diploma, December 12, 1899, CWS Papers.

27. "In Memory of Anne E. Wilson," undated newspaper article, Biographical File, CWS Papers.

28. Undated and untitled newspaper clipping, CWS Papers (Box 29).

29. Ibid.

Chapter 2: Public Acclaim, Private Sorrow

1. Diary of Cora Wilson Stewart, January 17, 1923, CWS Papers (Box 51).

2. Mount Sterling *Advocate*, August 13, 1901, CWS Papers (Box 29).

3. Undated and untitled newspaper clipping, CWS Papers (Box 29); Diary of Cora Wilson Stewart, January 17, 1923, CWS Papers (Box 51).

4. Diary of Cora Wilson Stewart, January 17, 1923, CWS Papers (Box 51); "Cora Wilson Stewart 'The Children's Friend' Candidate for School Superintendent of Rowan County," CWS Papers (Box 29).

5. Diary of Cora Wilson Stewart, January 17, 1923, CWS Papers (Box 51); "Cora Wilson Stewart 'The Children's Friend' Candidate for School Superintendent of Rowan County," CWS Papers (Box 29); author's interview with Norman Welles, September 2, 1972, Morehead, Kentucky.

6. Untitled, undated newspaper clipping, CWS Papers.

7. Ibid.

8. Ibid.

9. Ibid.

10. Undated and untitled newspaper clipping, CWS Papers (Box 46).

11. Undated and untitled speech, CWS Papers (Box 46).

12. Morehead, *Rowan County News*, May 10, 1956; interview with Ivan Stewart, November 26, 1990, CWS Oral History.

13. Interview with Ivan Stewart, November 26, 1990, CWS Oral History.

14. Interview with Ivan Stewart, November 26, 1990; interview with Mrs. Virginia Prewitt, December 7, 1990; interview with Herbert Stewart, December 11, 1990; interview with James Stewart, January 20, 1991; interview with Alice Stewart O'Hara, November 5, 1990, all in CWS Oral History.

15. Alex Stewart to Cora Wilson, *Rowan County Marriage Bonds Book #4*, p. 319, September 24, 1902.

16. Cora Stewart vs. Alex Stewart, *Rowan Circuit Court Order Book*, #11, March 7, 1904, pp. 96–97.

17. Cora Wilson to Alex Stewart, *Rowan County Marriage Bonds,* Book 7, June 22, 1904, p. 87.

18. Undated and untitled newspaper clipping, CWS Papers (Box 29); Diary of Cora Wilson Stewart, January 17, 1923, CWS Papers (Box 51).

19. Thomas D. Clark, *A History of Kentucky,* rev. ed., (Lexington: John Bradford Press, 1960) , pp. 360–61; Frank L. McVey, *The Gates Open Slowly: A History of Education in Kentucky* (Lexington: University of Kentucky Press, 1949), pp. 207–9; Kentucky Department of Education, *Second Whirlwind Campaign, 1909* (Frankfort, 1909), pp. 3–47.

20. Undated and untitled newspaper clipping, Biographical File, CWS Papers.

21. Interview with Virginia Williams, October 12, 1990, in CWS Oral History Project.

22. "Cora Wilson Stewart, the Children's Friend," in CWS Papers; Morehead, *The East Kentucky Citizen,* October 30, 1909.

23. Diary of Cora Wilson Stewart, December 30, 1922.

24. Court order against A. T. Stewart, March 23, 1910; Cora Wilson Stewart vs. Alexander Stewart, "Petition in Equity," Rowan County Court, March 23, 1910, Biographical File, CWS Papers; "Deposition of C. C. Nichols," March 23, 1910;" Deposition of Mrs. E. B. McGlone," March 23, 1910, both in CWS Papers (Box 29).

25. "Judgment Against A. T. Stewart," Rowan Circuit Court Book #13, June 8, 1910, pp. 16–17.

26. Interview with Ivan Stewart, November 26, 1990; interview with Mrs. Virginia Prewitt, December 7, 1990; interview with Herbert Stewart, December 11, 1990; interview with James Stewart, January 20, 1991; interview with Alice Stewart O'Hara, November 5, 1990, all in CWS Oral History Project.

27. Mrs. T. J. Munary to CWS, April 11, 1910; Mrs. C. Leathermore to CWS, April 19, 1910; Brainard Platt to CWS, December 2, 1910; G. F. Frield to CWS, December 2, 1910, all in CWS Papers.

28. Mrs. B. F. Clay to CWS, August 10, 1910, CWS Papers.

29. D. F. Gray to CWS August 10, 1910, CWS Papers.

30. Lutie Palmer to CWS, September 7, 1910, CWS Papers.

31. Mattie Dalton to CWS, October 12, 1910, CWS Papers.

32. Ibid.

33. Ibid.

34. Ibid.

35. Ibid.

36. Mattie Dalton to CWS, July 13, 1911, October 12, 1910, all in CWS Papers.

37. Mattie Dalton to CWS, October 19, 1910, CWS Papers.

38. *New York Tribune* January 4, 1923, CWS Papers.

Chapter 3: Beginnings in the Moonlight

1. G. F. Friel to CWS, December 2, 1910; Brainard Platt to CWS, November 30, 1910; Margaret Jartness to CWS, April 9, 1910; Mattie Dalton to CWS, October 19, 1910; W. J. Vaughn to CWS, January 5, 1911, all in CWS Papers.

2. Edward Reisner to CWS, February 25, 1911; C. C. May to CWS, May 17, 1910; Mattie Dalton to CWS, January 9, 1910, all in CWS Papers.

3. Louisville *Courier Journal,* January 26, 1913; Edward Reisner to CWS, February 23, 1911; H. Van Antwerp to CWS, March 28, 1911; R. S. Eubank to CWS, April 9, 1911, all in CWS Papers.

4. George Roberts to CWS, April 7, 1911, CWS Papers.

5. Louisville *Courier Journal*, January 26, 1913.

6. R. S. Eubank to CWS, April 9, 1911, CWS Papers.

7. M. O. Winfrey to CWS, June 16, 1911, CWS Papers.

8. Mattie Dalton to CWS, April 14, 1911, CWS Papers.

9. Jessie O. Yancey to CWS, July 5, 1911, CWS Papers.

10. Richmond Hamm to CWS, June 30, 1911, CWS Papers.

11. J. H. Booth to CWS, June 30, 1911, CWS Papers.

12. Everett L. Dix to CWS, June 3, 1911, CWS Papers.

13. Mrs. Desha Breckinridge to CWS, December 20, 1911, CWS Papers.

14. Edgar C. Riley to CWS, August 13, 1911, CWS Papers.

15. Edgar C. Riley to CWS, August 13, 1911, CWS Papers; Cora Wilson Stewart, *Moonlight Schools* (New York: E. P. Dulton, 1922), p. 11.

16. Stewart, *Moonlight Schools*, p. 11.

17. Ibid. pp. 11–13.

18. Ibid., p. 13

19. U.S. Census Bureau, *Thirteenth Census of the United States, 1910*, vol. 2, p. 749.

20. Williamsport, Pennsylvania, *Grit*, February 2, 1913; Lexington *Herald*, February 18, 1912; Louisville *Courier Journal*, February 18, 1912; Stewart *Moonlight Schools*, pp. 14–15.

21. Williamsport, Pennsylvania, *Grit*, February 2, 1913; Lexington *Herald*, February 18, 1912; Louisville *Courier Journal*, February 18, 1912; Stewart, *Moonlight Schools*, pp. 14–15.

22. Stewart, *Moonlight Schools*, pp. 16–18.

23. Information Sheet (n.d.), Biographical File, CWS Papers.

24. Ibid.

25. George W. Chapman to CWS, October 30, 1911, CWS Papers.

26. E. C. McDougle to CWS, October 31, 1911, CWS Papers; Williamsport *Grit*, February 2, 1913; Lexington *Herald*, February 18, 1912; Louisville *Courier Journal*, February 18, 1912; U.S. Bureau of Education, *Illiteracy in the United States and an Experiment for its Elimination* (Washington, 1913), p. 28.

27. Malcolm Knowles, *The Adult Education Movement in the United States* (New York: Holt, Rinehart and Winston, 1962), pp. 52–54.

28. Cora Wilson Stewart, "Address Before the Southern Educational Association," December 1, 1911, Houston, Texas, in CWS Papers.

Chapter 4: Moonlight Schools Spread

1. Flemingsburg, *Times-Democrat*, October 5, 1913.

2. J. S. Hobdy to CWS, April 13, 1912; J. P. Womack to CWS, April 26, 1912; Charles G. Mapin to CWS, July 10, 1912, all in CWS Papers.

3. A. C. Monahan to CWS, April 22, 1912, CWS Papers.

4. R. H. Wilson to CWS, April 16, 1912; Wallace Lund to CWS, March 20, 1912; *Paducah News-Democrat*, March 30, 1912, all in CWS Papers.

5. Cora Wilson Stewart, "President's Address to the Kentucky Education Association" (Louisville, 1912), pp. 47–49.

6. Ibid., p. 48.

7. Ibid.

8. Cora Wilson Stewart, *Moonlight Schools* (New York: E. P. Dutton, 1922), p. 44.

9. Louisville *Courier Journal*, December 29, 1912; Williamsport, Pennsylvania, *Grit*, February 2, 1913; "Information sheet" (n.d.), Biographical File, all in CWS Papers.

10. Jay O' Daniel to CWS, August 4, 1912, CWS Papers.

11. Stewart, *Moonlight Schools*, pp. 45–46.

12. Louisville *Courier Journal*, December 29, 1912.

13. U.S. Bureau of Education, *Illiteracy in the United States and an Experiment for It's Elimination* (Washington Government Printing Office, 1913), p. 29.

14. Stewart, *Moonlight Schools*, p. 28.

15. Louisville *Courier Journal*, December 29, 1912.

16. Stewart, *Moonlight Schools*, p. 55; "Census Persons Over Twenty Years of Age Who Cannot Read and Write (1918)," CWS Papers (Box 4).

17. Williamsport, Pennsylvania, *Grit*, February 2, 1913; Flemingsburg *Times-Democrat*, October 5, 1913; Stewart, *Moonlight Schools*, p. 124.

18. CWS to James B. McCreary, December 16, 1913, CWS Papers.

19. Lexington *Herald*, February 12, 1914.

20. *Frankfort Journal*, February 12, 1914.

21. "Adult Illiteracy in the United States," *Congressional Record*, March 3, 1914, p. 6–24.

22. Lexington *Herald*, February 18, 1914.

23. Mattie Dalton to CWS, March 2, 1914; Lida E. Gardner to CWS, February 18, 1914, both in CWS Papers.

24. "Adult Illiteracy in the United States," *Congressional Record*, March 3, 1914. pp. 6 –24.

25. Ibid.

26. Ibid.

27. Ibid.

28. Ibid. pp. 6–24.

Chapter 5: Beginnings of the K.I.C.

1. T. J. Coates to CWS, February 23, 1914, CWS Papers.

2. John F. Smith to CWS, February 12, 1914, CWS Papers.

3. Mrs. Lafon Riker to CWS, February 9, 1914, CWS Papers.

4. Kentucky Illiteracy Commission, *First Biennial Report, 1914–1915* (Louisville, 1916), pp. 2–9.

5. CWS to James B. McCreary, February 18, 1914, CWS Papers.

6. K.I.C., *First Report*, pp. 8–11.

7. Ibid. p. 10.

8. Jackson *Times*, April 24, 1914; Corbin *Times*, July 17, 1914; Lexington *Herald*, April 26, 1914; Kentucky Illiteracy Commission, *Report, 1916–1920* (Louisville, 1920), pp. 6–7.

9. K.I.C., *First Report*, p. 18; K.I.C., *Report, 1916-1920*, pp. 6–7.

10. James B. McCreary to CWS, September 9, 1914, CWS Papers.

11. Cora Wilson Stewart, *Moonlight Schools* (New York: E. P. Dutton, 1922), p. 67.

12. Lexington *Herald*, October 15, 1914.

13. *Elizabethtown News*, October 1, 1914.

14. London *Sentinel*, June 28, 1915; Whitley *Republican*, June 30, 1915.

15. James B. McCreary to CWS, February 10 and February 16, 1915, CWS Papers.

16. *The Mountaineer*, February 20, 1915, in CWS Papers.

17. Ibid.

18. K.I.C., *First Report*, p. 13.

19. Ibid. p. 12.

20. Ibid., p. 26.
21. Ibid., p. 28.
22. Ibid., p. 29.
23. Ibid., p.30.
24. Ibid., p. 33.
25. Ibid., p. 34.
26. Ibid., p. 44.
27. Ibid., p. 42.
28. Ibid., p. 40.
29. Ibid., p. 50.
30. Ibid., p. 54.
31. Ibid., p. 61.
32. James B. McCreary to CWS, February 16, 1915; CWS to B. F. Johnson, February 24, August 28, 1915; CWS to J. W. Carrahan, December 24, 1915, all in CWS Papers.
33. Cora Wilson Stewart, *Country Life Reader: First Book* (Richmond: B. F. Johnson, 1915), pp. 3–4.
34. Stewart, *Country Life Reader: First Book*, p. 7.
35. Stewart, *Moonlight Schools*, p. 126.
36. Stewart, *Moonlight Schools*, pp. 128–30.
37. Stewart, *Moonlight Schools*, pp. 126–30.
38. Stewart, *Moonlight Schools*, p. 135.
39. Ibid., pp. 134–35.
40. Stewart, *Moonlight Schools*, p. 135; CWS to Lois Willis, September 15, 1915, CWS Papers (Box 27).
41. K.I.C., *First Report*, p. 25.
42. Ibid., p. 20.
43. Ibid., p. 21.
44. Ibid., p. 22.

Chapter 6: A Growing Crusade

1. James. B. McCreary to CWS, January 1, 1916, CWS Papers.
2. Lowell W. Harrison, ed., *Kentucky's Governors, 1792-1985* (Lexington: University Press of Kentucky, 1985), p. 122–26.
3. Paducah *Evening Sun*, January 8, 1916; Louisville *Courier Journal*, January 6, 1916.
4. Somerset *Semi-Weekly News*, January 10, 1916, in CWS Papers.
5. Owensboro, *Daily Messenger*, January 16, 1916; Lexington *Herald*, January 11, 1916; *Elizabethtown News*, January 14, 1916, both in CWS Papers.
6. Louisville *Herald*, January 11, 1916.
7. Frankfort, *State Journal*, January 14, 1916.
8. Woodford, *Sun*, January 20, 1916.
9. *Elizabethtown News*, January 14, 1916.
10. Mattie Dalton to CWS, January 21, 1916, CWS Papers.
11. James B. McCreary to CWS, February 9, 1916; Joseph Tumulty, to CWS, February 8, 1916, both in CWS Papers.
12. Lexington *Herald*, February 18, 1916.
13. Mattie Dalton to CWS, February 17, 1916; James B. McCreary to CWS, February 18, 1916, both in CWS Papers.
14. Lexington *Herald*, February 19, 1916; Lexington *Leader*, February 19, 1916.

15. James B. McCreary to CWS, February 23, 1916, CWS Papers.

16. *Acts of the Kentucky General Assembly*, 1916.

17. J. H. Garvin to CWS, January 11, 1916, CWS Papers (Box 30).

18. Louisville *Herald*, April 14, 1916; Lexington *Herald*, February 18, 1916; Owensboro *Inquirer*, February 15, 1916; Emma Morehead to CWS, February 17, 1916; Kentucky *Times Star*, June 30, 1916, all in CWS Papers.

19. Diary of Cora Wilson Stewart, December 31, 1916, CWS Papers.

20. Ibid.

21. Cora Wilson Stewart, "The Elimination of Illiteracy," *Address to the National Education Association,* July 3, 1916, pp. 56–58.

22. Ibid., pp. 56–58.

23. Ibid., pp. 56–58.

24. Diary of Cora Wilson Stewart, December 31, 1916.

25. B. F. Johnson to CWS, January 4, 1917, CWS Papers.

26. CWS to B. F. Johnson, January 6, 1917, CWS Papers.

27. Lexington *Leader*, February 4, 1917.

28. Glasgow *Times*, March 13, 1917.

29. Lexington *Herald*, February 4, 1917.

30. Walton *Advertiser*, March 17, 1917, CWS Papers.

31. Ibid.

32. Ibid.

33. Owensboro *Inquirer*, July 19, 1917.

34. The Christian *Sun*, July 25, 1917, in CWS Papers.

35. Interview with Virginia Williams, October 12, 1990 in "CWS Oral History Project"; Biography File, in CWS Papers.

36. CWS to Homer Wilson, February 12, 1940, in CWS Papers.

37. Will of Jeremiah Wilson, *Rowan County Will Book A,* pp. 140–41.

38. CWS to F. T. Novel, January 20, 1917, CWS Papers.

39. Cora Wilson Stewart, *Moonlight Schools* (New York: E. P. Dutton, 1922), pp. 126–31.

40. *Journal of Education*, January 11, 1917.

41. Glasgow *Times*, April 20, 1917; *Shelby News*, December 25, 1917, both in CWS Papers.

42. Cora Wilson Stewart, *Country Life Reader: Third Book* (Richmond: B. F. Johnson, 1917), p. 1.

43. ibid.

Chapter 7: World War I and Its Impact

1. Cora Wilson Stewart, *Moonlight Schools*, (New York: E. P. Dutton, 1922), pp. 81–82; Calhoun *Star*, July 20, 1917; Nashville, *Southern Agriculturist*, July 1, 1917.

2. Unpublished manuscript, "Illiteracy in the United States Army," p. 11, in CWS Papers.

3. Ibid., p. 12.

4. Stewart, *Moonlight Schools*, p. 123.

5. Ibid., pp. 92–93.

6. K.I.C. Report, 1916–1920; Glasgow *Times*, August 13, 1917; Cadiz *Reporter*, August 16, 1917; both in CWS Scrapbook, CWS Papers (Box 55).

7. CWS to Woodrow Wilson, August 23, 1917, CWS Papers (Box 28); CWS to J.C.W. Beckham, August 25, 1917, CWS Papers (Box 29).

8. Hazard *Herald*, October 13, 1917, Scrapbook, CWS Papers (Box 55).

9. Louisville *Courier Journal*, August 24, 1917.

10. Ibid.

11. Mayfield *Times*, September 2, 1917, CWS Papers.

12. Hickham *Courier*, September 2, 1917; Glasgow *Times*, August 28, 1917; Jeffersonville *Jeffersonian*, October 25, 1917; Frankfort *State Journal*, September 13, 1917, all in CWS Papers.

13. Kokomo *Tribune*, November 2, 1918; Richmond *Register*, October 26, 1918; Louisville *Courier Journal*, October 22, 1917, all in CWS Papers.

14. "Illiteracy in the U.S. Army, " p. 15.

15. Ibid., pp. 15–17.

16. Ibid., p. 17.

17. Ibid., p. 18.

18. Cora Wilson Stewart, *Moonlight Schools*, p. 102; Indianapolis *Independent*, August 5, 1918.

19. *Acts of the Kentucky General Assembly*, March 28, 1918, pp. 154–56.

20. CWS to Robert Bingham, January 2, 1918, CWS Papers.

21. CWS to William Feagin, March 13, 1918, CWS Papers.

22. Lela Mae Stiles to CWS, March 5, 1917, CWS Papers.

23. CWS to P. P. Claxton, March 20, 1918, CWS Papers.

24. Labor *Herald*, March 2, 1918; Louisville *Courier Journal*, May 31, 1918, both in CWS Papers.

25. Warren C. Callahan to CWS, April 22, 1918, CWS Papers.

26. B. F. Johnson to CWS, June 1, 1918, July 19, 1918; CWS to B. F. Johnson, October 26, 1918; CWS Diary, January 4, 1918, all in CWS Papers.

27. A. E. Winship to CWS, July 12, 1918, CWS Papers.

28. A. E. Winship to CWS, July 11, 1918, CWS Papers.

29. J. G. Crabbe to CWS, July 13, 1918, CWS Papers.

30. Cora Wilson Stewart, "War-Modified Education and Illiteracy," *Proceedings of the National Education Association (June 1918)*, p. 118.

31. Ibid. p.120.

32. National Education Association, *Bulletin of the National Education Association (June 1919)*, p. 34.

33. John Higham, *Strangers in the Land: Patterns of American Nativism, 1860-1925* (New Brunswick, N.J.: Rutgers University Press, 1955), pp. 245–47.

34. New York *Tribune*, July 27, 1919, CWS Papers.

Chapter 8: High Tide of the Kentucky Campaign

1. Nat B. Sewell, "Report on the Kentucky Illiteracy Commission, December 24, 1918," in CWS Papers.

2. Kentucky Illiteracy Commission, *Moonlight School Course of Study (Patriotic Number)* 1918, in CWS Papers.

3. Ibid., p. 12.

4. Ibid., pp. 16–17.

5. Nout B. Sewell, "Report on the Kentucky Illiteracy Commission, December 24, 1918."

6. Report of Susan Kimrall, July 22, 1918, CWS Papers.

7. Report of Bessie Cartwright, July 29, 1918, CWS Papers.

8. *The Moonlighter*, November 11, 1918.

9. *The Moonlighter*, August 19, 1918.

10. *The Moonlighter*, August 12, 1918.

11. B. F. Johnson to CWS, August 24, 1918, CWS Papers.

12. B. F. Johnson to CWS, October 18, 1918, September 17, 1918; CWS to B. F. Johnson, October 25, 1918, all in CWS Papers.

13. Sarah Smither to CWS, January 25, 1919; CWS to A. J. Gray, February 5, 1919, both in CWS Papers.

14. J. L. McBrien to CWS, December 19, 1918, CWS Papers.

15. CWS to Robert Bingham, December 30, 1918, CWS Papers.

16. Ibid.

17. Louisville *Times*, April 19, 1919.

18. Louisville *Courier Journal*, April 23, 1919, May 18, 1919, both in CWS Papers.

19. Lexington *Leader*, June 24, 1919.

20. Louisville *Courier Journal*, May 19, 1919.

21. Report of Moary A. Norris, August 18, 1919, CWS Papers.

22. Report of Ira Pruden, July 22, 1919, CWS Papers.

23. *The Moonlighter*, October 6, 1919; the *Shelby News*, December 11, 1919; the Shelby *Sentinel*, December 26, 1919, all in CWS Papers.

24. Report of Rose Blessing Craft, July 14, 1919, CWS Papers.

25. The *Shelby News*, December 25, 1919, in CWS Papers.

26. Report of Sallie Ford, August 17, 1919; report of J. C. Williams, October 10, 1919; report of May McEllister, September 18, 1919, all in CWS Papers.

27. Report of Z. T. Osborne, July 21, 1919, CWS Papers.

28. Report of Mary A. Norris, August 18, 1919; report of J. C. Williams, October 8, 1919; report of Sallie Bell, October 8, 1919, October 21, 1919, all in CWS Papers.

29. Report of Sallie Bell, October 7, 1919; report of Mary A. Norris, August 18, 1919, both in CWS Papers.

30. Report of Ora Pruden, in *The Moonlighter*, October 6, 1919, CWS Papers.

31. Report of Ira Pruden, July 22, 1919, CWS Papers.

32. Report of Mary A. Norris, August 18, 1919, CWS Papers.

33. Report of Joseph B. Ross, August 25, 1919; report of Elizabeth Baker, August 2, 1919, both in CWS Papers.

34. *The Moonlighter*, October 6, 1919, CWS Papers.

35. *The Moonlighter*, September 22, 1919, CWS Papers.

36. Owensboro *Inquirer*, July 17, 1919, September 18, 1919; Henderson *The Gleanor*, July 18, 1919, all in CWS Papers. .

37. Burlington, Vermont, *Free Press*, April 26, 1919; Philadelphia *Inquirer*, March 2, 1919; New York *Evening Telegraph*, December 4, 1919; *Christian Science Monitor*, February 15, 1919; Lexington *Herald*, November 24, 1919. all in CWS Papers. John Higham, *Strangers in the Land: Patterns of American Nativism, 1860-1925* (New Brunswick, N.J.: Rutgers University Press, 1955), p 255–59; see Robert K. Murray, *Red Scare: A Study in National Hysteria, 1919-1920* (Minneapolis: University of Minnesota Press, 1955) for a thorough view of the postwar red scare.

38. New York *Tribune*, July 27, 1919.

39. The Towner Educational Bill (H.R. 154000), 65th Congress, Third Session; "Resolution of Illiteracy Conference of the Southern States" (Columbia, S.C., December 1–2 , 1919); New York *Tribune*, July 27, 1919, all in CWS Papers.

40. Nashville *Tennessean*, October 5, 1919; *Christian Science Monitor*, September 30, 1919; Everette Dix to CWS, October 2, 1919; S. E. Knares to CWS, September 30, 1919; Curtiss Airplane Corporation, September 30, 1919, all in CWS Papers; Lexington *Herald*, March 13, 19, 1920.

41. Jackson *Times*, October 17, 1919.

42. Kentucky Illiteracy Commission, *Report, 1916-1920*, p. 7. The 1920 U.S. Cen-

sus indicated that illiteracy had decreased by 53,070 since 1910. The U.S. Census Bureau asked individuals if they could write in any language, regardless of ability to read. The K.I.C. relied on reports from teachers, illiteracy agents, and superintendents, and letters written to Stewart. *U.S. Census Bureau, Fourteenth Census of the United States, 1920*, vol. 3, p. 10, 366.

43. Lexington, *Herald*, March 2, 1920.

44. Lowell W. Harrison, ed. *Kentucky's Governors 1792–1985* (Lexington: University Press of Kentucky, 1985) pp. 128–30.

45. Lexington *Herald*, March 5, 7,10, 1920; Lexington *Leader*, 5,11,1920

46. Lexington *Herald*, March 10, 1920.

47. George Colvin to various superintendents, March 2, 1920; *Christian Science Monitor*, April 14, 1920; Lexington *Herald*, March 13, 1920, all in CWS Papers.

48. *Christian Science Monitor*, April 14, 1920, CWS Papers.

49. Lexington *Herald*, March 10, 1920.

50. Ibid.

51. Lexington *Herald*, March 13, 1920.

52. Ibid.

53. Lexington *Herald*, March 11, 1920.

54. Lexington *Leader*, March 12, 1920.

55. Ibid.

56. Lexington *Herald*, March 13, 1920.

57. Ibid., pp. 8–9.

58. Kentucky Illiteracy Commission, *Report, 1916-1920*, p. 7.

59. *Historical Census of the United States of America*, pp. 354–65.

60. CWS to Lida Hafford, August 30, 1920, CWS Papers.

Chapter 9: Freelance Crusader

1. CWS to John V. Conway, August 24, 1920, CWS Papers.

2. Atlanta *Constitution*, March 14, 1920; Little Rock *Gazette*, March 12, 1920; *Christian Science Monitor*, April 5, 1920.

3. CWS to Sallie Ford, July 28, 1920, CWS Papers.

4. CWS to Alvin White, July 28, 1920, CWS Papers.

5. General W. H. Sears to Mrs. Jean A. Heathington, July 12, 1920; Lexington *Herald*, July 19, 1920, both in CWS Papers.

6. Harriet E. Corliss to Governor James B. Cox, July 20, 1920, CWS Papers.

7. CWS to Brainard Platt, July 24, 1920, CWS Papers.

8. General W. H. Sears to Mrs. Jean A. Heathington, July 12, 1920; J. W. Crabtree to CWS, July 17, 1920; CWS to Charl Williams, September 14, 1920; Pat Harrison to CWS, August 30, 1920; CWS to Mary C. Bradford, August 17, 1920, all in CWS Papers.

9. CWS to Lida Hafford, August 30, 1920, CWS Papers.

10. Pat Harrison to CWS, August 30, 1920, CWS Papers.

11. H. V. McChesney to CWS, August 21, 1920, CWS Papers.

12. CWS to Charl Williams, September 14, 1920, CWS Papers.

13. CWS to Hugh McGill, September 4, 1920, CWS Papers.

14. Ibid.

15. CWS to John Gryout, November 9, 1920, CWS Papers.

16. CWS to Robert G. Higdon, November 15, 1920, CWS Papers.

17. CWS to Mrs. J. Oscar Smith, November 11, 1920, CWS Papers.

18. Wesley M. Bagby, *The Road to Normalcy: The Presidential Campaign and Election of 1920* (Baltimore: Johns Hopkins Press, 1962), pp. 163–65; CWS to Sallie Lucas Jean, March 1, 1920, Mary Elliott Flannery papers, Special Collections, M. I. King Library, University of Kentucky. Hereinafter cited as Flannery Papers.

19. CWS to Sarah E. Luther, January 5, 1921, CWS Papers.

20. CWS to B. F. Johnson, April 21, 1921, CWS Papers.

21. B. F. Johnson to CWS, June 16, 1921, CWS Papers.

22. Louisville *Times*, April 21, 1921, CWS Papers.

23. Louisville *Times*, April 23, 1921, CWS Papers.

24. J. C. Preston to Arthur Chamberlain, August 6, 1921, CWS Papers.

25. CWS to J. C. Preston, November 14, 1921, CWS Papers.

26. CWS to Lela Mae Stiles, November 11, 1921, CWS Papers.

27. CWS to Lela Mae Stiles, November 6, 1921, CWS Papers.

28. "The Crusade Against Illiteracy and Its Founder Cora Wilson Stewart," p. 4, CWS Biographical File; Governor N. E. Kendall to CWS, November 9, 1921; CWS to Lela Mae Stiles, December 12, 1921; C. A. Filmer to CWS, May 5, 1921, all in CWS Papers; CWS to Mary E. Flannery, November 24, 1921, Flannery Papers.

29. Cora Wilson Stewart to Josephine C. Preston, December 1, 1921; CWS to Dr. A. E. Winship, December 5, 1921; CWS to Joy Elmer Morgan, February 7, 1922; CWS to J. W. Crabtree, February 17, 1922; CWS to Dr. Thomas E. Finegan, March 9, 1922, all in CWS Papers.

30. Cora Wilson Stewart to Josephine C. Preston, December 1, 1921; CWS to Dr. A. E. Winship, December 5, 1921; CWS to Joy Elmer Morgan, February 7, 1922; CWS to J. W. Crabtree, February 17, 1922; CWS to Dr. Thomas E. Finegan, March 9, 1922, all in CWS Papers; Diary of Cora Wilson Stewart, December 21, 1922, CWS Papers (Box 51).

31. CWS to Dr. W. B. Owens, July 15, 1922; CWS to Willis Lawson, May 29, 1922, both in CWS Papers.

32. CWS to Lela Mae Stiles, November 15, December 26, 1922; Dr. Augustus Thomas to CWS, December 21, 1922, all in CWS Papers.

33. CWS to Mrs. John D. Sherman, September 15, 1922; *Los Angeles Examiner*, November 26, 1922, both in CWS Papers.

34. CWS to Lela Mae Stiles, July 16, November 23, 1922, in CWS Papers.

35. CWS to Lela Mae Stiles, October 10, 27, 1922; CWS to Charles A. Duncan, March 14, 1922; Lela Mae Stiles to CWS, January 17, 1922, all in CWS Papers.

36. CWS Diary, December 31, 1922, CWS Papers.

37. Ibid.

38. CWS Diary, December 30, 1922, CWS Papers.

39. Ibid.

40. CWS to Lela Mae Stiles, December 9, 18, 1922, CWS Papers.

41. CWS to Lela Mae Stiles, December 1, 1922, CWS Papers.

Chapter 10: Fame and Frustration

1. CWS to Lela Mae Stiles, January 1, 1923, CWS Papers.

2. CWS to R. H. Wilson, February 20, 1923, CWS Papers.

3. George Colvin to M. L. Brittain, June 23, 1922, CWS Papers.

4. "Resolutions Annual Conference on Illiteracy, Northern and Southern States, Detroit, Michigan, May 1–2, 1923," in CWS Papers.

5. CWS to R. A. Nestos, May 28, 1923, CWS Papers.

6. CWS to S. K. Mendis, May 29, 1923, CWS Papers.
7. CWS to Mrs. Claude I. Jones, January 24, 1923, CWS Papers.
8. Mary K. Sherman to CWS, March 18, 1923, CWS Papers.
9. Columbus, Georgia, *Enquirer*, May 13, 1923, in CWS Papers.
10. CWS to Lela Mae Stiles, July 9, 1923, CWS Papers.
11. Ibid.
12. Ibid.
13. J. W. Riley to CWS, September 29, 1923, CWS Papers.
14. CWS to William J. Fields, September 29, 1923, CWS Papers.
15. CWS to Lela Mae Stiles, November 13, 1923, CWS Papers.
16. CWS to Henry J. Allen, November 8, 1923, CWS Papers.
17. Mrs. J. C. Layne to CWS, November 23, 1923, CWS Papers.
18. CWS to Lela Mae Stiles, December 3, 1923, CWS Papers.
19. CWS to Lela Mae Stiles, December 2, 1924, CWS Papers.
20. Ibid.
21. CWS to William J. Fields, December 6, 1923, CWS Papers.
22. CWS to Lela Mae Stiles, November 21, 1923, CWS Papers.
23. CWS to Mrs. Thomas Winter, December 14, 1923, CWS Papers.
24. CWS to Wil Lou Gray, December 18, 1923, CWS Papers.
25. CWS to Lela Mae Stiles, n.d., 1924, CWS Papers.
26. "Report of the Illiteracy Committee of the National Education Association" (July 1924); *Christian Science Monitor*, January 11, 1924; Washington *Herald*, January 12, 1924, all in CWS Papers.
27. "Illiteracy Report of the Illiteracy Committee of the National Education Association" (Washington, D.C.: National Education Association, 1924), p. 37.
28. CWS to A. H. Chamberlain, January 25, 1924, CWS Papers.
29. CWS to Lela Mae Stiles, January 20, 1924, CWS Papers.
30. *Congressional Digest*, vol. III, February 1924, pp. 159–60, in CWS Papers.
31. CWS to Mrs. John D. Sherman, March 19, 21, 1925; CWS to J. W. Crabtree, March 19, 1925, all in CWS Papers.
32. CWS to W. H. Sears, November 10, 1924, CWS Papers.

Chapter 11: Planning a National Crusade

1. CWS to Charl O. Williams, February 28, 1925; CWS to Mrs. Bruce Carr Jones, September 9, 1925; Charles H. Herlihy to CWS, December 12, 1924; CWS to Clarence Siple, January 27, 1925, all in CWS Papers.
2. CWS, "My Experiences in Forming the National Illiteracy Association," Biographical File, CWS Papers; Diary of Cora Wilson Stewart, December 31, 1925, CWS Papers.
3. Diary of Cora Wilson Stewart, January 1, 1926, CWS Papers.
4. Ibid.
5. Diary of Cora Wilson Stewart, December 31, 1925, CWS Papers.
6. Untitled notes of CWS, June 26, 1925, CWS Papers.
7. CWS to H. E. Goldsworthy, November 8, 1925; CWS to Sally Lucas Jean, November 6, 1925; Greensboro *Daily News*, July 20, 1925, all in CWS Papers.
8. CWS to E. C. Atkins, April 20, 1925; CWS to Joseph A. Sewell, April 20, 1925, both in CWS Papers.
9. CWS to H. E. Goldsworthy, November 8, 1925, CWS Papers.
10. CWS to Dr. Stephen B. L. Penrose, November 27, 1925, CWS Papers.

11. CWS to Charl Williams, February 28, 1925, CWS Papers.

12. *Christian Science Monitor,* July 2, 1925, CWS Papers.

13. Lela Mae Stiles to CWS, July 9, 1925, September 3, 12, 1925, CWS Papers.

14. Diary of Cora Wilson Stewart, January 1, 1926; "The Crusade Against Illiteracy and Its Founder Cora Wilson Stewart," p. 5, both in Biographical File, CWS Papers.

15. CWS to William Allen White, September 23, 1925, CWS Papers.

16. CWS to Sally Lucas Jean, November 6, 1925, CWS Papers.

17. CWS to Robert Deming, December 14, 1925, CWS Papers.

18. CWS to A. E. Winship, December 14, 1925, CWS Papers.

19. Robert C. Deming to CWS, December 18, 1925, CWS Papers.

Chapter 12: Birth of the N.I.C.

1. Diary of Cora Wilson Stewart, January 1, 1926, CWS Papers.

2. Ibid.

3. Ibid.

4. Ibid.

5. Ibid.

6. Ibid.

7. Diary of Cora Wilson Stewart, January 2, 1926, CWS Papers.

8. Diary of Cora Wilson Stewart, January 20, 1926, CWS Papers.

9. Diary of Cora Wilson Stewart, January 10, 1926, CWS Papers.

10. Ibid.

11. Houston *Chronicle,* February 26, 1926; CWS to William Allen White, February 26, 27, 1926, all in CWS Papers.

12. William Allen White to CWS, February 24, 1926, CWS Papers.

13. CWS to William Allen White, February 25, 1926, CWS Papers.

14. Calvin Coolidge to CWS, March 6, 1926, CWS Papers.

15. CWS to Sally Lucas Jean, March 8, 1926, CWS Papers.

16. CWS to William Allen White, April 14, 1926, CWS Papers.

17. CWS to William Allen White, May 1, 12, 1926, CWS Papers.

18. Grand Rapids, Michigan *Press,* May 31, 1926, CWS Papers.

19. CWS to William Allen White, June 15, 1926, CWS Papers.

20. Ibid.

21. Ibid.

22. William Allen White to CWS, June 21, 1926, CWS Papers.

23. CWS to William Allen White, June 19, 1926, CWS Papers.

24. CWS to William Allen White, June 26, 1926, CWS Papers.

25. CWS to William Allen White, August 30, 1926; CWS to Walter Ricks, August 10, 30, 1926, all in CWS Papers.

26. CWS to Mary Elliott Flannery, September 2, 1926, Flannery Papers.

27. CWS to William Allen White, August 30, 1926, October 20, 1926, both in CWS Papers.

28. CWS to William Allen White, October 20, 1926, CWS Papers.

29. CWS to William Allen White, December 2, 1926, CWS Papers.

30. CWS to Josephine C. Preston, December 1, 1926, CWS Papers.

31. C. Hartley Grattan, I*n Quest of Knowledge: A Historical Perspective on Adult Education* (New York: Association Press, 1955), pp. 277–78.

32. Ibid., pp. 278–80.

33. CWS to Robert Deming, December 14, 1925, January 23, 1926, both in CWS

Papers; Morse A. Cartwright, *Ten Years of Adult Education: A Report on a Decade of Progress in the American Movement* (New York: Macmillan, 1935), pp. 38–39.

34. CWS to Julia Harris, December 1, 1926, Julia Collier Harris Papers, Sophia Smith Collection. William Neilson Library, Smith College; CWS to William Allen White, June 19, 1926, CWS Papers.

35. Cartwright, *Ten Years of Adult Education*, pp. 50–56.

36. Joseph H. Stewart to CWS, December 17, 1926, CWS Papers.

Chapter 13: Growing Pains

1. Diary of CWS, December 31, 1926, CWS Papers.
2. Ibid.
3. Diary of CWS, January 1, 1927, CWS Papers.
4. Ibid.
5. Diary of CWS, January 25, 1927, CWS Papers.
6. Ibid.
7. CWS to William Allen White, April 15, 1927, CWS Papers.
8. N.I.C. Financial Statement, February 22, 1926–January 31, 1927, CWS Papers.
9. Diary of CWS January 17, 1928, CWS Papers.
10. CWS to William Allen White, January 26, 1927, CWS Papers.
11. CWS to Mrs. Phelps, April 24, 1928, CWS Papers.
12. CWS to William Allen White, April 3, 1928, CWS Papers.
13. CWS to Sally Lucas Jean, April 11, 1928, CWS Papers.
14. CWS to Julia Harris, March 17, 1927, CWS Papers.
15. CWS to Dr. R. E. Richter, January 14, 1928, CWS Papers.
16. Sally Lucas Jean to CWS, February 22, 1928, CWS Papers.
17. CWS to A. T. Burke, March 14, 1927, CWS Papers.
18. CWS to A. T. Burke, March 14, 1927, April 25, 1928, CWS Papers.
19. CWS to Mrs. Anna Dallinger, August 28, 1927, CWS Papers.
20. CWS to Roscoe Edlunds, March 3, 1927, CWS Papers; Cora Wilson Stewart, *Mother's First Book*, p. 6.
21. Stewart, *Mother's First Book*, p. 6.
22. Cora Wilson Stewart, untitled, unpublished manuscript, CWS Papers.
23. CWS to Mr. W. J. Rice, March 17, 1928, CWS Papers.
24. CWS to Roscoe Edlund, November 27, 1926, CWS Papers.
25. CWS to Henry J. Allen, March 20, 1928, CWS Papers.
26. CWS to William Allen White, October 3, 1928, CWS Papers.
27. Cora Wilson Stewart, "Report of the Illiteracy Committee of the National Council on Education" in *National Education Association: Proceedings of the Sixty-Sixth Annual Meeting held at Minneapolis, Minnesota, July 1–6, 1928*, vol. 66 (Washington, D.C.: National Education Association, 1928), pp. 248–49. Reprinted by permission.
28. Ibid.
29. CWS to Henry J. Allen, May 31, 1928, CWS Papers.
30. CWS to William Allen White, December 1, 1928; William Allen White, December 15, 1928, both in CWS Papers.
31. CWS to Evelyn Williams, December 22, 1928, CWS Papers.
32. Diary of Cora Wilson Stewart, January 1, 1929, CWS Papers.
33. Ibid.
34. CWS to William Allen White, February 26, 1929, CWS papers.
35. CWS to Roscoe Edlund, April 29, 1929, CWS Papers.

36. T. Harry Williams, *Huey Long* (New York: Alfred A. Knopf, 1969), p. 523.

37. T. H. Harris, to J. C. Preston, May 13, 1929, CWS Papers.

38. CWS to John Finley, May 6, 1929, CWS Papers.

39. Ibid.

40. Cora Wilson Stewart, untitled, undated manuscript, CWS Papers.

41. "Metropolitan Life Insurance Project," CWS Papers.

42. CWS to Henry J. Allen, October 17, 1929, CWS Papers; B. F. Johnson to CWS, June 30, 1929, both in CWS Papers.

43. CWS to Evelyn Williams, July 14, 1929, CWS Papers.

44. CWS to Henry J. Allen, October 17, 1929, CWS Papers.

45. CWS to Herbert Houston, October 28, 1929; French Strother to CWS, October 21, 1929, both in CWS Papers.

46. CWS to Herbert Houston, November 13, 1929, CWS Papers.

47. CWS to Herbert Houston, November 14, 1929, CWS Papers.

48. Cora Wilson Stewart, untitled notes, November 30, 1929, CWS Papers.

49. CWS to T. H. Harris, December 2, 1929, CWS Papers.

50. CWS to T. H. Harris, December 28, 1929, CWS Papers.

51. CWS to R. A. Nestos, December 28, 1929, CWS Papers.

Chapter 14: Struggle for Control

1. Key West *Citizen*, March 28, 1930; Santa Monica *Outlook*, March 18, 1930, both in CWS Papers.

2. Idaho Falls, Idaho, *Post*, March 30, 1930, CWS Papers.

3. Minnie Jean Nielsen, Summary of Activities, January 31, 1930–September 30, 1930, CWS Papers.

4. J. A. Benschoten, *Worlds Work*, December 1930.

5. *New York Times*, May 10, 1930.

6. Cora Wilson Stewart, "Report to the Office," February 1, 1930, CWS Papers.

7. Cora Wilson Stewart, "Report to the Executive Committee of the National Advisory Committee on Illiteracy" (n.d.).

8. CWS to Herbert Houston, February 20, 1930, CWS Papers.

9. CWS to R. A. Nestos, March 1, 1930, CWS Papers.

10. R. A. Nestos to CWS, February 22, 1930, CWS Papers.

11. CWS to Herbert Houston, March 11, 1930, CWS Papers.

12. CWS to R. A. Nestos, March 11, 1930, CWS Papers.

13. CWS to R. A. Nestos, March 12, 1930, CWS Papers

14. CWS to R. A. Nestos, April 4, 1930, CWS Papers.

15. CWS to R. A. Nestos, May 8, 1930; Herbert Houston to CWS May 2, 1930, CWS Papers.

16. CWS to Herbert Houston, May 23, 1930, CWS Papers.

17. M. S. Robertson to T. H. Harris, July 26, 1930, CWS Papers.

18. CWS Memo for conference with Dr. Gray, 1930, CWS Papers.

19. CWS "Memo," 1930, CWS Papers.

20. CWS to R. A. Nestos, May 31, 1930, CWS Papers.

21. CWS to T. H. Harris, August 20, 1930, CWS Papers.

22. Ibid.

23. CWS to T. H. Harris, August 26, 1930, CWS Papers.

24. M. S. Robertson to T. H. Harris, August 28, 1930, CWS Papers.

25. Edgar W. Knight, *Education in the United States*, 3d rev. ed. (Boston: Ginn, 1951), p. 577–79.

26. CWS to T. H. Harris, September 1, 1930, CWS Papers.

27. CWS to R. A. Nestos, September 1, 1930, CWS Papers.

28. CWS to Herbert Houston, September 16, 1930, CWS Papers.

29. CWS to T. H. Harris, October 2, 1930, CWS Papers.

30. CWS to T. H. Harris, October 4, 1930, CWS Papers.

31. CWS to T. H. Harris, September 30, 1930; T. H. Harris to CWS, October 3, 1930; Blake Nagel to CWS, September 29, 1930, all in CWS Papers.

32. CWS to T. H. Harris, October 28, 1930, CWS Papers.

33. CWS to Herbert Houston, November 6, 1930, CWS Papers.

34. CWS to Luther H. Hodges, November 25, 1930, CWS Papers.

35. CWS to Herbert Houston, November 6, 1930, CWS Papers.

36. R. A. Nestos to CWS, October 28, 1930, CWS Papers.

37. CWS to R. A. Nestos, November 1, 1930; United States Senate Joint Resolution 219, December 15, 1930; CWS to R. A. Nestos October 8, 1930, all in CWS Papers.

38. CWS to R. A. Nestos, October 8, 1930, CWS Papers.

39. CWS to Henry J. Allen, December 3, 1930, CWS Papers.

40. CWS to Herbert Houston, December 3, 1930, CWS Papers.

41. B. F. Johnson to CWS, October 15, 1930; B. F. Johnson to CWS, May 7, 1930, all in CWS Papers.

42. Diary of Cora Wilson Stewart, December 31, 1930, CWS Papers.

Chapter 15: The Great Depression and Moral Rearmament

1. CWS to R. A. Nestos, March 27, 1931, CWS Papers.

2. Gardena, California, *News*, November 12, 1932; Holyoke, Massachusetts, *Transcript*, April 29, 1931, all in CWS Papers.

3. *Meeting of the Department of Illiteracy, Fourth Biennial Conference of the World Federation of Education Associations (July 28, 1931)*.

4. CWS to R. A. Nestos, February 3, 1931; *Blackfeet News*, March 12, 1931; CWS TO Herbert Houston, January 31, 1931; Wyoming *State Journal*, March 9, 1931, all in CWS Papers.

5. "The Report of the Secretary of the Committee on Information," National Advisory Committee on Illiteracy (1931); CWS to Herbert Houston, March 31, 1931, both in CWS Papers.

6. Clutie Bloodworth to CWS, April 29, 1931, CWS Papers.

7. CWS to R. A. Nestos, April 13, 1931, CWS Papers.

8. "Minutes of the Executive Committee of the National Advisory Committee on Illiteracy" (May 18, 1931).

9. CWS to Luther H. Hodges, May 2, 1931, CWS Papers.

10. CWS to Cora S. Payne, October 24, 1932, CWS Papers.

11. "Moonlight Trysts for Education," *Literary Digest*, January 10, 1931, pp. 77–80.

12. "Mountaineer" (n.d., n.p.), CWS Papers.

13. CWS to Herbert Houston, September 7, 1931, CWS Papers.

14. Ibid.

15. CWS to Herbert Houston, September 8, 1931, CWS Papers.

16. CWS to various prison officials, undated, in CWS Box 52, CWS Papers.

17. F. C. Campbell to A. C. Cooley, May 24, 1932; Wyoming *State Journal*, March 9, 1932, both in CWS Papers.

18. CWS to Clutie Bloodworth, May 11, 1932, CWS Papers.

19. Ibid.
20. CWS to Clutie Bloodworth, June 4, 1932, CWS Papers.
21. CWS to Clutie Bloodworth, July 5, 1932, CWS Papers.
22. CWS to Dr. Daniel A. Polling, August 29, 1932, CWS Papers.
23. CWS to French Strother, August 29, 1932, CWS Papers.
24. CWS to Mrs. Ellis A. Yost, September 7, 1932, CWS Papers.
25. CWS to Mrs. Mary W. Dawson, October 10, 1931, CWS Papers.
26. CWS to R. A. Nestos, September 30, 1932, CWS Papers.
27. CWS to Clutie Bloodworth, October 15, 1932, CWS Papers.
28. Lyman R. Wilbur to members of the N.A.C.I., December 12, 1932, CWS Papers.
29. CWS to F. C. Button, March 6, 1933, CWS Papers.
30. CWS to Miss Hale, December 19, 1933, CWS Papers.
31. CWS Radio Address, December 10, 1933, CWS Papers.
32. CWS to Dr. J. Herbert Killey, December 14, 1933, CWS Papers.
33. CWS to Luther Hodges, August 28, 1934, CWS Papers.
34. L. O. Anderson, "The W.P.A. and Adult Education," *The School Executive* 55 (August 1936): 430; Arthur E. Bestor, "The A.B.C. of Federal Emergency Education," *The Journal of Adult Education* 6 (April 1934): 150–54; Frank Ernest Hill, *The School in the Camps* (New York: American Association of Adult Education, 1935), pp. 60–61. Roy Otis Chumbler, " A Study of Adult Education in Nineteen Kentucky Counties " (Master's thesis, University of Kentucky, 1938), pp. 58–59.
35. CWS to Ruth Bryan Owen, April 25, 1935, CWS Papers.
36. CWS to Governor Pearson, April 24, 1935, CWS Papers.
37. Memphis *Press-Scimitar* (n.d.); Cincinnati *Star*, April 26, 1935, both in CWS Papers.
38. Walter Houston Clark, *The Oxford Group: Its History and Significance* (New York: Bookman Associates, 1951), pp. 25–34; Allan W. Eister, *Drawing-Room Conversion: A Sociological Account of the Oxford Group Movement* (Durham: Duke University Press, 1950), pp. 10–11, 28–33. For the best account of the Oxford Movement and its founder, see Garth Lean, *On the Tail of a Comet: The Life of Frank Buchman* (Colorado Springs: Helmers and Howard, 1988).
39. CWS untitled, undated religious notes, CWS Papers.
40. Ibid.
41. CWS, untitled religious notes, May 3, 1934, CWS Papers, Box 38.
42. CWS, untitled, undated religious notes, CWS Papers, Box 38.
43. CWS to her sisters, July 29, 1934, CWS Papers Box 40.
44. CWS to Sally Lucas Jean, August 17, 1934, CWS Papers, Box 31.
45. Birmingham, England, *Evening Dispatch*, July 25, 1936, CWS Papers.
46. "Second World Assembly–Moral Rearmament" (July 21–31, 1939), CWS Papers.
47. Erwin Holt to CWS, January 16, 1937, CWS Papers.
48. Author's phone Interview with Arpha Burrell, May 2, 1992.

Chapter 16: Final Days

1. Author's phone interview with Arpha Burrell, May 2, 1992; author's phone interview with Marion McCrea, February 19, 1995; author's phone interview with Noi Doyle, February 19, 1995; author's phone interview with Roi Doyle Peers, April 8, 1995.
2. CWS to Marion McCrea, May 30, 1952, McCrea Papers.
3. CWS to Marion McCrea , January 7, 1953, McCrea Papers.

4. Marion McCrea interview, February 19, 1995.

5. *TV Guide,* May 18, 1954, pp. A–35.

6. Noi Doyle interview, February 19, 1995; Marion McCrea interview, February 19, 1995; E. P. Dutton, Co., to CWS, November 25, 1958, CWS Papers.

7. CWS to Marion McCrea, October 25, 1958, McCrea Papers.

8. Tryon, *Daily Bulletin,* December 3, 1958. "Certificate of Death for Cora Wilson Stewart," December 9, 1958.

9. Aura Jones to Marion McCrae, December 6, 1958, McCrea Papers.

Epilogue

1. "What Would I Do If I Had My Life to Live Over" (undated speech notes), in CWS Papers.

SELECTED BIBLIOGRAPHY

Personal Interviews

Burrell, Arpha. Telephone interview. May 2, 1992.
Doyle, Noi. Personal interview. Lexington, Kentucky, March 8, 1973.
Doyle, Noi. Telephone interview. February 19, 1995.
McCrae, Marion. Telephone interview. February 19, 1995.
Peers, Roi. Telephone interview. April 8, 1995.
Powers, Norma. Telephone interview. July 28, 1992.
Welles, Norman. Personal interview. Morehead, Kentucky, September 2, 1972.

Interviews from "Cora Wilson Stewart and the Moonlight School Oral History Project," Morehead State University:
O'Hara, Alice Stewart. November 5, 1990.
Powers, Norma. November 23, 1990.
Prewitt, Virginia. December 7, 1990.
Stewart, Herbert. December 11, 1990.
Stewart, Ivan. November 26, 1990.
Stewart, James. January 20, 1991.
Williams, Virginia. October 12, 1990.

Manuscripts

Mary Elliott Flannery Papers. Special Collections. M. I. King Library, University of Kentucky.
Julia Collier Harris Papers. Sophia Smith Collection. William Allan Neilson Library, Smith College.
Linda Neville Papers. Special Collections. M. I. King Library, University of Kentucky.
Cora Wilson Stewart Papers. Special Collections. M. I. King Library, University of Kentucky.
Thomas R. Underwood Papers. Special Collections. M. I. King Library, University of Kentucky.
William Allen White Papers. Manuscript Division. Library of Congress, Washington, D.C.

United Nations Publications

Gray, William Scott. *The Teaching of Reading and Writing.* Paris: UNESCO 1969.
United Nations Educational, Scientific and Cultural Organization. *Functional Literacy: Why and How.* Paris, 1970.
_____. *Learn and Live: The Way Out of Ignorance for 1,200,000,000 People.* Paris, 1951.
_____. *World Congress of Ministers of Education on the Eradication of Illiteracy.* Paris, 1966.

Government Publications

State of Kentucky. *Acts of the Kentucky General Assembly.* Frankfort, 1914, 1916, 1918.
_____. *Journal of the Regular Session of the Kentucky Senate, 1914.* Frankfort, 1914.
State of Kentucky. Department of Education. *County Teachers Institute Manual.* Frankfort, 1911.
_____. *Second Whirlwind Campaign, 1909.* Frankfort, 1909.
State of Kentucky. Kentucky Illiteracy Commission. *Facts Concerning the Moonlight School Work.* Frankfort, 1916.
_____. *First Biennial Report, 1914–1915.* Frankfort, 1916.
_____. *Moonlight School Course of Study, Patriotic Number (1918).* Frankfort, 1918.
_____. *Report, 1916–1920.* Frankfort, 1920.
State of Mississippi. Mississippi Illiteracy Commission. *Illiteracy in Mississippi: Blot It Out!* Jackson, 1916.
State of North Carolina. Board of Health. "Certificate of Death: Cora Wilson Stewart." December 9, 1958.
United States. Department of Commerce. Bureau of the Census. *Tenth Census of the United States, 1880.* Washington, 1880.
_____. *Twelfth Census of the United States, 1900.* Washington, 1900.
_____. *Thirteenth Census of the United States, 1910.* Washington, 1910.
_____. *Fifteenth Census of the United States, 1930.* Washington, 1930.
_____. *Sixteenth Census of the United States, 1940.* Washington, 1940.
United States. Department of the Interior. *Bureau of Education. Illiteracy in the United States and an Experiment for Its Elimination.* Washington, 1913.
United States. Works Progress Administration. *Educational Activities of the Works Progress Administration.* Washington, 1939.

Educational Publications

Kentucky Education Association. *Proceedings of the Fortieth Annual Session.* Louisville, 1911.
National Education Association. *Addresses and Proceedings of the Fifty-Sixth Annual Convention of the National Education Association (1918).* Washington, 1918.
_____. *Addresses and Proceedings of the Sixty-Sixth Annual Meeting Held at Minneapolis, Minnesota, July 1–6, 1928.* Vol. 66. Washington, 1928.
_____ *Illiteracy Report of the Illiteracy Commission of the National Education Association.* July 1924. Washington, 1924.

_____. *World Conference on Education*, June 28–July 6, 1923. Washington, D.C., 1923.
Southern Educational Board. *Educational Conditions in the Southern Appalachians.* Knoxville, 1902.

Newspapers

Christian Science Monitor, 1919.
Lexington *Herald*. 1911–1920.
Lexington *Leader*. 1911–1920.
Louisville *Courier Journal*. 1911–1920, 1958.

New York Times. 1887.
Rowan County News (Morehead). 1956.

Books

Bremmer, Robert H. *American Philanthropy*. Chicago: University of Chicago Press, 1960.
Brown, Harlan R. *In the Foothills of the Cumberlands: A History of Eastern Kentucky*. Ashland, Ky.: Graber Printing, 1959.
Cartwright, Moses A. *Ten Years of Adult Education: A Report on a Decade of Progress in the American Movement*. New York: Macmillan, 1935.
Chambers, Clarke. *Seedtime of Reform: American Social Service and Social Action, 1918–1933*. Minneapolis: University of Minnesota Press, 1963.
Clark, Thomas D. *A History of Kentucky*. Rev. ed. Lexington: John Bradford Press, 1960.
_____. *Three Paths to the Modern South, Education, Agriculture and Conservation*. Athens: University of Georgia Press, 1965.
Clarke, Walter Houston. *The Oxford Group: Its History and Significance*. New York: Bookman Associates, 1951.
Cleugh, Mary F. *Educating Older People*. London: Tavistock, 1962.
Coon, Charles. *Facts about Southern Educational Progress*. Durham: Seeman Printing, 1905.
Dabney, Charles William. *Universal Education in the South*. 2 vol. Chapel Hill: University of North Carolina Press, 1936.
Dottrens, Robert. *L'enseignement de l'écriture*. Paris: Editions Delachaux & Niestle, 1931.
Eister, Allan W. *Drawing-Room Conversion: A Sociological Account of the Oxford Group Movement*. Durham: Duke University Press, 1950.
Ely, Mary L., ed. *Handbook of Adult Education in the United States*. New York: Institute of Adult Education, Teachers College, Columbia University, 1948.
Embree, Edwin R. *Julius Rosenwald Fund: Review of the Two-Year Period 1931–1933*. Chicago: Julius Rosenwald Fund, 1933.
Flexnor, Eleanor. *Century of Struggle: The Woman's Rights Movement in the United States*. Cambridge: Belknap Press, 1959.
Goldberg, Samuel. *Army Training of Illiterates in World War II*. New York: New York Bureau of Publications, Teachers College, Columbia University, 1951.
Graham, Otis L. *An Encore for Reform: The Old Progressives and the New Deal*. New York: Oxford University Press, 1967.
Grattan, Clinton Hartley. *In Quest of Knowledge: A Historical Perspective on Adult Education*. New York: Association Press, 1955.
Gray, William Scott. *The Opportunity Schools of South Carolina: An Experimental Study*. New York: American Association for Adult Education, 1932.

Greer, Thomas H. *American Social Reform Movements: Their Pattern Since 1865*. New York: Prentice Hall, 1949.

Hamlett, Barksdale. *History of Education in Kentucky*. Frankfort: Kentucky Department of Education, 1914.

Harlan, Louis R. *Separate and Unequal: Public School Campaigns and Racism in the Southern Seaboard States, 1901–1915*. Chapel Hill: University of North Carolina Press, 1958.

Harris, T. H. *The Memoirs of T. H. Harris*. Baton Rouge: Bureau of Educational Materials and Research, College of Education, Louisiana State University, 1963.

Hartman, Edward G. *The Movement to Americanize the Immigrant*. New York: Columbia University Press, 1948.

Henson, Herbert Hensly. *The Oxford Group Movement*. New York: Oxford University Press, 1936.

Higham, John. *Strangers in the Land: Patterns of American Nativism, 1860–1925*. New Brunswick, N.J.: Rutgers University Press, 1955.

Hofstader, Richard. *The Age of Reform, From Bryan to Roosevelt*. New York: Alfred A. Knopf, 1955.

Isenberg, Irwin. *The Drive Against Illiteracy*. New York: H. W. Wilson, 1964.

Johnson, Walter. *William Allen White's America*. New York: Henry Holt, 1947.

Kandel, Issac L. *The Impact of War upon American Education*. Chapel Hill: University of North Carolina Press, 1948.

Kephart, Horace. *Our Southern Highlanders*. New York: MacMillan, 1926.

Knight, Edgar W. *Education in the United States*. 3d rev. ed. Boston: Ginn, 1951.

Knowles, Malcolm. *The Adult Education Movement in the United States*. New York: Holt, Rinehart and Winston, 1962.

Landis, Benson. *Rural Adult Education*. New York: Macmillan, 1933.

Laubach, Frank C. *Teaching the World to Read: A Handbook for Illiteracy Campaigns*. New York: Friendship Press, 1947.

Ligon, Moses Edward. *A History of Public Education in Kentucky*. Lexington: University of Kentucky Press, 1942.

Lean, Garth. *On the Tail of a Comet: The Life of Frank Buchman*. Colorado Springs: Helmers & Howard, 1988.

McVey, Frank L. *The Gates Open Slowly: A History of Education in Kentucky*. Lexington: University of Kentucky Press, 1949.

Mowry, George. *The California Progressives*. Berkeley: University of California Press, 1951.

Pinnock, Theodore James. *Results of an Exploratory Study of Functional Illiterates in Macon County Alabama*. Tuskeegee: Tuskeegee Institute, 1965.

Riegel, Robert E. *American Women: A Study of Social Change*. Rutherford,Madison, Teaneck, N.J.: Fairleigh Dickinson Press, 1970.

Robinson, Edgar Eugene, and Paul Edwards, eds. *The Memoirs of Ray Lyman Wilbur*. Stanford: Stanford University Press, 1960.

Scott, Anne Firor. *The Southern Lady: From Pedestal to Politics*. Chicago and London: University of Chicago Press, 1968.

Sinclair, Andrew. *The Better Half: The Emancipation of the American Woman*. New York: Harper & Row, 1965.

Stewart, Cora Wilson. *Moonlight Schools*. New York: E. P. Dutton, 1922.

Tindall, George. *The Emergence of the New South, 1913–1945*. Vol. 10 of *A History of the South*. Edited by Wendell Holmes Stephenson and E. Merton Coulter. Baton Rouge: Louisiana State University Press, 1967.

White, William Allen. *The Autobiography of William Allen White*. New York: Macmillan, 1946.

Williams, T. Harry. *Huey Long*. New York: Alfred A. Knopf, 1969.

Woodward, C. Vann. *Origins of the New South, 1877–1913*. Vol. 9 of *A History of the South*. Edited by Wendell Holmes Stephenson and E. Merton Coulter. Baton Rouge: Louisiana State University Press, 1951.

Articles

"Adults at Study." *Time*, September 17, 1934, pp. 60–62.

Anderson, Mrs. Leonard O. "The W.P.A. and Adult Education." *The School Executive* 55 (August 1936): 429–30, 450–51.

Berg, Paul Conrad. "Illiteracy at the Crossroads." *Adult Leadership* (June 1960): 47–48.

Bestor, Arthur E. "The A.B.C. of Federal Emergency Education." *Journal of Adult Education* 6 (April 1934): 150–54.

Blum, John M. "Nativism, Anti-Radicalism, and the Foreign Scare, 1917–1920." *Midwest Journal* 3 (Winter 1950–51): 46–53.

Coben, Stanley. "A Study of Nativism: The American Red Scare of 1919–1920." *Political Science Quarterly* 79 (March 1964): 52–75.

Coe, George A. "What Sort of School Is a C.C.C. Camp." *Social Frontier* (May 1935): 24–26.

"Education in the Civilian Conservative Corps." *School Review* 42 (December 1931): 729–31.

Fairchild, Henry Pratt. "The Literacy Test and Its Making." *Quarterly Journal of Economics,* 31 (May 1917): 447–60.

"40,000 v. 2,000,000." *Time*, August 27, 1934, 49.

Fox, Ester. "Considerations in Constructing a Basic Reading Program for Functionally Illiterate Adults." *Adult Leadership* (May 1964): 7–8.

Henry, Lyle K. "The Civilian Conservation Corps as an Educational Institution." *School and Society,* January 11, 1936, 62–66.

Lemons, Stanley J. "Social Feminism in the 1920s: Progressive Women and Industrial Legislation." *Labor History* 14 (Winter 1973): 83–91.

Link, Arthur S. "The Progressive Movement in the South, 1870–1914." *North Carolina Historical Review* 23 (April 1946): 172–95.

Lloyd, A. L. "Background of Feuding." *History Today* 2 (July 1952): 451–57.

Moran, Edward T. [Cora Wilson Stewart]. "The Rowan County War." *World Wide Magazine* 9 (August 1902): 321–30.

O'Neill, William L. "Feminism as a Radical Ideology." *Dissent: Explorations in the History of American Radicalism*. Edited by Alfred F. Young. Dekalb: Northern Illinois University Press, 1968.

Perkins, John S. "Extent and Nature of the Federal W.P.A. Educational Programs." *School and Society,* (January 23, 1937), 134–36.

Punke, Harold H. "Literacy, Relief and Adult Education in Georgia." *School and Society,* October 12, 1935, 514–17.

Scott, Anne Firor. "After Suffrage: The Southern Woman in the Twenties." *Journal of Southern History* 30 (August 1964): 298–318.

Tager, Jack. "Progressives, Conservatives, and the Theory of Status Revolution." *Mid America* 48 (July 1966): 162–75.

Van Deusen, Henry P. "Apostle of the Twentieth Century: Frank N. D. Buchman." *Atlantic Monthly* 154 (July 1934): 1–24.

————. "The Oxford Group Movement." *Atlantic Monthly* 154 (August 1934): 240–52.

Witty, Paul A. "Campaign Against Illiteracy—A War We Must Win." *National Parent Teacher* 53 (November 1958): 20–23.

Unpublished Sources

Allen, Lindsey E. "History of W.P.A. Educational Programs in Kentucky." Master's thesis, University of Kentucky, 1964.

Chapman, Mary Lucile. "The Influence of Coal in the Big Sandy Valley." Ph.D. diss., University of Kentucky, 1945.

Chumbler, Roy Otis. "A Study of Adult Education in Nineteen Kentucky Counties." Master's thesis, University of Kentucky, 1938.

Cross, Roscoe C. "The Public Life of James Bennett McCreary." Master's thesis, University of Kentucky, 1925.

Estes, Florence. "Cora Wilson Stewart and the Moonlight Schools of Kentucky, 1911–1920." Ed.D. diss., University of Kentucky, 1988.

Harris, Meriel Daniel. "Two Famous Kentucky Feuds and Their Causes." Master's thesis, University of Kentucky, 1940.

Reynolds, James R. "Moonlight Schools in Rowan County." Paper presented at seminar, Morehead State University, 1958.

Travelstead, Chester Coleman. "Adult Education in Kentucky." Ph.D. diss., University of Kentucky, 1950.

*J*NDEX